ESSAYS ON THE ECONOMIC HISTORY OF THE MIDDLE EAST

Middle Eastern Studies Occasional Publications
1. The Middle Eastern Economy
2. Modern Egypt
3. Towards a Modern Iran
4. Zionism and Arabism in Palestine and Israel
5. Palestine and Israel in the 19th and 20th Centuries
6. Essays on the Economic History of the Middle East

ESSAYS ON THE ECONOMIC HISTORY OF THE MIDDLE EAST

Edited by
Elie Kedourie and Sylvia G. Haim

LONDON AND NEW YORK

First published 1988 in Great Britain by
FRANK CASS & CO. LTD.

Published 2015 by Routledge
2 Park Square, Milton Park, Abingdon, Oxfordshire OX14 4RN
711 Third Avenue, New York, NY 10017

First issued in paperback 2015

Routledge is an imprint of the Taylor and Francis Group, an informa business

Copyright © 1988 Frank Cass & Co. Ltd.

British Library Cataloguing in Publication Data

Essays on the economic history of the Middle East.
1. Middle East. Economic conditions
I. Kedourie, Elie II. Haim, Sylvia G.
330.956'052

ISBN 13: 978-1-138-88394-9 (pbk)
ISBN 13: 978-0-7146-3318-3 (hbk)

Library of Congress Cataloging-in-Publication Data

Essays on the economic history of the Middle East.

(Middle Eastern studies occasional publications; 6)
1. Middle East – Economic conditions. I. Kedourie, Elie. II. Haim, Sylvia G. III. Series.
HC415.15.E87 1987   330.956   87-38225
ISBN 0-7146-3318-6

All rights reserved. No part of this publication may be reproduced in any form or by any means, electronic, mechanical, photocopying, recording or otherwise, without the prior permission of Frank Cass and Company Limited.

CONTENTS

Notes on Contributors — vii

Foreword — ix

1. Despotism and the Disintegration of the Iranian Economy 1500–1800
   Ahmad Seyf — 1

2. Silk and Socio-economic Changes in Lebanon, 1860–1919
   Kais Firro — 20

3. Reflections on a Subsistence Economy: Production and Trade of the Mahdist Sudan, 1881–1898
   Yitzhak Nakash — 51

4. Land Tenure and Taxation in Iran, 1800–1906
   Ahmad Seyf — 70

5. Recent Trends in Agricultural Development in the Near East
   A. A. El-Sherbini — 93

6. The Oil Nationalization Movement, the British Boycott and the Iranian Economy 1951–1953
   Kamran M. Dadkhah — 104

7. The Costs of Foreign Investment: The Case of the Egyptian Free Zones
   Leslie Sklair — 132

8. Labour Migration to the Arab Gulf in the 1980s
   Masudul Alam Choudhury — 157

9. Saudi Arabia's Industrialization Strategy: A Question of Comparative Advantage
   Robert E. Looney — 177

10. One Arab State, Many Arab States: The Impact of Population Growth and Oil Revenues
    Gad G. Gilbar — 196

NOTES ON CONTRIBUTORS

Ahmad Seyf studied at the universities of Glasgow, Manchester and Reading where he completed his Ph.D. on 'Some Aspects of Economic Development in Iran 1800 – 1906' and is currently teaching economics at the United States – International University – Europe, Bushey, Herts.

Dr Kais Firro is lecturer at the Department of Middle Eastern History at the University of Haifa and Head of the Druze Section at the Gustav Heinemann Institute of Middle Eastern Studies.

Yitzhak Nakash obtained his B.A. and M.A. degrees in Middle Eastern history from the University of Haifa. He is now a Ph.D. candidate at Princeton University.

Dr Abdel-Aziz El-Sherbini is presently an adviser on strategic planning to the Government of Egypt. He is also a freelance management consultant. After completing his graduate studies at the University of Chicago, he lectured at several universities in Egypt and other Middle Eastern countries. In 1965 he entered the UN system and held senior posts in several UN organisations until his mandatory retirement in August 1986. He is the author of *Food Security Issues in the Arab Near East* (Pergamon Press, 1979) and many articles in Arabic, English and French.

Kamran M. Dadkhah received his Ph.D. from Indiana University and, at present, is Assistant Professor in the Department of Economics, Northeastern University, Boston, USA.

Leslie Sklair is Senior Lecturer in Sociology at the London School of Economics. His contribution to this book stems from a research project under the working title 'Development effects of foreign investment: a comparison of the Republic of Ireland, Egypt, China and Mexico'.

Dr Masudul Alam Choudhury is Associate Professor of Economics at the University College of Cape Breton, Sydney, Nova Scotia, Canada, where he also edits the international academic journal, *Humanomics*.

NOTES ON CONTRIBUTORS

Dr Choudhury's most recent books are, *Contributions to Islamic Economic Theory: A Study in Social Economics* (The Macmillan Press Ltd., 1986), *Islamic Economic Co-operation* (The Macmillan Press Ltd., forthcoming), *The Paradigm of Humanomics* (Bangi, Malaysia: The National University of Malaysia Press, forthcoming).

Robert Looney is Professor of National Security Affairs at the United States Naval Postgraduate School at Monterey, California. He is the author of 14 books on economic development issues and has served as economic advisor to the governments of Iran and Saudi Arabia.

Gad G. Gilbar is associate professor of Middle Eastern Economic History at the University of Haifa, and senior research fellow at the Dayan Center for Middle Eastern and African Studies, Tel Aviv University. He was fellow of the Institute for Advanced Studies at the Hebrew University of Jerusalem (1978–79) and visiting scholar at the Center for Middle Eastern Studies, Harvard University (1981–82). His recent publications include (co-ed.) *Studies in Islamic Society* (Haifa and Leiden, 1984), and (ed.) *Ottoman Palestine 1800–1914: Studies in Economic and Social History* (Leiden, 1988).

FOREWORD

This is the sixth volume in the series of occasional publications to appear under the auspices of *Middle Eastern Studies*. It is also the second collection dealing with Middle-Eastern economics and economic history. The first, *The Middle Eastern Economy*, which appeared in 1977, was a reprint of a special number of *Middle Eastern Studies* devoted to the subject – no. 3 of volume 12. The contents of the present volume, by contrast, are published here for the first time. The ten papers which make up the volume were submitted at various times recently by their authors to *Middle Eastern Studies*, and accepted for publication by the Editors. But it has seemed to them that rather than publish the articles individually in different numbers of the Journal, it would be useful and profitable to group them together in a single volume.

Of the ten chapters, three (chapters 2, 3 and 4) consider various topics relating to the economic history of the Lebanon, the Sudan and Iran in the nineteenth century, and chapter 1 surveys the relation between government and economy in Iran during the sixteenth–eighteenth centuries. Four of the remaining chapters deal with recent and contemporary issues in the economy of Iran, Egypt, the Gulf and Saudi Arabia (chapters 6–9), while the two other chapters (5 and 10) survey region-wide developments in agriculture, demography and oil revenues.

The economic history of the Middle East remains, for many reasons, a difficult subject, in which comparatively little work is done, and it gives the Editors particular pleasure to have been able in some measure to promote and, they hope, to advance the subject which, from the inception of *Middle Eastern Studies* in 1964, has always occupied a distinctive place within its pages.

E.K.
S.G.H.

1

Despotism and the Disintegration of the Iranian Economy, 1500–1800

Ahmad Seyf

The object of this paper is to examine briefly the economic development in Iran in the period between the emergence of the Safavid's despotism in 1501, and the collapse of the Zand dynasty and the establishment of the Qajars at the end of the eighteenth century. It is maintained that this period represents the most significant phase of Iranian history. Not only did the decline which beset the economy from the end of the seventeenth century coincide with a rapid expansion and growth in Europe, but available evidence indicates that the Iranian economy appeared to be less backward during the first half of the sixteenth century than it was at the turn of the nineteenth century. In other words, around the year 1800, the Iranian economy was already in crisis which intensified in the course of the nineteenth century, eventually paving the way for the Constitutional Movement of 1906–11.

The economic history of Iran for this period has yet to be written, and this paper tries to give a rough sketch of major developments during two distinct phases. First, a period of relative prosperity and growth, from the 1580s up to 1650; and a period of decline and falling living standards which followed and continued throughout the eighteenth century.

To begin with, there exists evidence indicating that following the establishment of the Safavid dynasty in 1501, some improvements were made during the reign of its founder, Ismail (1501–24). These included measures in the field of distribution as well as those aimed to revive the productive capacity of the economy. The Venetian traveller, Duarte Barbaso, who spent several years in Iran during this period, wrote that not only did he keep 'nothing for himself', but

> If he finds any persons who make no use of their wealth and do no service therewith to any, then he [Ismail] takes it from them

and distributes it equally to the worthy men of his army whom he knows to be in want, and to the real owner of the property he gives as much as to each one of them. Hence some Moors call him 'the Leveller' ...[1]

It is also on record that the corvée in 'building roads and irrigation works was very extensive' during this period;[2] implying that either the extent of lands under cultivation increased or lands already under cultivation were more intensively used; both of which, however, tended to increase output. Whatever the case may be, it goes some way towards explaining Ismail's policy of reducing the rate of taxation on the peasantry to one-sixth of the produce (the original rate not specified).[3] Given greater expenditure on roads and irrigation works, it may be reasonable to argue that despite the reduction in the rate of taxation, the mass of revenue probably increased as a result of these measures aimed to improve the public works. Otherwise, it would not have been possible to increase expenditure at a lower rate of taxation.

Tahmasp I (1524–76) who succeeded Ismail did not follow the same policy, especially during the second half of his reign. It is probable that the internal disorder which followed Ismail's death contributed to check the progress. To which, of course, the detrimental effects of Perso-Ottoman conflicts during 1533–55 must be added. However, Tahmasp is said to have increased the rate of taxation and introduced new dues, for example, *toufir* and *tafavot*.[4] Yet, for the last 14 years of his rule he did not pay the salaries of his soldiers, let alone maintain the public works. The contemporary sources claim that no one complained and all were ready to serve the king, which seems improbable unless they had been given a free hand to extract as much as possible from the ordinary people, i.e. the peasantry.[5] As a sign of economic decline, it is worth mentioning that despite the increase in the rate of taxation and the introduction of new dues, the total revenue of the State is estimated to have declined from five million gold coins in the early 1550s to about three million in 1571.[6] At a constant rate of taxation, this decline implied a 40 per cent reduction in the taxable production. Considering the increase, it is likely that the decline was probably higher. It is most improbable that a decline of this magnitude would happen without serious effects on the population and on the productive power of the economy. Over and above civil and foreign wars, which would have had some negative impact on the economy, it can also be argued that the rapacious appropriation of resources and material wealth contributed rather significantly to the crisis. In other words, during the second half of his rule Tahmasp, while appropriating a greater portion from the producers, did little or nothing to expand the productive capacity. This view is supported by the fact that despite a reduced State revenue, upon Tahmasp's death in 1576, it was discovered that there was in his treasury 3800 million *dinars* of gold and silver coins, 600 ingots of gold and silver (30.5 lbs. each), 200 kharwars of silk (650 lbs. each), 30,000 pairs of fine and expensive garments and a complete set of arms for 30,000 soldiers.[7] Small wonder that there were widespread rebellions in the province of Gilan and in Tabriz during 1571–3.[8] It is possible that the above figures overstated the hoard, but it seems almost certain that a large proportion of the surplus had been hoarded. A contemporary observer noted that Tahmasp's main concern was to accumulate riches with 'thousands and thousands of tricks that are unworthy of men, not to speak of kings'.[9] This enormous treasure plainly implied that the surplus produce which was mainly in the hands of the State was indeed unproductively saved instead of being recycled into the economy. It should also be added that taking a large amount of money out of circulation tended to slow down exchange i.e. internal and external trade. As a further sign of economic decline, let us recall that towards the end of Tahmasp's rule insecurity prevailed in the country and inevitably made unsafe the trade routes to Hormoz and to Aleppo which upset the overall commercial prospect. A British trade mission which went to Iran via Russia in 1571 concluded that 'any immediate effort to continue the trade was inadvisable'.[10] On the other hand, the policy of increasing the rate of taxation while little was done to enhance production was bound to impoverish the masses of people. Edward, an English merchant who went to Iran in 1568 remarked that 'the people in general' were 'too poor to buy English cloth'.[11]

The prevailing insecurity, itself a sign of economic crisis, was also an indication of a weakened central authority which seemed unable to manage an economy in crisis. The most probable consequence of this combination was deeper socio-economic crisis, greater negligence in the provision, let alone expansion, of much needed public works. The situation worsened in 1571 as a result of the outbreak of a devastating plague and widespread famine around the same time, and this tends to support the hypothesis of a deep economic crisis. No exact idea can be formed of the actual effects of the plague and famine on population, but in the case of the latter it is on record that in various parts of the country cannibalism had been observed.[12]

From 1576 till 1587, no improvement appears to have occurred; instead, as a result of continuous civil disorders and the increasingly oppressive taxation, the productive capacity had probably declined even further. The mass of the peasantry must have been the ultimate victims, because despite the overall decline of the economy some taxes were said to have been raised five times between 1570 and 1587.[13] This process of decline, however, appears to have come to an end during the reign of Abbas I (1587–1629) who not only re-established the authority of the central government but, in order to consolidate its position and power, undertook a number of measures to revive the economy. These included the repair of the decayed irrigation systems i.e. *qanats*, and the building of new ones. Reforms were introduced in various fields, such as land tax, and the rate of taxation was reduced to its pre-1570 level. Internal tranquillity was restored, which in itself may indicate the beginning of the process of economic recovery.[14] By vigorously campaigning against robbers, and at the same time constructing roads and caravanserai, and restoring and expanding irrigation works, Abbas encouraged production and the development of trade. On internal peace and security, from the time of Abbas and throughout most of the seventeenth century one traveller after another expressed his admiration for the safe condition of the Iranian caravan routes, and there were no complaints of those extortions on the part of the local rulers so familiar from travels in the Ottoman Empire. As Coverte, writing in 1612, noted: 'And there [in Iran] a man may travel without danger of robbing, for it is there a strange thing to hear of a thief.'[15] In 1618 the English agent, Baker, described the route between Isfahan and Jask (a port on the Persian Gulf coasts) in the following manner:

> [We are] confident that these parts are so free from any thieves and robbers, that in this particular it is hardly paralleled by any of our Christian governments and exceeded by none, insomuch that Banyans (who carry neither weapon offensive nor defensive) go about freely and frequently pass with their ready money throughout the whole Persian territory. (spelling modernized)[16]

It is perhaps reasonable to argue that the picture given by these merchants is fairly accurate, because otherwise their own interests or the interests of the companies they represented might have been endangered. It seems obvious that such a peaceful society reflected a relatively prosperous economy. To support this view, let us point out that, in fact, seventeenth century travellers often spoke of major irrigation projects, and Chardin reported that irrigation by *qanats* was free, implying that these were constructed and maintained by the government.[17] Attempts were also made to redirect the Karun River (in Khuzestan) to irrigate the central provinces, especially Isfahan. But this project was not successful in

Abbas' time. Considerable efforts were made to build new roads and to repair and expand the existing ones. For example, Herbert, who travelled in Iran during 1627–9, on his way to Qazvin from Isfahan, wrote:

> The most part of the night we rode upon a paved causeway, broad enough for ten horses to go abreast, built by extraordinary labour and expense over a part of a great desert.[18]

270 kilometres (about 160 miles) of such roads were constructed in the province of Mazandran on the Caspian shores.[19] Herbert like other travellers of the early seventeenth century often refers to the cheapness and abundance of provisions,[20] whereas towards the end of the seventeenth century and during the eighteenth century scarcity and high prices of food are often recorded.[21]

In addition to the cheapness and abundance of provisions, cash crops, especially silk, were produced in large quantities. We are told that the customs duties on silk exports are estimated to have been 40 million *dinars*.[22] It may be an overestimation, but let us recall that in the early seventeenth century Iranian raw silk 'was the second biggest European import from Asia'.[23] Olearius, who spent nearly three years in Iran during the 1630s, estimated the total silk crop at a little less than 4.4 million lbs.[24] To see the true scale of expansion in the silk production, it should be remembered that the largest quantity ever produced during the nineteenth century never exceeded 2.2 million lbs. (in 1864).[25] The ability to allocate large amounts of land and labour to the production of cash crops without falling food supply or rising inflation not only implies that both land and labour were in large supply – as a result of expanding irrigation works and population growth respectively – but may also indicate that productivity in the food-producing sector was probably rising faster than population growth. In other words, capital/labour/output ratios increased faster than the growth in the population. This hypothesis can also be supported by the growth and expansion of Iranian towns during this period. For example, Tabriz is said to have been an important centre for trade as well as textiles and weapon manufactures with a population estimated at 300,000.[26] Reducing this estimate by one-third, the population of Tabriz during these years was still higher than it was at the turn of the twentieth century. To see the extent of the development of Tabriz, one can compare this estimate, or the reduced figure, with those of 30,000 for 1810, 100,000 for 1850, 120,000 for 1866/7 and finally 180,000 for as late as 1899.[27] The city of Isfahan was said to have had 80,000 inhabitants at the end of the sixteenth century, but in the 1620s Herbert estimated its population at 200,000 and Olearious in the late 1730s suggested the remarkable figure of 500,000.[28] Assuming Herbert's estimate to be by and large relatively more reliable, this compares with those of 60,000 for 1811, 100,000 for 1849/50, 60,000–70,000 for 1884, 82,000 for 1893 and finally 100,000 for as late as 1899.[29]

Furthermore, there exists evidence indicating that the rural population was increasing too. It was reported that in Central Iran, an area of 4,500 square kilometres (less than 1,760 square miles) contained 1,500 villages in the 1660s, whereas the number was only 800 during the first half of the fourteenth century.[30] Chardin claimed that not only was the number increasing but 'the peasantry around Isfahan appeared to be better off than the French peasants'.[31]

Owing to a relatively prosperous agriculture and well-maintained and safe roads, trade seems to have expanded during this period too. In addition to Isfahan and Tabriz, many other towns favourable to foreign trade or favoured by the Iranian despots expanded and accommodated merchants of various nationalities. For example, Gambroon (Bandar Abbas) is said to have been transformed from a 'small village' to 'a city of great commerce' in which resided 'English, Dutch, Danes, Portuguese, Armenians, Georgians, Muscovites, Turks, Indians, Jews and Banian merchants'.[32] The native traders, trading most probably on Shah's behalf, were said to have had trading agents in countries as distant as Sweden and China.[33] The number of Indians living in Isfahan was estimated at 20,000, whereas towards the end of the seventeenth century and during the early eighteenth century the emigration of Iranian peasantry to India is suggested to have been one of the causes of population decline in Iran.[34] There is evidence indicating that large scale emigration probably took place, because we are told that during 1698–1701 taxes on the peasantry, artisans and even the merchants were raised sharply and three new taxes were introduced.[35]

In contrast to the description often given by the nineteenth century observers of the situation in Iranian towns, Herbert while in Shiraz in the late 1620s wrote, 'in all my life I never saw people more jocund and less quarrelsome'.[36] For the sake of comparison, the following was written on the same town by Consul Abbott in 1849/50: 'Idleness and the want of useful occupation for a large proportion of the inhabitants appear to be the principal cause of their mischievous and turbulent character.'[37] Writing on the city of Qom, Herbert noted:

> The city has about two thousand houses, most of them of more than common structure – well built, well formed, well

furnished. The streets are spacious; the bazar beautiful; but the city is now unwalled.[38]

Kashan, a town 'abundantly peopled' was also a major centre of textile handicrafts:

> An English merchant who was there [in Kashan] about the year 1600, spares not to aver that there was then more silk brought in one year into Kashan than broadcloths are into London ... The Caravanserai in this city is very noble – nay I may say an unparalleled fabric of that kind.[39]

On the basis of our foregoing discussion, it seems reasonable to conclude that the economy was functioning rather successfully under Abbas I. The surplus mainly in the hands of the State was by and large injected into the economy to maintain and expand irrigation works, roads, caravanserais and the like, an interesting combination which encouraged production and trade. Under these circumstances population also tended to grow.

Such a close circular relationship between population, production, revenue and public works has a built-in vulnerability. A break at any point suffices to cause the collapse of the entire system. The reason for this lack of self-propelled dynamism must be sought in the dual function of despotism as a system of government in which, in an economy based on surplus extraction from the direct producers, the State plays a prominent role in economic affairs. In other words, despotism encourages production while that production serves its purposes. At the same time, however, it destroys individuals' abilities to accumulate and often prevents a widely diffused power base from emerging. This was even more forcefully true for the despotic government under Abbas I. The Shah not only had the monopoly of foreign trade; 'besides, by a customary law he makes himself heir to whom he pleases; so that few rich men die but he claims a propriety, none daring to call his claim in question'.[40] This passage clearly indicates the distortion of the process of capital accumulation by the individual in Iran. The question, however, was not whether there was private property, but whether it was allowed to expand and regenerate itself. The answer can only be in the negative. It is true that when a despotic power was firmly established, as it was under Abbas I, 'the country is so secure, and travellers can scarce find a more quiet place than Persia'.[41] But by the same token, it was also true that the State was able to exercise unlimited power against the individual. Let us recall that the despots usually enjoyed the power of life and death; condemn without hearing; dispose of men's persons and estates when and as they please without any respect of right, especially at men's deaths where there is any considerable estate, the heir not presuming further than to inventory ...[42]

This power was not ceremonial; on the contrary, Iranian history provides numerous examples of its reality. It was this unlimited power which enabled Abbas to order the execution of Morshed Qoli Khan, the man who paved the way for his accession to the throne, and of all his friends and relatives. Sanson, who spent eight years in Iran during the second half of the seventeenth century, mentioned the following impressive evidence of the situation. The son of the great Mongol, who was on an official visit to Iran, was asked by the Shah what he thought of his Lords and other officers. To which the prince replied that he thought they had every one a very good mien; but he was amazed to see not one old man amongst them.[43] Even examples from the nineteenth century when despotism in Iran was relatively weak and to a large extent lacked the means to exercise unlimited power, seem to confirm the point. The executions of Haj Ibrahim Kalantar, Ghaim Magham, Amir Kabir, all powerful grand Vazirs with reformist tendencies, cannot simply be coincidental.

In sum, the insignificant role played by individuals in the improvement of productive capacity can be attributed to two factors. First, the preeminence of the State meant that the surplus appropriated by the individual was relatively small. Second, the absence of a legal and institutional framework for property rights led those who had acquired some surplus to hoard rather than to invest, since to invest would have exposed them to the rapacity of the despot. Understandably, hoarding as an attempt to conceal one's riches cannot be quantified, but there is overwhelming evidence indicating that its scale was relatively large.[44] Money 'saved' and protected in this manner would contribute little or nothing to expand the productive capacity of the economy. In this and similar cases, money tended to remain as mere hoarded use-value, a sort of consumption temporarily postponed, rather than 'a measure of value, and ... medium of circulation'. In other words, 'gold and silver thus become of themselves social expression for superfluity or wealth'.[45]

Under this condition, however, a crisis in the economy would almost inevitably follow the collapse of the central authority. This seems to have been the situation in Iran following the death of Abbas I in 1629. Particular mention must be made of the rebellion in Gilan which immediately followed. The province of Gilan was declared *khaleseh* (state owned) from 1592, and Mazandran four years later in 1596.[46] During the period of disorder, the rebels attacked among others the major silk-producing centres of Lahijan and Rasht. The silk crop of 1629 and 1630 suffered badly and no deliveries from the 1629 crop of silk had yet arrived in Isfahan by February 1630.[47] Continued civil disorders on the one hand and the renewed conflict with the Ottoman Empire on the other meant that not only was production further disrupted but, more important perhaps, the surplus – which inevitably declined *pari passu* with a decline in the production – was more and more allocated to maintenance of the war effort rather than of the fragile public works. Later in the century, Chardin noted (probably during his second journey in the late 1670s) that the number of irrigation works, especially *qanats*, had declined, and the peasantry, particularly from the South, were emigrating to India in large numbers in search of more tolerable conditions of life.[48] In contrast to what the travellers wrote during the first half of the seventeenth century, towards the end of this century it was said that 'in many places ... the poverty and misery of the peasantry is beyond description'.[49] Around the same time it was also said that the number of *qanats* in the province of Azarbaijan alone had declined by 400 during the previous 60 years.[50] The government in turn increased the rate of taxation to sustain its revenue. As the surplus expropriated from the peasantry was not productively expended, the eventual impact of an increase in taxation was greater impoverishment of the peasantry and a further depression of demand for non-farm products. The overall decline in the economy manifested itself in various forms, and, as a case in point, a corresponding decline in external trade became apparent from the 1670s. During the first six or seven years of the rule of Shah Solayman (1666–94) the customs revenues from Bandar Abbas and Lingeh (the two main trading ports on the Gulf coast) varied between 9.1 to 11 million *dinars*, whereas during the reign of Abbas II (1642–66) it was said to have been about 24.5 million *dinars*.[51] As no changes appear to have taken place in the rate of duties, the decline in the revenue indicates a decline of external trade which, in turn, reflected a decline in production and in the size of exchangeable surplus. As for the decline in the economy, there were external factors too. Fryer, who visited Iran during 1672–81, suggested that 'the discovery of the sea route' to India by the Europeans may have also contributed to the decline of the Persian economy. In his view, the decline of Isfahan was undoubtedly caused by this discovery, because 'it was the storehouse and general market for Indian wares as well as its own', whereas by then 'it became a lake, in which riches do now stagnate, not circulate, or at least not with the force they did before'.[52]

The overall situation reached a critical point towards the end of the century and was hardly under any control during the eighteenth century. It seems that worsening economic conditions led to a decline in the population too. This was probably quite considerable, because by 1710 the Shah was forced to issue a decree forbidding peasants' mobility.[53] Nevertheless, the economy received its most serious blow in 1722 when Afghan rebels captured the capital, Isfahan, following which there was a period of chaos and disorder. As Lambton pointed out, 'the period of Afghan domination is remarkable only for the ruin which it brought about especially in Isfahan and the neighbourhood'.[54] In support of this point, it was reported that in the province of Isfahan alone, more than 1000 villages were totally destroyed and subsequently depopulated.[55] The scale of destruction was so great that the district had not recovered by the second half of the nineteenth century, and Mounsey put the total number of inhabited villages at only 100 in the 1860s.[56]

As a result of the confusion, the irrigation system, i.e. *qanats*, dikes and dams suffered very badly, and the famous dam of band-e-Soltan in Marv was completely destroyed.[57] In addition to Isfahan, Shiraz, Yazd, Tabriz and Qazvin were also plundered and are said to have lost about two-thirds of their population.[58]

The collapse of the central authority opened the way for many years of disturbances, wars and misery. The country was also invaded by its two powerful neighbours, the Ottoman Empire and Russia. These two countries took advantage of the confusion in Iran and concluded a treaty in 1723 which provided for the partition of the north-west of Iran. The Russians promptly occupied Baku and Darband as well as Gilan and threatened the districts adjacent to the Caspian Sea. The Ottomans, on the other hand, declared war on Iran and a strong army led by the Pasha of Baghdad occupied Kermanshah, and Luristan. In short, the most populous and productive provinces of Iran, Gilan, Mazandran, Azarbaijan and Kermanshah came under foreign occupation.[59] Civil wars, foreign occupation and consequent disruption of production was so considerable that it gave rise to a severe famine during 1735–36, and the decline in the purchasing power of the mass of population led to a further depression in trade which in turn adversely affected handicrafts.[60]

The state of confusion and civil war continued for 14 years, until 1736, when a new dynasty, Afshariyeh under Nader came into being. Regardless of the decline in the productive capacity of the economy, Nader Shah (1736–47) embarked on endless wars not only to establish himself as the absolute ruler but also to revive the 'Persian Empire', while the material bases for such achievement were no longer present. The consequence of such a naive policy was that the direct producers, the peasantry, already downtrodden to an absolute minimum, were further squeezed. The revenue, instead of being invested to repair and possibly expand the much-damaged public works, and especially the irrigation system, had been largely wasted in his criminal destruction of India. His plunder, estimated variously at £87.5 to £120 millions, was by and large hoarded in Kalat-e Naderi and did not influence the development of the Iranian economy.[61] What his 'success' in India achieved, however, was to raise his desire for further military campaigns, which inevitably led to more excessive taxation.[62] Some idea of the extent of oppression may be formed from the following passage:

> In Kerman, for example, in 1736 the people were so denuded of supplies by the expeditions which he [Nader] had planned for the recapture of Qandhar that there was a famine for seven or eight years.[63]

Not only were the fruits of labour taken away from the people by force; a considerable proportion of the labour force was employed for unproductive purposes:

> In February 1738 men and women of the Kerman district [who were already suffering from famine] were compelled to act as porters to Qandhar owing to shortage of draught animals.[64]

In 1744, a French traveller, Otter, was told horrifying stories about the ongoing oppression and he came across peasants whose cattle, flocks and all other movable belongings had already been carried off by the Shah's collectors.[65] In his preparation for military campaigns, Nader is said to have dispatched groups of soldiers to destroy villages and take peasants as prisoners.[66] Not only the peasantry, the merchants too were squeezed and had good reasons to complain. Like his predecessors, Nader monopolized the foreign trade of the country thus depriving the merchants of this source of revenue. Elton reported that

> this year [1739] all goods that arrived at Rasht were obliged to be sold there, and that the Shah would not permit anyone to buy them except his own merchants; ... Also that the Shah had engross'd all the raw silk to himself.[67]

The internal trade appears to have been in his hands too. Nader is said to have had one or more 'Court merchants' in every city and he was 'in a manner, the sole trader in all Persia' as 'none but the Shah's *kupecheen* [Court merchant] could buy any goods imported'.[68]

In addition to much reduced opportunities for the merchants, they were heavily taxed. Pierson, the East India Company's Agent in Isfahan, reported in 1747 that 'the Armenian merchants of Isfahan' were greatly oppressed and this 'reduced the trade to its lowest ebb, as no merchant dared to purchase anything for fear of being thought rich'.[69] Pierson was not alone in drawing attention to Nader's oppressive trade policies, the Agents at Kirman and Bandar Abbas also reported to the same effect.[70] As to the likely effects of this policy, a 'distinguished merchant' conjectured: 'If the king goes on at this rate, in another year we must make money of wood, for neither gold nor silver will appear except in his treasuries'.[71]

There is evidence to suggest that the shortage of money was quite drastic, the main reason being that in order to meet his increasing military expenditure Nader issued orders to collect taxes at a far higher level than previously in *money*. For example, the money demanded from Rasht and its surrounding villages in 1747 was twice as much as taxes levied and collected from the entire province of Gilan in 1743.[72] Nader's brutal rule killed off any incentive to undertake investment and his oppressive taxation left the great majority of the people very little to spend either on consumption (except on the bare necessities of life) or investment. As a result, both production and consumption were adversely affected. The State itself was too busy with military campaigns to pay much attention to the improvement of the already declining public works. With further decline of these works, agricultural production was bound to suffer further. This is to say that not only was there less to consume but also less surplus to be exchanged with or supplied to the urban centres. A decline in internal as well as external trade followed. A merchant in Qazvin described the situation in the early 1740s in the following terms:

> Qazvin had then 12,000 houses inhabited, and now it has only 1,100, see from this eminence how this poor city is in ruin. Nor is Isfahan much better; that city had formerly 100,000 houses well inhabited ... but incredible as it may seem to you, I am assured that only 5,000 houses are now inhabited. I have formerly been in Isfahan with a caravan of 30,000 crowns value and in less than three months returned home with my capital, and a profit of 4,000; now I could not sell 3,000 crowns in ten months.[73]

It was perhaps as a result of this development that travellers who visited Iran during the eighteenth century gave a more depressing picture than that painted by early seventeenth-century travellers. Hanway, a British merchant who spent several years in Iran during Nader's rule, wrote, 'the people everywhere complained aloud, that the Shah had reduced them to the extremest misery'.[74] Every peasant household was forced to dispatch one of its members to serve in the army. If a village ignored this order, it was likely to face complete destruction.[75] Furthermore, if a soldier died in an epidemic, was killed in action or deserted the army, the inhabitants of his village would have had to pay a heavy fine.[76]

When oppressive measures are practised, there must either be rebellion or emigration, both of which must adversely affect the population and the economy. In the case of the latter, it was reported that Nader's oppressive taxation 'induced thousands of our people to fly for shelter into India; and though we hate the Turks more than we do the Christians; yet it is incredible what number of our people have taken refuge in Turkey'.[77] The emigration and the decline of the internal trade, as mentioned earlier, seemed to have affected urban life in Iran. To illustrate this, let us recall that Herbert estimated the population of Qazvin at 20,000 families or 200,000 in the late 1620s, whereas Hanway was told that the number of inhabited houses declined from 12,000 to 1,100 in the 1740s, and he added that three-quarters of the town was in ruin and 'old women appeared in several of the shops which in former times was not practised'.[78] Noticing the decline in the population, Hanway enquired why such a vast country had so few inhabitants. He was told by an Iranian:

> It is true, our country is ruined; but it cannot be otherwise; for the Shah has supported all his forces in one continued campaign of four years, by the taxes drawn from his people, who have but little left to support themselves.[79]

It is not possible to determine whether the incentive was to flee from the town to the farming areas, i.e. a redistribution of population, or to become nomads. In view of the evidence indicating rebellions by nomads in several provinces of Iran during 1743–46,[80] one may be led to assert that the most likely result was greater nomadism. This, in turn, could be interpreted to imply an absolute decline in population as nomadism was unlikely to be able to sustain a dense and rising population.

On the overall condition of the economy as a whole and the peasantry in particular, Hanway wrote:

> As we approached the very few villages that remained, the inhabitants taking us for soldiers or robbers, which was much the same, fled into the mountains, and left us to provide for ourselves.[81]

Other eighteenth century sources gave a similar description. Elton who travelled in Iran in 1739 pointed out, 'people who have lately come from Isfahan, indifferently tell us, that it is almost drained of inhabitants'.[82] Elton's report was supported by Otto, who travelled from Baghdad to Isfahan in 1737 and described the state of the peasantry and common people as by no means enviable and, when he returned to Baghdad in 1739, he reported a further deterioration.[83] A Russian traveller, V. Beratishuv, wrote in 1743 that 'hunger and poverty are to be seen everywhere, the inhabitants of many towns and villages fled out of desperation. From Tabriz to Hamadan [a distance of about 365 miles] I have not seen even a single inhabited village'.[84]

As to further evidence of the decline of population and agriculture during this period, reference can be made to the whole question of state revenue under Nader. Despite his cruelty in collecting taxes, the total revenue in his time is said to have been only one-third of what it had been during the last Safavid Shah.[85] At the same time, as revenue was a certain proportion of total produce and also as there is no evidence indicating a reduction in the tax ratio, it can be argued that the decline in the total revenue was indicative of a corresponding decline in total production. This argument is considered reasonable because Nader's rapacious appropriation of resources and material wealth was bound to reduce the productive capacity of the economy. For the sake of illustration, let us recall that prior to, and during, his campaign against India, Nader's standing army was estimated to have been 200,000 strong with an annual total expenditure of 20 million crowns (excluding contingent expenses).[86] At the same time, it was also said that, prior to his conquest of India, provinces under his rule were supposed to bring into the treasury the sum total of less than 10.5 million crowns, i.e. less than 55 per cent of his military expenditure.[87] Yet, we know that this army was kept and the campaign continued for four years, implying an extra taxation of more than 38 million crowns in four years, provided that there was no other expenditure. Judging by the descriptions given by eighteenth century travellers on the manner in which these taxes were collected, it seems reasonable to conclude that Nader's department of finance, or to use Engels' term, 'plunder at home', was in fact plundering the peasantry and the merchants in order to maintain his department of war, 'plunder at home and abroad'. His neglect of the department of public works, 'provision for reproduction', however, paved the way for his downfall.[88] In other words, at a constant, if not declining, production level more and more was expropriated from the peasantry to be used for the execution of endless military campaigns. There is no evidence that the merchants and artisans lived under better conditions. According to Hanway, 'though Gilan was reputed to be under the least unhappy circumstances of any province in Persia, yet the villages were in a very ruinous condition'.[89] Elton indicated that the foreign trade of Iran suffered: 'French, English, Dutch, used to have agents at Isfahan and only the Dutch are still there'.[90] Hanway also reported on instances in which foreign merchants initially intending to go to Iran went to Khiveh and Bokhara instead, because the situation in Iran was said to be unsafe and unsatisfactory. He added that the export of raw silk by Russian and Armenian merchants was one-tenth of its usual quantity.[91] The English merchants left Iran altogether in 1749, and the table below shows the value of raw silk exported by them during the last few years of their residence in the country.

TABLE 1
THE VALUE OF RAW SILK EXPORTED BY THE ENGLISH MERCHANTS
FROM IRAN: 1743-49[88]

Year	Value in Crowns
1743	120,000
1744	50,000
1745	62,500
1746	50,500
1747	30,000
1748	12,000
1749	33,000

Nader was assassinated in 1747, and there were civil wars and internal disorders again for several years. It was only during the latter years of the reign of Karim Khan Zand (1750-79) that the country enjoyed a brief period of relative peace and tranquillity. He is said to have reduced the rate of taxation, and took measures to encourage handicrafts. Irrigation networks in the south, especially in the province of Fars, were partly repaired. Merchants, particularly Armenians, were granted privileges in an attempt to expand trade.[93] Karim Khan died in 1779 and his death was followed by a period of anarchy and bloody civil wars between various rival factions, until Agha Mohammad Khan Qajar, the founder of the Qajar dynasty, established his rule in the mid-1790s. The brutality with which the new dynasty was founded is beyond any description. There was hardly any province which escaped immense destruction. The following account compiled from a pro-Qajar chronicle is self-explanatory:

> In 1784, His Majesty [Agha Mohammad] having marched in the direction of Irak [in central Iran] first took the city of Qom and next advanced to Kashan and from hence to Isfahan ... [He] ordered an expedition against the mountain tribes of Bakhtiari, Ferahani and Guzazi; he quite destroyed their entrenched posts, and made great numbers of them the prey of his triumphant sword ... In the year 1786 ... advanced into Gilan, and reduced that country ... In 1789, ... advanced to reduce Fars ... and about the end of the year 1205 *Hejri* [1790] ... he formed the project of reducing Azarbaijan ... On the very first attack, His Majesty destroyed [the town of] Sarab, and having kindled the fire of plunder and devastation, consumed in the flames all the houses of that region ... In 1792, Kerman, Bam and Narmashir were reduced ... [and] ... ordered the fort of Shiraz ... to be demolished ... [He then] moved to Astarabad ... great number of Turkamans were put to death or reduced to slavery ... and in the highways were built minarets constructed with their heads ... After this [he] formed in the year 1793 the project of reducing Khorasan ... [In 1794] the army advanced to Ganja and completely reduced the district of Shakki and Shirwan.[94]

When Kerman was finally captured in 1794, Agha Mohammad is said

> not to have been satisfied until 35,000 pairs of eyes had been handed to him upon a dish, while every fine building was razed to the ground, and 30,000 women and children were carried off into slavery.[95]

It is true that the city of Kerman was rebuilt on a new location during the first quarter of the nineteenth century but, to illustrate the extent of the destruction, Pottinger, writing in 1810, claimed to have visited minarets constructed with human heads still standing outside the city of Bam.[96]

CONCLUSION

This study has examined some aspects of economic development in Iran between 1500 and 1800, and has identified two distinct phases. First, a period of relative prosperity and growth under Abbas I, which continued for a few years after his death in 1629. Second, a period of decline and falling living standards beginning in the mid-seventeenth century and continuing throughout the eighteenth century. What made this process still more disastrous was that the decline took place at a time

DESPOTISM AND THE IRANIAN ECONOMY 1500-1800

when western Europe was being transformed both economically and politically, thus widening the gap between the stationary, if not absolutely declining Iran and a West that was moving quickly towards the accumulation of capital and the adjustment of its social and political systems to new economic needs. During this period, the State occupied a dominant position and exercised a decisive influence on the socioeconomic life of Iran. The cardinal attribute of sovereignty, for Iranian political thinking, was the Shah's unlimited right to exploit all sources of income within his realm as Imperial possession. It followed that there could be no stable hereditary nobility in Iran, because there was no security of property on which such a nobility could be based. Wealth and honour were effectively coterminous with the State, and individual's rank was simply a function of his position within it. It further followed that, on the one hand, the necessity of highly capital- (as well as labour-) intensive public works (mainly irrigation works) for agricultural development, and on the other, the appropriation of a major part of the surplus by the State or through the State organs, meant that the State had a vital economic function, in contrast to western Europe during the same period. It thus seems reasonable to argue that whenever the central authority was secure and functioned efficiently (as between the 1580s and 1650s), the surplus was by and large utilized productively, i.e. reinvested, and the economy prospered. Likewise, when this was not the case (as from the 1650s onwards), the collapse of the central authority or its rapacious appropriation of the surplus would normally have led to a situation where less surplus tended to be produced in the next round, when a smaller fund was available for the maintenance and expansion of essential public works. If we also take into account the civil wars of the eighteenth century, especially during the last quarter of the century, it is possible to argue that by the turn of the nineteenth century, the Iranian economy was much weaker than it had been two hundred years previously.

NOTES

1 Quoted in J. J. Saunders (ed.), *The Muslim World on the Eve of Europe's Expansion*, New Jersey 1966, pp. 36-7.
2 I. P. Petrushevsky, N. V. Pigulevskaya, N. V. Yakubovsky, A. U. Striyeva, A. M. Belnitsky, *Tarikh-e Iran az Dowre-ye Bastan ta Payan Sade-ye Hezh-dahom-e Miladi*, trans. by K. Keshavarz, Tehran 1975, p. 481 (hereafter *TI*).
3 Ibid. p. 481.
4 Ibid. p. 488.
5 Bastani Parizi, *Siyasat va Iqtesad-e Asr Safavi*, Tehran 1969, pp. 47-9.
6 *TI*, p. 489.
7 Ibid. p. 488.

8   Ibid., pp. 488–94.
9   N. Steensgaard, *The Asian Trade Revolution of the Seventeenth Century*, Chicago, 1974, p. 103.
10 W. Foster, *England's Quest of Eastern Trade*, London, 1966, p. 43.
11 Ibid., p. 38.
12 *TI*, p. 489.
13 Ibid., p. 512.
14 Ibid., p. 528.
15 Steensgaard, *The Asian Trade Revolution*, p. 68.
16 Ibid., p. 68.
17 *TI*, p. 533.
18 T. Herbert, *Travels in Persia ... 1627–29*, New edition, London, 1928, p. 143.
19 *TI*, p. 522.
20 Herbert, *Travels*, pp. 46, 59, 201.
21 *TI*, pp. 534, 598.
22 Ibid., p. 535.
23 Steensgaard, *The Asian Trade Revolution*, p. 367.
24 N. Curzon, *Persia and the Persian Question*, London 1892 (reprinted Cass, 1966), vol. 1, p. 367. Petrushevsky using the same original sources gives the total output of silk in 1637/38 as a little less than 3.9 million lbs. See his *Keshavarzi va Monasebat-e Arzi dar Iran-e Ahd-e Moghul*, trans. by K. Keshavarz, Tehran, 1966, vol. 1, p. 290.
25 A. Seyf, 'Silk Production and Trade in Iran in the Nineteenth Century', *Iranian Studies*, vol. xvi (1983), nos. 1–2, p. 62.
26 *TI*, p. 491.
27 See A. Kinnier, *A Geographical Memoir of the Persian Empire*, London, 1813, p. 151. Lady Sheil, *Glimpses of Life and Manners in Persia*, London, 1856, p. 56. A. H. Mounsey, *A Journey Through the Caucasus and the Interior of Persia*, London, 1872, p. 94. E. Lorini, *Persia Economica Contemporanea ...*, Rome, 1900, p. 383.
28 *TI*, p. 523. Herbert, *Travels*, p. 126. Curzon, *Persia*, vol. 2, p. 23.
29 Curzon, *Persia*, vol. 2, p. 43. K. E. Abbott, 'Trade, Manufactures and Production of Various Cities ...' in FO 60/165. Dickson, 'Persia', in *Parliamentary Accounts and Papers 1884/85 LXXVI*. H. Schindler, *The Eastern Persia, Irak*, London, 1896, p. 120. Lorini, *Persia*, p. 383.
30 *TI*, p. 533.
31 Ibid., p. 530.
32 Herbert, *Travels*, p. 43. The list of foreign merchants residing in Amol is given on p. 178.
33 *TI*, p. 541.
34 Ibid., pp. 536, 544.
35 Ibid., p. 571.
36 Herbert, *Travels*, p. 74.
37 Abbott, 'Trade, Manufactures', in FO 60/165.
38 Herbert, *Travels*, p. 216.
39 Ibid., pp. 217–19.
40 Ibid., p. 226.
41 Ibid., p. 229.
42 Ibid., p. 227.
43 P. Sanson, *The Present State of Persia, 1683–91*, London, 1695, pp. 64–5.
44 See for example, M. Ravandi, *Tarikh-e Ijtema'i Iran*, Tehran, 1977, vol. 3, pp. 311–12.
45 K. Marx, *Capital*, Moscow, 1977, vol. 1, pp. 130–1.
46 *TI*, p. 513.
47 Steensgaard, *The Asian Trade Revolution*, p. 386. See also *TI*, pp. 554–7.
48 *TI*, p. 536.
49 Ibid., p. 572.
50 Petrushevsky, *Keshavarzi va Monsebat*, vol. 1, p. 216.
51 *TI*, p. 574.

52. J. Fryer, *A New Account of East India and Persia – Being Nine Years of Travels, 1672–81*, New edition, London, 1915, vol. 3, pp. 24–5.
53. *TI*, p. 573.
54. A. K. S. Lambton, *Landlord and Peasant in Persia*, Oxford, 1969, p. 129.
55. *TI*, p. 597.
56. Mounsey, *A Journey*, p. 182.
57. *TI*, p. 597.
58. Ibid., p. 598.
59. Ibid., pp. 587–92. Like most of the Soviet historians whose works appeared in *farsi* (Persian), the authors give a distorted account of the situation. Neither the Tsar nor Lenin would ever have dreamt that Soviet historians would present the invasion as an attempt 'to save the Christians', or 'to help the *Gilanese* to fight against the Afghans', see p. 588.
60. Ibid., p. 598.
61. J. Hanway, *An Historical Account of the British Trade over the Caspian Sea*, London, 1754, vol. 1, p. 170. A. A. Amin, *British Interests in the Persian Gulf*, Leiden, 1967, p. 16.
62. M. R. Aroonova, K. Z. Ashrafian, *Doulat-e Nader Shah Afshar*, trans. by H. Moumeni, Tehran, 1977, pp. 267–97.
63. Lambton, *Landlord*, p. 132.
64. Ibid., p. 132.
65. Hanway, *Historical*, vol. 1, p. 141.
66. Aroonova/Ashrafian, *Doulat*, p. 88.
67. Spilman (ed.), *Journey*, pp. 7–8.
68. Ibid., pp. 26–7.
69. Gambroon Diary, quoted in A. A. Amin, *British Interest*, p. 19.
70. Ibid., p. 19.
71. Hanway, *Historical*, vol. 1, pp. 157–8.
72. Aroonova/Ashrafian, *Doulat*, p. 109.
73. Hanway, *Historical*, vol. 1, p. 156.
74. Ibid., p. 141.
75. Aroonova/Ashrafian, *Doulat*, pp. 89–90.
76. Ibid., p. 109.
77. Hanway, *Historical*, vol. 1, pp. 156, 296.
78. Ibid., pp. 156, 158. Herbert, *Travels*, p. 202.
79. Hanway, *Historical*, vol. 1, p. 164.
80. *TI*, pp. 610–12.
81. Hanway, *Historical*, vol. 1, p. 160.
82. J. Spilman (ed.), *A Journey Through Russia into Persia in the Year 1739*, London, 1742, p. 38. This is, in fact, Elton's travel account.
83. Lambton, *Landlord*, p. 132.
84. Aroonova/Ashrafian, *Doulat*, p. 275.
85. Ravandi, *Tarikh*, vol. 3, p. 166.
86. Hanway, *Historical*, vol. 1, pp. 171, 297.
87. Ibid., p. 297.
88. For these departments, see Engels to Marx, 6 June 1853, in, Marx–Engels, *Selected Correspondence*, Moscow, 1975, p. 76.
89. Hanway, *Historical*, vol. 1, p. 150.
90. Spilman (ed.), *Journey*, p. 38.
91. Hanway, *Historical*, vol. 1, pp. 13, 355. The silk production of Gilan declined considerably and was said to have been only one-sixth of its former volume. See ibid., vol. 1, pp. 289–92.
92. Ibid., p. 350.
93. *TI*, p. 615.
94. Abdur-Razzaq b. Najaf Quli, *The Dynasty of the Qajars*, trans. by H. J. Brydges, London, 1833, pp. 18–24.
95. Burzon, *Persia*, vol. 2, p. 243.
96. H. Pottinger, *Travels in Baluchistan and Sind*, London, 1816, trans. by S. Goudarzi, Tehran, 1970, p. 255.

2

Silk and Socio-Economic Changes in Lebanon, 1860–1919

Kais Firro

One of the factors that seriously affected the socio-economic and ethnic structure of modern Lebanon was the agriculture, trade and industry of silk. In attempting to evaluate the influence of this factor on the development of Lebanon we have to turn to the nineteenth century, when the production of silk encompassed most of Mt. Lebanon's population and many of the Biqa' Valley's farmers and the coastal population of Beirut and Tripoli.

For the student of the modern history, economics and socio-ethnics of Lebanon, therefore, the study of silk production is important, since it involves a complex multiplicity of issues affecting Lebanese society.

The production of silk on Mt. Lebanon, in the Biqa' Valley and on the coast dates back to the seventeenth century. The nineteenth-century changes that occurred in the world silk markets and the economic penetration of the West into the region caused the expansion of silk production. New areas were taken up by the growing of mulberry trees and changes took place in the trade and manufacture of silk. This brought about the domination of the silk sector by the French market and capital. Most of the raw silk and cocoons were exported to France. Local mills were set up after 1840 and operated thanks to French capital. Direct contact, however, between the producers of silk cocoons and the French merchants was generally limited. The farmers sold their cocoon yields in advance to the mills or to the trading houses in Beirut and Tripoli. The silk trade and industry thus created a new, bourgeois, class.

This study will examine the impact of these changes on socio-economic and ethnic relations in Mt. Lebanon. The period covered by the discussion is from 1860 to 1919; the analysis, however, will necessarily refer to the years prior to and after this period. Silk of Mt. Lebanon and other areas of the region was known as Syrian silk. The term Syria is used in this study in the broad sense which includes the Lebanon of today.

one to see the constant differential in cocoon prices between the two ports. The difference was the outcome of the added value on cocoon prices devolved on the French merchants by those in Beirut. It may be assumed that an added value was also devolved on the Beirut merchants from the time of the purchase of the cocoons from the producers.

Cocoon prices were characterized by many fluctuations from year to year and even from month to month, as the price tables in Ducousso and in the French and English consular reports, as well as the reports of the Marseilles and Lyons Chambers of Commerce, all bear testimony. Table 4 attempts to track these prices from 1840 to 1911.

In order to ascertain the gap in cocoon prices between their first sale by the producers and their sale on the French market, a comparison should be made of the prices in the markets of Beirut and Marseilles. The *Compte Rendu* reports of the Marseilles Chamber of Commerce show that prices fluctuated there more than they did in Beirut. Thus in the 1870s the average price was about FF 16.5 per kilo, but prices actually swung between FF10 and FF30 per kg. Even if only one year

TABLE 4
PRICE OF AN *OKE** OF FRESH COCOONS IN BEIRUT MARKETS IN OTTOMAN PIASTERS**
5-Year Average

Period	Price	Period	Price
1836–1840	11.0***	1876–1880	23.0***
1841–1845	12.0***	1881–1885	23.4**
1846–1850	11.5***	1886–1890	22.7
1851–1855	20.5***	1891–1895	19.0
1856–1860	32.0***	1896–1900	20.0
1861–1865	31.0	1901–1905	22.0***
1866–1870	39.0	1906–1910	23.4
1871–1875	26.5***	1911	20.2

Sources: (1836–40), Ducousso, *op. cit.*, p. 108.
        (1841–60), Chevallier, *La société du Mont Liban*, p. 30.
        (1861–1911), Ducousso, *op. cit.*, pp. 110–11.
*   One *oke* = 1280 grams approximately.
** One piaster = 10/44 French francs approximately. It should be noted that the piaster devalued against the franc during the course of the period investigated: in 1889, it was 10/40 and in 1945, 10/42. There was also a difference between the official and the real value of the Piaster.
*** The average was based on partial prices, since the tables for these years were not complete.

of that decade is taken, it will be seen that prices changed from month to month. Nevertheless, the overall price curve for Marseilles over this entire period generally resembled that of Beirut: a rise lasting from 1850 to 1870, a fall at the beginning of the 1870s that lasted to the end of the century, when prices more or less stabilized (at around FF10 per kg.). A comparison of prices between the two markets shows that the value added was triple. If the average price in the 1870s was about FF4.3 per kg. (24.4 Piasters per *oke*) in Beirut, it was FF16.5 per kg. in Marseilles. In the 1890s, the average price in Beirut was FF3.2 per kg.; in Marseilles, FF9. In the first decade of the twentieth century, Beirut averaged FF3.4 and Marseilles FF10 per kg.[15]

Even when the cost of transportation and insurance in shipping the cocoons from Beirut and Tripoli to Marseilles is added to the price, the gap between the two markets still remains wide. Freight and insurance cost FF0.143–0.163 per kilo.[16] If to this is added the difference between the selling price on the Beirut markets and the buying price from the farmers, one can only conclude that the trade in cocoons produced by the farmers actually produced huge profits for the merchants.[17]

The developments that took place, especially in the second half of the nineteenth century, turned farmers into producers just of cocoons; and very few of these cocoons were spun in the simple mills of the farmers or even in the large mills that continued to operate according to traditional methods in the large cities of Syria. With the introduction of modern mills to Mt. Lebanon, there took place a significant decrease in local spinning.

The process started in 1840, when a merchant from Marseilles by the name of Nicolas Portalis established the first spinning mill in the village of Btater in the Jurd area of Mt. Lebanon. Portalis, who began his business in Egypt during the reign of Mohammad Ali, moved his activities in the East to Beirut with the aid of capital supplied by a wealthy Alexandrean merchant named Pastre. Portalis introduced into Lebanon the first mill that operated with the new techniques. The choice of the village of Btater was made in order to circumvent the Ottoman prohibition against Christian foreigners' purchasing land in the Empire. Portalis received the patronage of one of the Druze Sheikh Yusif Abd al-Malek. The site choice was also rooted in the geographical location of the village close to the Beirut–Damascus road in the heart of an area that was rich in silk-growing, water, trees (for heating the spinning pools), and Christian work ethic (most of the population in the region was Christian, despite its being under Druze *muqata'aji* control).

SILK IN LEBANON, 1860-1919

Portalis' spinning mill opened the door for other foreign entrepreneurs. An Englishman by the name of Scott set up the second mill a year later in the village of Chemlan in the Al-Gharb region on the land and with the patronage of the Druze *muqata'aji* Sheikh Mohammad Arslan. By 1851 Mt. Lebanon could count a number of modern spinning mills, which symbolized the start of a new process in the silk industry and influenced the economic and social life of the inhabitants.[18] The new mills led to a significant increase in the quantity of raw silk exported from Syria to France. Prior to the establishment of these mills, silk spun according to the traditional methods supplied the weaving mills of Aleppo, Damascus, Homs, and Hama and only a small proportion would reach Marseilles, under the designation Kesruwani silk (from Kesruwan) or Baladi silk.[19]

After 1864, a relatively peaceful period set in on Mt. Lebanon, which was the important centre for Syrian silk, and brought about the construction of still more spinning mills. Table 5 describes this development.

The spinning mills of Mt. Lebanon, especially those in the mixed areas — that is, the Shuf and Matn Mountains — constituted nearly three quarters of all such mills in the entire area called Syria in French sources. According to the French consular report of 1908, approximately 115 spinning mills were operating in Syria in 1907,[20] of which 75 were concentrated in this region. The rest were scattered on Mt. Lebanon and in near-by areas, distributed as follows:

Beirut	3 mills
Shuf	27
Matn	48
Keruwan	7
Batrun	9
Kurah	12
'Akar and Safitah	6
Zahleh	3
Total	115

By the start of World War I, according to Ducousso, only some 155-174 spinning mills were operating of the 194 that had been set up in Syria. Most were concentrated on Mt. Lebanon, especially the Shuf and Matn Mountains, as follows:[21]

Beirut Villayet	19 mills
Shuf	22
Matn	110
Kesruwan	9
Batrun	1
Kurah	13
Total	174

TABLE 5
NUMBER OF SPINNING MILLS IN LEBANON
1840–1914

Year	Total No.	No. in operation	French mills	English mills	Local mills	No. of pools	No. of employees
1840 (1)	1*	1	1	–	–		
1852 (2)	9*	9	5	2	2		830–850
1858 (3)	52*	?	12	–	40		
1867 (4)	67	?	10	2	55		
1871 (5)	85	?	10	2	73	4,000	3,500
1885 (6)	105	?	5	?2	98		
1893 (7)	126	?	8	?2	116	7,638	
1895 (8)	130	?	8	?2	120	8,000	
1900 (9)	150	?	9	?2	139	8,500	
1913 (10)	194	155	3	?2	189	10,886	

* Data are for Mt. Lebanon only.

Sources: (1) Chevallier, *La Société du Mont Liban*, p. 210.
        (2) Issawi, *op. cit.*, pl. 57. The number of workers refers to 1850 and is according to Chevallier, *op. cit.*, p. 219.
        (3) Farley, James Lewis, *Two Years in Syria*, London 1858, p. 224.
        (4) Ducousso, *op. cit.*, p. 125.
        (5) F.O. *British Consular Report, Beirut, March 1872*, p. 843. The number of employees refers to 1875 and appears in report of 31 Dec. 1875.
        (6) Ducousso, *op. cit.*, p. 127.
        (7) *Moniteur Officiel du commerce*, Beyrouth, No. 196, 1894 and *British Consular Report, Beirut*, No. 1626, 23 July 1895.
        (8) *Moniteur Officiel du commerce*, Beyrouth, 15 Décembre 1896, p. 348.
        (9) Verney & Dambmann, *op. cit.*, pp. 648–9. According to other sources, the number of pools was 9,000; see Bourgand, *op. cit.*, p. 38.
        (10) Ducousso, *op. cit.*, pp. 132, 156.

All reports of the period cite the fact that the number of mills in operation at the end of the 1890s was fewer than the number established. The French consul reported in 1908 that the number of mills was diminishing each year. In 1907, the number decreased no less than 10 per cent from that of the previous year. The number of pools that were operated also became fewer, declining from 7,500 in 1906 to 6,500 in 1907.[22] By 1913, there were only 8,669 pools being worked of a total of 10,866[23] that had been set up.

Although the number of locally owned mills increased, French-owned mills continued to be the largest ones up to the First World War; they also had the greatest output capability owing to the large number of pools in each mill and the newest machinery. The average number of pools in locally owned mills was 50; the number in French mills averaged more than 120 and, in some instances, there were as many as 200 pools or more. Ducousso's table of Syrian mills shows that in 1913 there were 9,450 pools, of which 1,150 − some 12 per cent − belonged to the large French-owned mills,[24] and this was at a time when but three of the 194 mills in Syria were French owned. Between 1900 and 1905 there had been eight French mills, but these boasted a total of 832−850 pools.[25]

The decrease in the number of French mills toward the end of the period being investigated was brought on by difficult management problems: absentee owners residing in France who employed local managers but did not give them a free hand in an industry that operated according to demand in France and the fluctuations of the local cocoon market.[26]

The small number of French-owned mills continued, nevertheless, to produce fine silk − *soie grège à grand extra*. Its quality was superior to that of the other mills in Syria.[27] The French mills were technologically modern. For example, the Palluat and Testenoire mills in the village of Qrayyeh in the Matn region, which had been established in 1862, were the first to employ mechanical power and modern methods of heating the pools. Those mills were sold in 1900 to the trading house of Veuve Guérin et fils. Improvements and new equipment were introduced in 1903 and 1908.[28]

The three French-owned mills that remained by the beginning of World War I manufactured no more than 10 per cent − or 34,900 kg. − of the overall output of Syrian silk.[29] While the French mills were becoming fewer in number, the number of Lebanese-owned mills was growing, particularly from the 1870s. Two explanations account for this trend: (1) local silk brokers and merchants managed during the 1850s and 1860s to accumulate capital, which they invested in building their own mills;[30] (2) capital from Lyons continued to finance the silk trade, including the local spinning mills. A Lebanese/Syrian who wanted to build a 40-pools mill could do so with a capitalization of FF8,000−10,000. This sum, however, was insufficient to operate the mill and for that he needed capital that he would receive yearly in credit and which he would pay off during the course of the year, generally in the form of silk.[31] At times, local mill owners would receive the necessary capital from Beirut bankers; the loan bore an interest rate of 10 per cent or more and a mortgage on the property was secured as collateral. Beirut bankers and money-lenders thus became an important link in the silk trade because, for their loans, they too received silk, which they exported to Lyons.[32]

SOCIAL CHANGES

The establishment of spinning mills by the local population — generally those who were silk merchants and agents — brought about revolutionary social changes in Lebanon. There is no doubt that Lebanese feudalism began its decline prior to 1861 as a result of the weakening status of the sheikhs during the time of Bachir al-Shehabi II (1788–1840), as a result of the farmers' revolt, and as a result of the formal abrogation of feudalism in the organizational agreement ('Le Réglement Organique') of *mutasarrifiyah* (semi-autonomy) of 1861.[33] The silk trade and the construction of mills after 1861, however, completed this decline, led to a new bourgeois class, and perpetuated Christian ascendancy in Lebanon.

The weakness of the Druze *muqata'ajis*, which continued to be tied to land wealth, was felt even before 1861. In 1850, the Druze prince Amin Arslan expressed his concern and the concern of his community at the involvement of the merchants and spinning mills, which in his opinion undermined the situation in the area to the benefit of the Christian population.[34]

Documents from the private Archives of the Jumblatt family illustrate the dependence of the *muqata'ajis* on merchants. In 1843, Nu'man Jumblatt, one of the most powerful *muqata'ajis*, was indebted to the *hawajahs* (merchants): Mikhail Seidah, Bsharah Atallah, Griffor and Niqula Murad. He pledged to pay off his debts in the silk season. In one of the debt contracts Nu'man mortgaged a portion of his land in Shuifat Village.[35] This was two decades earlier. After 1861, the process of decline in the economic power of the *muqata'ajis* grew more rapid. At the same time, there crystallized a bourgeois class that was connected with the silk trade and was mainly Christian. This class set up almost 780 silk-exporting companies in Beirut, in addition to spinning mills, which were spread over Mt. Lebanon.

An examination of the names of these companies shows that they were bought in the main by Lebanese Christians, with the number of foreign-owned companies not exceeding six. The most conspicuous of the Lebanese families in these ventures were: Bassul, Far'un, Sabbagh, Fayad, Lahud, Haik, Bustani, Khayyat, Khuri, Naqqash and others. The Bassul company alone exported toward the end of the period being investigated almost 63,000 kg. of silk annually, the Far'un company 34,800 kg.; both of these quantities exceeded the shipments of French firms like Veuve Guérin et fils, which exported 27,600 kg. a year. Lahud company exported almost 10,000 kg. a year and the Fayad and Sabbagh companies exported close to 7,500 kg. each.[36] Thus the four largest Lebanese companies could export approximately 30 per cent of all Syrian silk exports.

These merchants were involved in all economic activities connected with the silk trade. Some of them were even capitalist farmers and mill owners. The most striking example of the families that were involved in all areas of the silk trade was the Lahud family, which set up in Jebayl a 100-pool mill and who through their income from the silk trade and the profits from the mill increased their ownership of mulberry plantations in the vicinity of Jebayl and managed with their money to tie up the young farmers.[37]

The Fayad family owned three export companies and three mills in the Shuf Mountains. The Far'un family had, in addition to an export company, ten mills: three in the village of Mashta, three in Qubiyat, two in Safitah, and two in Andqiyat.[38] Most of the local mill owners in the vilayet of Beirut and Lebanon Mountain that are listed in Ducousso's book[39] are Christian, with only a few Druze or Sunnis. Of the 23 mills in the Shuf, two were owned by Druzes (Sa'id Hamdan and Mohammad Salim Dau in the village of Dair-Kuchi and Sa'id Abu Isma'il in B'aqlin village). The remainder were owned by local Christians, the most notable among whom were the Khuri family, with partnership in four mills, the Fayad, Baddura, and Ni'mi families, with two each; and the Awn family, which was in partnership with the Khuri family in two large mills and owned a large mill of its own in Damur.

Christians owned nine mills in Kesruwan, the most prominent of them being Elias Qasis, who owned two of the three largest in the area. Christians owned 12 mills in the Kurah area.

Of the 104 spinning mills in the Matn area, only five belonged to Druzes: the mill in Qurnail village belonged to Ahmad Husayn Abu al-Husn, that in Bzabdin village belonged to Ali Abu Ali, in Salima village two mills belonged to the Misri family, a mill in al-Metayn village belonged to Bachir Nuwahid. Christians owned 95 mills, the most notable owners being the Zalzal family and the Aql family, with three each; and Yusuf Francis Tu'mi with three, two of which were the largest in the area after the French-owned mills.

In the vilayet of Beirut, there were 18 mills. Four small mills, each with one pool, belonged to Moslem owners. The rest were owned by Christians, the most prominent being the Far'un and Shiha families, who together possessed nine mills, which were among the largest in Syria.

The spinning mills may have had local Lebanese ownership, but they operated with French capital. In early May of each year, they needed money in order to transmit advances to the farmers, who sold their cocoon yields in advance to the mills. The large sums were necessary for the cocoon purchase period, and the money transfers took place between May and July.[40]

The silk trading houses in France, particularly those in Lyons, would each year transfer to Beirut and to other cities some FF6–7.5 million, which was half the required capital for purchasing the Syrian cocoons, in order to provide the mills with advances.[41] These transfers constituted close to a third of the total value of Syrian silk that reached Lyons.[42] The French trading houses in Lyons, Marseilles and Paris would supply the credit to cocoon growers and the mills according to the type of relationship they had with businesses in Beirut and Sidon. Trading houses represented in Lebanon by an agency of their own – like Veuve Guérin et fils (Lyons), which owned a large mill in Qrayyeh in the Matn; or a trading house like Terrail Payen et Cie (Lyons), which was represented in Beirut by Eynard; or Meyrieux Peillon et Cie (Marseilles), which was represented by Mourgue d'Alque Ney et Cie; or Boutet Frères et Cie (Paris) which was represented by the Nasr family – all these could give advances directly to the mills and receive silk in exchange. As for a trading house that had representation in Lebanon but no money locally, money would be transferred to bankers or mills and silk shipments received in return. These two systems were utilized with the large mills. As for the others, however – those which constituted the majority and belonged to local residents – they received the money needed for their activities through private bankers, but this cost them more than did credit received by means of the two other systems.

The private banker – *sarraf* – took as collateral for his advances mortgages on the assets of the mills and charged a rate of interest that amounted to 7–9 per cent; the mill was obliged to sell this banker silk, the value of which was double or triple the sum of the credit given. In addition, the mills paid a 2 per cent agent's commission on the sale of the silk in Lyons. The banker had to supply the trading house in France with silk in exchange for the credit he received. His final calculations were made at the expense of the mills. Thus he would receive from the mills another payment for his exchange-rate losses and also obligate the mills with a special payment of silk that was to be deposited with him in order to adjust his bill to the final sale to the Lyons trading house.[43]

Thus the Lyons trading houses provided the principal stimulus to the manufacture and trade of silk. In 1871, the owners of these firms, merchants and industrialists, organized an association, to which almost 80 members belonged, within the framework of the French Textile Union.[44] It should be noted that the silk merchants of Lyons were aided by the reports of the French consul-general in Beirut. These detailed reports began to arrive in Lyons from 1865. In 1883, the association of silk merchants set up a communications office with Beirut in order to receive information on the trade and industrial situation there.[45]

The Lyons trading houses in effect controlled Syrian silk manufacture and trade. They supplied the required capital both for trade and for spinning. They fixed the prices in Syria in accordance with the price of silk on the world market. In such a process, composed of a series of stages, the cocoon producers and the mill owners came out with less profit and were more vulnerable with every price decrease. The silk and cocoon exporters, meanwhile, and the Beirut bankers, who were the brokers between the silk manufacturers and the cocoon producers, were less hurt by price decreases. The middlemen could compensate for their losses when prices fell through a 'cleansing' of their accounts with the mills and the cocoon producers. The mill owners, who were exposed to the risks inherent in price fluctuations, could compensate for part of their losses through a clearing of accounts with the cocoon producers. There is no doubt that the nature of the silk trade, which extended for a period of three to six months and sometimes more and which was conducted by selling in advance and by means of credit given to the end of the trade period, enabled the brokers and mill owners to make up their losses at the expense of the farmers, the producers of the cocoons.

In addition to the farmer–cocoon producer class, the Lebanese workers, both male and female, who came from the rural population, also profited little from an industry and trade that could manifest huge profits. The salary of mill employees was not uniform, but changed according to skill and job and season. A mill employed on average about three managers, each responsible for a part of the work process; three or four children for collecting wastes and doing other small jobs; a woman responsible for sorting the silk; and one spinner for each pool (with an average of 50 pools per mill in Syria).[46] The spinners, whether male or female, were divided into four categories in accordance with their work skill, the salary of each category being different from one another. A description of this division of labour and wages is given in Table 6.

The average daily salary of women in the mills was FF0.53–0.73. This average matches the general salary of women in the Ottoman

TABLE 6
DIVISION OF LABOUR IN LEBANESE SPINNING MILLS AND DAILY WAGES

Job	No. employed	Wage per employee in summer (piasters)	Wage per employee in summer (FF)	Wage per employee in winter (piasters)	Wage per employee in winter (FF)
Manager	1	8–12	1.36–2.04		
Pool heater	1	8–10	1.36–1.70		
Wastes collector	3–4	1–3	0.17–0.51		
Wastes sorter	1	2.5–4.5	0.43–0.77	3.5–4	0.60–0.68
Master spinner	one of these per pool	5–6	0.85–1.02	3.5–4	0.60–0.68
Spinner, Grade B	one of these per pool	4.25–4.5	0.72–0.77	3–3.25	0.51–0.55
Spinner, Grade C	one of these per pool	3–4	0.51–0.68	2.5–3	0.42–0.51
Apprentice	one of these per pool	1–2.5	0.17–0.42	1–1.75	0.17–0.30

Source: 'L'industrie de la Soie à Beyrouth et au Liban', M.O.C., Beyrouth 16 Décembre 1907 – M.O.C., Beyrouth 16 Janvier 1908, pp. 55–8. Ducousso, *op. cit.*, pp. 156–7.
* A piaster was worth FF0.17 in the mills; its value outside ranged between FF0.18 and FF0.22. A work day in the summer consisted of 13 hours; in the winter, 9–10 hours.

Empire who worked in weaving or agriculture. At the end of the nineteenth century, women's salaries in agriculture and weaving in the areas of the Empire averaged FF0.50–0.75 per 10-hour working day. Only in certain areas were the wages lower, as in Ankara and Adana, where they averaged FF0.35–0.50 per day.[47] The average salary of men working in spinning mills reached FF1.36–1.87 per day, putting it somewhat above the average wages of those in weaving and agriculture, which paid FF1.20–1.50 and FF1.00–1.50 per day, respectively.[48]

Except for the large French-owned mills, the spinning mills did not operate throughout the year: some were open for nine months, others for as little as three. Thus the annual income for a Lebanese mill worker amounted, in dry figures, to FF90–150. By way of comparison, industrial workers in France earned a yearly income at the end of the nineteenth century and the beginning of the twentieth of FF1,200 and more. The Lebanese workers were in fact an example of those who supplied Western industries with processed raw material.[49]

Toward the end of our period, the number of workers in the silk mills of Lebanon amounted to 14,000, of whom 12,000 were women.[50] The total figure is a large one, considering the fact that the entire population of Mt. Lebanon numbered 200,000–250,000 by the end of the century.[51] In addition, such a number of salaried workers in one sector was considered high in an agricultural country like Syria (or the Ottoman Empire as a whole).

Even though the income of the workers in the spinning mills was low, there is no doubt that it constituted a certain addition to the family income of Mt. Lebanon farmers. Most of the mill workers came from farming families who grew cocoons or other crops. Some of the workers themselves never completely neglected agriculture, as the mills did not operate year round in the main. Nevertheless, the spinning mills no doubt brought about the proletarianization of the farmers of Mt. Lebanon.

Work in the mills had an ethnic character. Most workers were Maronite Christians, Orthodox or Catholic. Druzes numbered only about 1,000 of the total number. Of the 13,000 Christians, some 8,500 were Maronite, 2,500 Orthodox, and 2,000 Catholic.[52] This ethnic proportion did not correspond to the population distribution. Whereas the percentage of Christians in the mills came to 92.8 per cent, their percentage among the population of Mt. Lebanon was 79.7 per cent. The percentage of Druzes in the mills – 7.2 per cent – was lower than their percentage of the population, 12.4 per cent. Of the 174 active mills in Lebanon at the end of the period there were fully 132 concentrated in the Matn and Shuf areas. If one considers that these areas contain the entire Druze population of the time and that the large French mills which employed more than 2,000 workers were also found in these two areas, then one can readily see that the percentage of Druze mill employees was indeed quite tiny compared to the Christian. Tables 7 and 8 present the division of the population according to area and ethnic group and give the percentage of mill employees among each group.

Table 8 demonstrates that the silk industry in Lebanon was a Christian industry; both the owners and the mill workers were mainly Christian – fully 93 per cent in each case. Even in the mixed areas of Matn and the Shuf, where the Christians constituted 66.6 per cent of the population, some 92 per cent of mill owners and of their employees were Christian. Although the Druzes comprised 26.3 per cent

TABLE 7
DISTRIBUTION OF LEBANESE POPULATION BY AREA AND RELIGION ACCORDING TO OTTOMAN REGISTER OF 1888, CALCULATED BY CUINET AND McCARTHY*

		AREA DISTRIBUTION		
Qada	% of Total	Ottoman Register	McCarthy	Cuinet
Shuf	24.0	47,966	56,494	95,936
Matn	23.2	46,390	54,639	92,792
Kersruwan	19.9	39,680	46,735	79,455
Batrun	15.9	31,770	37,419	63,568
Jezzin	5.4	10,864	12,796	21,743
Zahlih	4.2	8,292	9,766	16,674
Kurah	6.0	11,127	14,127	23,990
Dair al-Qamar	1.4	2,712	3,294	5,372
Totals:				
Ottoman Register		119,668		
McCarthy			235,169	
Cuinet				399,530
% of Total		100.0	100.0	100.0

Sources: McCarthy, J. 'The population of Ottoman Syria and Iraq', *A.A.S.*, Vol. 15, No. 1, March, 1981, p. 23. Cuinet, V., *Syrie, Liban et Palestine*, Paris, 1896, p. 211.

* Both Cuinet and McCarthy calculated the population by relying on the Ottoman Register; therefore, their percentages were identical.

of the population of these areas, they owned but 5.3 per cent of the mills and made up only 7.8 per cent of the workers. To these statistics can be added the Beirut merchants and brokers, the overwhelming majority of whom were Christian. The inescapable conclusion is that the silk manufacture and trade sector commenced the social and economic change that corresponded with perpetuating the political

TABLE 7 (continued)

RELIGIOUS DISTRIBUTION OF CUINET

Muslims		Catholics					Other Christians		
Sunni	Shi'i	Maronite	Greek	Armenian	Syrian	Latin	Syrian & Greek Orthodox	Protestant	Druze
8,972	1,044	28,268	7,312				9,000	600	40,140
268	1,590	56,380	6,752			14	18,112	68	9,608
748	6,800	68,600	1,148	30	30	55	2,044		
740	4,352	53,040	872			18	4,356	10	
344	2,920	11,812	6,232				356	15	64
144	60	2,676	11,436			45	2,268	45	
2,360	80	3,640	16			2	17,892		
		4,664	704						
7,995	9,922	135,259	20,298		12		31,923	393	29,367
13,576	16,846	229,680	34,470	30	30	138	54,203	738	49,812
3.4	4.2	57.5	8.6		0.1		13.6	0.2	12.4

ascendancy of the Christians, as it manifested itself in the agreements of 1861 and 1864, which laid the foundation for the *Mutasarrifyah* of Mt. Lebanon.

The flourishing or the decline of silk weaving in Syria was doubtless a function of the world silk market as well as of the production of cocoons in Syria. This industry, however, was also affected by changes that took place in the labour market on Mt. Lebanon, where most of the mills were constructed. At the end of the nineteenth and beginning

TABLE 8
POPULATION, SPINNING MILLS AND MILL EMPLOYEES IN MT. LEBANON AND IN MATN & SHUF REGIONS

	Population According to McCarthy			Mills and Employees in 1911			
		N.	%	Mills	%	Mill Employees	%
Mt. Lebanon:							
	Maronite	135,259				8500	
	Greek Orthodox	31,923				2500	
	Greek Catholic	20,298				2000	
	Total Christian	187,480	79.6	144	93.0	13,000	92.9
	Druze	29,367	12.4	7	4.5	1,000	7.1
	Other	18,322	7.9	1	0.6		
Total Mt. Lebanon		235,169	100.0	155*	100.0	14,000	100.0
Matn & Shuf							
	Christian	74,014	66.6	121	91.7	11,900**	92.2
	Druze	29,228	26.3	7	5.3	1,000	7.8
	Other	7,890	7.1	1	0.7		
Total Matn & Shuf		111,132	100.0	132*	100.0	12,900	100

Sources: Population – McCarthy, *op. cit.*, p. 23
Mills and Employees – Ducousso, *op. cit.*, pp. 132, 156, 216–23

* To this figure there have to be added another 3 mills, foreign-owned, which constituted 1.9 per cent of all mills on Mt. Lebanon and 2.3 per cent of all mills in the Shuf and Matn.

** The number of mill employees in the Shuf and Matn was calculated from the number of pools (8,044 of 8,669 pools) on Mt. Lebanon of the twentieth century, both the French and English consular reports began to attribute the industry's decline to the emigration of the work force from Mt. Lebanon. This migration had two destinations: America and Beirut.

In 1800, the city of Beirut was a relatively small port city of 6,000 population. By the end of the nineteenth century, it had become one of Syria's largest cities, its population having reached 120,000–130,000 (see Table 9).

TABLE 9
POPULATION OF BEIRUT, 1800–1914

Year	Population
1800	6,000
1830	9,000
1860	46,600
1863	60,000
1865	80,000
1870	70,000
1875	80,000
1895	120,000
1908	136,000
1914	130,000

Source: Chevallier, *La Société du Mont Liban*, pp. 52–292.

It is true that the increase in the population of Beirut continued throughout the nineteenth century and into the twentieth; however, this growth intensified after 1875 because of the events that took place in Mt. Lebanon in the 1860s. Toward the end of the century, the migration to Beirut intensified. Thus the French consular reports in the 1890s started to emphasize the rapid development of the city. One such report in 1894, describing this development at the end of the 1880s and start of the 1890s, stated that some 250–300 houses were built each year, or approximately a house a day.[53] Another consular report estimated the population of Beirut in 1895 at 130,000 to 140,000 and attributed the increase to the exodus from the interior or Mt. Lebanon.[54] The English consular reports also stressed the rapid construction of the 1890s[55] and pointed to the rise in the percentage of the Christian population of the city, and the drop in the Moslem population, owing to the immigration from Mt. Lebanon. By 1894, the number of Christians (70,000) surpassed the number of Moslems in Beirut, which then had a total population of 120,000.[56]

Emigration further intensified in the 1890s and at the start of the twentieth century. According to one English consular report, nearly 4,500 Christians left the country in 1892, most of them from Mt. Lebanon: 2,500 went to Brazil, 500 to other countries in South America, 500 to North America, 500 to Australia and 500 to New Zealand and other areas. The same report cites the fact that the emigration was continuing apace despite the restrictions placed in the way of would-be migrants by the Ottoman regime and despite the problems they met with at their destinations. Few of the migrants, who were mainly from the poorer classes, remained abroad. Their purpose was to accumulate as much money as possible over a four- or five-year period and then return to their villages.[57]

Despite the restrictions and the difficulties, emigration continued strong, and in 1893 some 3,000 left from Beirut and 4,000 from Tripoli.[58] In 1896, 5,500 Lebanese, most of them Christian, sailed from Beirut to emigrate abroad; for the first time, the number included Druzes. The destination of most was South America.[59] The number of emigrants leaving from Beirut came to 13,000 in 1899, most of them from Mt. Lebanon and only a small number from the city of Beirut itself. More than two thirds of the emigrants went to the United States, Canada, Brazil, and Argentina; the rest to Australia, South Africa, and various Pacific Ocean island countries.[60] The United States took tough measures in 1900 against migrants in its 'Regulations against Paupers', which limited the entry of foreigners. Nevertheless, nearly 10,000 Lebanese emigrants went that year to South America.[61]

In the 1890s most of the migration was temporary, as described above. In the twentieth century, however, it became permanent, as entire families left Lebanon. The average number of departures came to 4,000–5,000 a year.[62] The continuous emigration from the 1880s resulted in the departure from Mt. Lebanon of one third of its population.[63] By 1908, the number of permanent Lebanese immigrants came to 100,000.[64]

The emigration from Mt. Lebanon explains, according to the French consular reports, the relative decline of the silk industry at the end of our period.[65] In 1907, there were only 115 mills in operation of the 174 established on Mt. Lebanon. The number of mill workers grew smaller from year to year; in 1907 it was 10 per cent smaller than in the previous year.[66] Ducousso also attributes the decline of the mills to this emigration, which by 1911 had led to a decrease of 15–20 per cent in the number of spinning mill employees in Syria.[67]

Even though cocoon production in Syria did not drop between 1890 and 1913 compared to previous years (see Table 2), the continued emigration did to some extent harm production in that some of the migrants came from the population of cocoon growers.[68] By the time of World War I, emigration had definitely hurt the silk industry[69] and aroused the concern of the Lyons silk merchants.[70]

What caused the Lebanese to migrate in such large numbers? Did the changes that were and had been taking place in the growing and manufacturing of silk given any impetus to the migration? Was the decline in the price of silk and cocoons during the 1890s sufficient motivation?

Thomas Philipp, in his article on Syrian migration to Egypt, attributes the emigration of the Lebanese to the complex of changes that were taking place in society owing to the integration of Lebanon into the world economy. The silk trade and industry in Lebanon were among the sectors affected by this integration. The crises in the silk industry do not in themselves explain the emigration, since similar crises also occurred during the eighteenth century. The changes that took place in the second half of the nineteenth century, however, deepened the integration of the cocoon producers and Syrian merchants into the world silk market; these changes made them more dependent on the world market and prevented them from influencing the prices that were set in France. Thus the migration was an integral part of all the changes that befell the silk industry. Summing up the principal motives for emigration, Philipp wrote that economic pressure was the main reason for the emigration from Syria and Lebanon during the last third of the nineteenth century.[71]

The question remains, though: was there indeed economic pressure in Lebanon that propelled emigration? Was the economic situation on Mt. Lebanon more difficult than in other areas of Syria, to the extent that the majority of Syrian emigrants came from Mt. Lebanon? Why did not that same economic pressure motivate the Druzes to emigrate in the same proportions as the Christians? Why were most of the emigrants from Syria and Lebanon during that period Christian?[72] Was the economic situation of the Christians in Syria more difficult than that of the rest of the population?

The use of the term 'economic pressure', without being defining, gives the impression that conditions in the areas from which there was large-scale migration were worse than in other areas of Syria. In order to better understand the effect of the economic factor on this migration, one has to ask not only why people migrate, but also why they do not. This question transfers the discussion of migration from the economic aspect to other aspects that can, at times, prove more important. Peterson comments on this in his article on the social aspects of migration, by pointing out that in most of the general models dealing with migration, the assumption exists that these mass movements are characterized by economic forces, but that this assumption is not always correct.[73] As to the motives of the Lebanese migration, it is possible to make a far-reaching assumption that the Christians emigrated precisely because they possessed the economic means enabling them at least to pay the fare to America or Australia or other places. Thus the motivation for the emigration of the Christians from Lebanon was complex; it cannot be explained simply by 'economic pressure'.

The Christians in Lebanon were affected more than the rest of the population of Syria by Western penetration into the region. This penetration not only started the economic changes, it also led to normative alterations among the Christians that were reflected in changes in their way of life and expectations for the future. The silk industry, tied as it was to the world silk market, created a kind of monoculture on Mt. Lebanon that was accompanied by a decline in the traditional agricultural crops. By World War I, the income from raising cocoons and from work in the silk mills amounted to 75 million piasters or close to FF17 million. By contrast, revenue from all other branches of agriculture amounted to 30 million piasters (nearly 6.8FF million).[74] The agriculture, trade, and manufacture of silk expanded the use of money on Mt. Lebanon, which process was not mirrored in other agricultural areas of Syria. Furthermore, the agriculture and manufacture of silk were characterized by relatively frequent ups and downs in consequence of the many fluctuations in the prices of cocoons and silk. Price decreases had great effect on the rural population, which was tied to the world market. The agricultural area of Lebanon was limited: of the general area of 320,000 hectares of Mt. Lebanon, the Lebanese worked only 17,500 hectares during this period, or but 5.5 per cent of the area. As it was, the cultivable land constituted only 20,000 hectares or 6.25 per cent of the area,[75] which did not give the dense population[76] much alternative. Lebanon could not supply its population with food and was dependent for its grain on the Biqa' and on Hauran. Every drop in silk industry revenue meant a decrease in grain-buying power. The rises and falls in silk prices understandably produced psychological tension among the Lebanese. The population that worked with silk accustomed itself to such changing conditions, which were fraught with risks.

Under such conditions, the migration adventure became a viable, magnetic alternative. The United States, Latin America, Australia, and other places drew the Lebanese immigrants and inflated their expectations. Despite the fact that these hopes were not always realized and that there were even disappointments,[77] emigration continued with all its risks because it began to bear fruit. Many immigrant Lebanese transferred money back home or returned with the money to live in their homeland differently from the way they formerly lived. The large money transfers raised the income level of Mt. Lebanon and contributed to the relative enriching of its population in comparison to other rural populations in Syria. According to the English consular reports, the money transfers of the Lebanese migrants at the beginning of the 1890s ranged between 10 million and 12 million piasters a year, or FF2.27 to FF2.72 million.[78] The same sources reported that by 1913, the amount of these transfers had risen to between 50 million and 75 million piasters, or FF11.35−17.025 million.[79] Most of the transfers came to Mt. Lebanon. Ruppin estimates that money transfers to the *Mutasarrifiyah* of Lebanon amounted to 90 million piasters yearly before World War I. This sum is equivalent to 20,430,000 francs, which constituted 41 per cent of the total annual income of the Mutasarrifiyah of the Mountain.[80] It approximately equalled the revenue from the export of Syrian silk.[81]

There is no doubt that the large money transfers to Mt. Lebanon saved many Lebanese from dependence on silk monoculture, as these sums exceeded the annual income from raising cocoons and spinning silk, activities which produced only 34 per cent of the total income of the Mountain. Thus in analysing the reasons for the continuing migration, there must be an understanding of the dynamics of this migration. A successful wave of migration invites other migration waves. The 'economic pressure' of Mt. Lebanon, then, should not be understood as the given situation for the whole period of this study nor as the cause for the migration.

The migration of the Druzes was modest prior to the war, especially when compared to the Christians. During this period, though, the Druzes did migrate to Hauran as a result of the complex of changes that took place on Mt. Lebanon during the nineteenth century. For one thing, the Druzes lost their political and economic standing on Mt. Lebanon. For another, the Druzes did not produce a new wealthy class that was connected with the silk trade. Even the Druze *muqata'ajis* did not integrate into the class of newly rich that created the economic integration with the West. The Druze *muqata'ajis* and the Druze farmers continued to work in agriculture. They were among the cocoon growers and so were vulnerable to crises in the trade and manufacture of silk. A combination of economic and political factors brought about the emigration of many Druzes to Hauran. During the second half of the nineteenth century, Hauran became the Druze centre in Syria. Thus the name of Jabal (Mt.) Druze was shifted from Mt. Lebanon to Mt. Hauran.[82]

The growing of silk in Lebanon shook the traditional socio-cultural frameworks of Mt. Lebanon; it led to social mobility, of which migration was one of the symptoms. If the motivation to emigrate was the complex of changes that befell the area, the silk industry, with all its implications for the economic, social and political life of the people, was a most important factor in this complex of changes that created the dynamics of emigration.

* * *

If the silk industry had a decisive effect on socio-economic change in Mt. Lebanon before World War I, the decline of this sector during the war brought real suffering to the area. The same integration that created dependence on the economy of the West caused the Lebanese to suffer during the war. The farmers who produced cocoons and silk in Lebanon and were accustomed to receiving their wages from this work upon the conclusion of the silk trade process were hurt the most, as the war halted this trade.[83] The war severely affected the normal life of the Lebanese. The cessation of the silk trade brought about a halt in the credit that the cocoon producers used to receive as advances. The Lebanese farmers, who were dependent on their food supply from other areas, could not buy their grain. The dependence on one crop prior to the war and the difficulty in making a rapid change from growing mulberry trees to growing grain and other commodities made it impossible for the Lebanese to satisfy their grain needs, since the Ottoman regime forbade the transport of grain to Mt. Lebanon during the war lest it fall into the hands of their enemies. Of the 175,000 hectares of cultivated land on Mt. Lebanon, only 7,533 hectares — 4.3 per cent — were allocated to wheat growing. The wheat yield did not exceed 12,728,800 kg. If one excludes from this figure the portion intended for new planting, there remained only 11,598,850 kg. of wheat for the consumption of the population of the area, which during the war numbered more than 300,000 people. The annual consumption of Lebanese grain per head was thus about 34 kg., or a mere 95 grams per day.[84]

The prevention of the entry of grain during the war created a grain shortage and led to starvation among the poor classes. Typhus broke out, and many people left for Hauran and the coastal plain in order to seek work and food. According to Croizat, who was sent to Syria in 1919 by the Lyons and Marseilles chambers of commerce, some 40 per cent of the Lebanese population had left the Mountain or died of starvation. On the coastal plain and in the Biqa', the mulberry trees began to be uprooted in order to clear the land for growing grain. On the Mountain, where the land was poor and the changing over of the area difficult, the farmers had to seed the plantations with grain.[85]

The war hit the silk trade hard. Trade was stopped in the Biqa' area, the mulberry trees disappeared almost completely, as witnessed by Beriel, who visited Syria after the war. Even on the coast, except for the area of Damur, the mulberry trees were uprooted in order to clear the land for other crops. On the Mountain, even though many mulberry plantations remained after the war, the farmers stopped tending them and turned to grain and vegetables. Only in the Zghortah area did there remain relatively good plantations for growing silk anew.[86]

The result of all this was a significant decrease in Syrian silk exports to Lyons after the war. The percentage of Syrian silk in Lyons silk imports fell from 6 per cent in 1913 to 2 per cent in 1919–20.[87] Even in 1922, when Syria managed to rehabilitate some of this industry, the percentage of Syrian silk consignments reaching Lyons did not exceed 2.4 per cent.[88] After the war, Syria was unable to return to the level of cocoon production that it had attained before the war. Despite attempts by the French to revive Syrian silk and despite the relative improvement in cocoon production between 1924 and 1930, silk agriculture in Syria became moribund. Table 10 describes the situation.

TABLE 10
FRESH COCOON PRODUCTION IN SYRIA (FRENCH MANDATE), 1930–34 (000 kg)

Year	Production	Year	Production	Year	Production	Year	Production
1910	6,100	1919	500	1924	2,860	1929	3,460
1911	6,000	1920	800	1925	2,900	1930	3,550
1912	6,000	1921	1,800	1926	2,960	1931	2,760
1913	6,100	1922	1,900	1927	3,185	1932	1,762
1914	6,100	1923	2,200	1928	3,350	1933	1,400
						1934	1,300

Source: Latron, 'La production et le commerce de la soie du Levant', *l'Asie Française*, Paris, Février 1935, p. 79.

Most of the Lebanese spinning mills were closed down; by the 1920s, there remained only some 1,000 pools in operation, with silk production down 10 per cent from what the mills had produced before the war.[89] These mills were unable to spin the quantity of cocoons produced. Many cocoons thus remained in the country. By the 1930s, there remained only the mills in the villages of Bayt-Meri, Bchamun, Ma'aser-Bayt-ed-Din, Ayn-Traz, Qrayyah and Bikfayya.[90]

The Syrian silk industry, which had put its imprint on Lebanese history for a hundred years, may be said to have died in the 1930s. It was an industry that had brought about revolutionary changes in the socio-economic life of Mt. Lebanon and the adjoining areas in the nineteenth century.

CONCLUSION

Because of the agriculture, manufacture, and trade in silk, Mt. Lebanon and the adjoining areas on the coast and in the Biqa' Valley underwent, during the second half of the nineteenth century and beginning of the twentieth century, a process that changed its socio-economic structure. During this period, these areas completed their full integration into the Western economy, silk being the chief cause of this integration. The silk and silk cocoon trade in Lebanon was controlled by the silk trading houses of Lyons and Marseilles. The French supplied the capital needed for the trade, the spinning mills, and even the agriculture of silk. In return, they received almost all the yield of raw silk and of cocoons. The cocoon producers, the merchants, and the brokers who exported the silk were all harnessed to French capital. Thus silk depended on the economic influence of the French in Syria.

The growing demand for silk in the markets of Lyons and Marseilles led to an expansion of the growing of mulberry trees and of cocoons to such an extent that the silk sector became a monoculture, particularly on Mt. Lebanon. The expansion of the trade and the establishment of the mills on Mt. Lebanon and the coastal area produced a newly rich class that was tied to French capital and influenced by the French way of life. This new class was predominantly Christian, so that the silk industry wore an ethnic look and perpetuated Christian dominance in the economy and society, which has had its effects on Lebanese history to this date. It is in this sense that silk aided other factors in bringing about the fall of the Druze ascendancy on Mt. Lebanon, which had been based on an agricultural and feudal society, and the start of an era of Christian ascendancy, based on the manufacture and trade of silk.

SILK IN LEBANON, 1860-1919

In spite of the relative economic prosperity that silk created, the sector itself was a cause of suffering for many groups, particularly the farmer population that grew cocoons. The crises that attacked the sector as a result of the many price fluctuations of the commodity often shook the normal life of this population, which was dependent on the silk market and on the supply of food from other areas. This dependency was one of the principal reasons for the period of hunger that struck Mt. Lebanon during World War I. The mobility that silk created in the population that was involved in the agriculture and manufacture of silk was not restricted to the socio-cultural sphere. It also included massive emigration across the sea, which in itself led to revolutionary changes in the economic, social, and cultural life of the Lebanese.

NOTES

1 A.M. Bourgaud, *Lyon et le commerce des soies avec le Levant*, Lyon, 1901, p. 34; A. Martineau, *Le Commerce français dans le Levant*, Paris, 1902, p. 160; G. Ducousso, *L'industrie de la soie en Syrie*, Paris and Beyrouth, 1913 and 1918, pp. 117–18. According to other estimates, the land covered by mulberry trees amounted to 28,000 hectares; see: Paul Huvelin, 'Que vaut la Syrie', Chambre de Commerce de Marseille (C.C.M., hereafter) Congrès Français de la Syrie 3, 4, et 5 Jan. 1919, Section économique, p. 18. There are even some estimates that go up to 30,000 hectares of covered land: Bériel, 'La Sériculture au Liban', *L'Asie Française*, supplément No. 5, Paris 1927, p. 119. According to Owen, in the 1890s mulberry were planted on about half of the cultivated land in Mt. Lebanon and its adjacent slopes, R. Owen, *The Middle East in the World Economy 1800–1914*, London and New York, 1981, p. 249.
2 Achard, 'Notes sur la Syrie', *L'Asie Française*, supplément No. 4, 1922, p. 97.
3 P. Clerget, *Les Industries de la soie en France*, Paris, p. 64.
4 B. Labaki, 'La filature de la soie dans le Sendjak du Mont Liban: Une Expérience de croissance industrielle dépendante, 1810–1914', *Arabica* (29), 1982, p. 85.
5 Ducousso, op. cit., pp. 184–91 and Owen, op. cit., p. 252.
6 C.C.M., *Compte rendu de la situation industrielle et commercialle* (hereafter, C.R.), Cocoons, p. 59 and 1870, p. 66.
7 The Syrian silk market was called *qaysariya*. It is possible to find such a place in most Syrian cities (Aleppo, Damascus, Beirut, Tripoli, Sidon, and others).
8 Martineau, op. cit., p. 146.
9 Ducousso, op. cit., pp. 63–71 and Owen, op. cit., pp. 154, 252.
10 Ibid., p. 105 and D. Chevallier, 'Lyon et la Syrie en 1919, Les bases d'une intervention', *Revue Historique*, Paris 1960, p. 296.
11 Ducousso, op. cit., p. 106 and Owen, op. cit., p. 154.
12 Ibid.
13 C.F. Volney, *Voyage en Syrie et en Egypte pendant les années 1782, 1784 et 1885* (2 vols, Paris, 1787) vol. II, p. 265.
14 D. Chevallier, *La Société du Mont Liban à l'Epoque de la révolution industrielle en Europe*, Paris, 1971, pp. 283–8 and Owen, op. cit., p. 253.
15 The average prices in Marseilles markets were computed from the Chamber of Commerce reports: C.R., Cocoons 1870–1914. The price in francs per kg. in Beirut markets was based on the following computation: 1 *oke* = approx. 1280 grams; 1 piaster = 10/44 French francs, approx.
16 Ducousso, op. cit., p. 112.

17 Ibid., p. 110. In addition to the gap between the buying price of the brokers and the selling price in Beirut or at the spinning mills, the price was influenced by several other expenditures, such as brokers' fees, freight rates, *étoffage* (stuffing), and ventilation charge, which came to more than 1 piaster per *oke*.
18 On the mills and their effect, see: Chevallier, *La Société du Mont Liban*, pp. 210–32.
19 Ducousso, op. cit., p. 124.
20 *Moniteur officiel du commerce* (hereafter M.O.C.), Beyrouth, 16 Jan. 1908.
21 Ducousso, op. cit., pp. 132, 155–6.
22 M.O.C., Beyrouth, 16 Jan. 1908.
23 Huvelin, op. cit., p. 26.
24 Ducousso, op. cit., pp. 217–31.
25 Verney et Dambmann, *Les puissances étrangères dans le Levant, en Syrie et en Palestine*, Paris 1900, pp. 648–9 and M.O.C., No. 569, Tripolie, 1906.
26 Ducousso, op. cit., pp. 127–9.
27 Ibid., p. 133.
28 Ibid.
29 J. Thobie, *Intérêts et impérialisme français dans l'empire Ottoman 1895–1914* (Publication de la Sorbonne), Paris, 1977, p. 493.
30 It might be noted that many Lebanese mill-owners were also silk and cocoon merchants.
31 M. Croizat, 'Rapport sur la sériculture en Syrie', Chambre de Commerce de Lyon (C.C.L.), 1919, p. 6.
32 Chevallier, 'Lyon et la Syrie', pp. 294–5.
33 For a discussion of the political changes during the time of Bachir al-Chehabi II, see S. Salibi Kamal, *The Modern History of Lebanon*, New York, 1965, Ch. II–III. On the farmers' revolt, see Y. Porath, 'The peasant revolt of 1858–61 in Kisrawan', A.A.S., vol. 2, Jerusalem, 1966, pp. 76–157. On the settlement of 1861–4 and Lebanese feudalism, see I. Harik, *Politics and Change in a Traditional Society, Lebanon, 1711–1845*, Princeton University Press, U.S.A., 1968; I. Harik, 'The *Iqta*' System in Lebanon, a comparative political view', *The Middle East Journal* XIX, 1965, pp. 405–42.
34 Chevallier, *La société du Mont Liban*, pp. 235–8.
35 Documents from the private archives of the Jumblatt family published by Hichi H. Salem, *al-Murasalat al-ijtima'iyah wal-iqtisadiyah li zu'ama' Lubnam khilal thalathat qurun 1600–1900* (The social and economic correspondence of Lebanese leaders during three centuries 1600–1900), 3 vols., Beirut 1980–1981, vol. II, pp. 98–105 and vol. III, pp. 89–90 (in Arabic).
36 Ducousso, op. cit., pp. 233–5.
37 Chevallier, 'Lyon et la Syrie', pp. 296–7.
38 Ducousso, op. cit., pp. 217–31.
39 Ibid.
40 Thobie, op. cit., p. 495.
41 Ducousso, op. cit., p. 17.
42 Chevallier, 'Lyon et la Syrie', p. 295.
43 Thobie, op. cit., pp. 496–7 and Verney et Dambmann, op. cit., pp. 648–9.
44 L. Guencau, 'Lyon et le commerce de la soie' (Thèse), Paris, 1923, pp. 71–8. P. Clerget, *Les industries de la soie en France*, Paris, 1925, p. 48.
45 Chevallier, 'Lyon et la Syrie', pp. 276–7.
46 'L'industrie de la soie à Beyrouth et au Liban', *M.O.C.*, 16 Jan. 1908, pp. 56–8.
47 Verney et Dambmann, op. cit., p. 479.
48 Ibid.
49 Until 1904, a work day in France was 10 hours; from 1908, it came down to 8 hours. The daily wage of industrial workers at the start of the 20th century in the area of Paris averaged FF 7–8 for men and FF 5.40–6.15 for women; in other areas of France, it was FF 4.50–5.25 for men and FF 3.50–4.00 for women. Ch. et A. Ambrosi, *La France 1870–1975*, Paris, N.Y., Barcelona, Milan, 1976, pp. 80–1.
50 Ducousso, op. cit., pp. 155–6 and Labaki, op. cit., p. 81.

51 The population estimates for Mt. Lebanon differ from source to source. According to the French Cuinet it numbered 399,530 at the end of the 19th century (Cuinet (V), *Syrie, Liban et Palestine*, Paris, 1896, p. 211); according to Ruppin, it was 400,000 at the beginning of the 20th century, including 100,000 migrants (A. Ruppin, 'Syrien als Wirtschaftsgebiet, Beihefte zum Tropenpflanzer', in Ch. Issawi, *The Economic History of the Middle East 1800–1914*, Chicago and London, 1966, p. 270). A more recent publication set this population at the end of the 19th century at close to 240,000 (T. McCarthy, 'The Population of Ottoman Syria and Iraq 1878–1914', *A.S.S.*, Vol. 15, No. 1, University of Haifa, March 1981, p. 23). Since the migration continued up to the First World War, it is possible to estimate the population of Mt. Lebanon at the end of the 19th century at close to 300,000.
52 Ducousso, op. cit., p. 156 and Labaki, op. cit., p. 81.
53 M.O.C. No. 196, Beyrouth, 1894.
54 Ibid., Beyrouth, 1er semestre 1897, p. 344.
55 Foreign Office (F.O. hereafter), Annual Series Diplomatic and Consular Reports on Trade and Finance (D.C.R. hereafter), Trade and Commerce of Beirut and the Coast of Syria, No. 1279, Beirut 1893.
56 Ibid., No. 1626, Beirut, 1895.
57 Ibid., No. 1279, Beirut, 1893.
58 Ibid., No. 1418, Beirut, 1894.
59 M.O.C., Beyrouth, 1er semestre, 1897, pp. 667–8.
60 F.O., D.C.R., No. 2442, Beirut, 1900.
61 Ibid., No. 2662, Beirut, 1901.
62 Chevallier, 'Lyon et la Syrie', p. 302.
63 M.O.C., No. 607, Beirut, 1907.
64 E. Safa, 'L'émigration Libanaise' (Thèse), Beyrouth, 1960, p. 177 and Wajih Kautharani, *al-Ittijahat al-jitima'iyah wal-siasiyah fi jabal Lubnan wal-machriq al-'arabi* (*Socio-political trends in Mt. Lebanon and the Arab-Orient*), Beirut, 1978, p. 101 (in Arabic); see also: Ruppin in Issawi, op. cit., p. 270.
65 M.O.C., No. 469, Beyrouth, 1905 and ibid., No. 569, Tripolie, 1906.
66 'L'industrie de la Soie', M.O.C., 16 Jan. 1908, pp. 56–8.
67 Ducousso, op. cit., p. 160.
68 M.O.C., No. 947, Beyrouth, 1911.
69 F.O., D.C.R., No. 4496, Beirut, 1910.
70 Chevallier, 'Lyon et la Syrie', p. 302.
71 T. Philipp, 'Demographic patterns of Syrian immigration to Egypt in the nineteenth century – an interpretation', A.A.S., Vol. 16, No. 2, July 1982, pp. 180–2.
72 Ruppin in Issawi, op. cit., pp. 269–73.
73 W. Peterson, 'Migration, Social Aspects', *International Encyclopedia of Social Sciences*, N.Y., 1968, pp. 282–3.
74 Ruppin in Issawi, op. cit., p. 271.
75 Achard, 'Notes sur la Syrie', *L'Asie française*, No. 4, Paris, 1922, p. 97; Huvelin, op. cit., p. 14; Lubnan, *Mabaheth 'ilmiyah wa ijtima'iyah* (Lebanon Scientific and Social Essays) published in 1918, examined and re-edited by Fouad E. Boustany, 2 vols, Beirut, 1970, vol. 2, p. 472.
76 The population density of Mt. Lebanon was the highest. During this period, the overall area consisted of 450,000 hectares and the population was close to 300,000 people; the density thus comes to one resident for each hectare and a half, or one per 15 km^2.
77 In 1892, the English consular report describes the warning of Lebanese migrants to Australia against going to that country because of the difficult living conditions there among the immigrants. F.O., D.C.R., No. 2179, Beirut, 1893.
78 Ibid., and ibid., No. 1626, Beirut, 1895.
79 Ibid., No. 5302, Beirut, 1914.
80 Ruppin in Issawi, op. cit., p. 271.
81 The average annual export of Syrian silk between 1888 and 1913, computed from the British Consular reports, was £850,000 (FF 21,420,000).

82 On the Druze migration, see Shibli 'Aisami, *Muhafazat-es Swaida* [The region of Swaida], Damascus, 1962, pp. 17–21 (in Arabic).
83 This situation has been aptly described by Croizat: 'Cette classe [paysanne], très pauvre et en même temps peu prévoyante, a l'habitude de vivre sur le travail à venir; elle loue ses services à un employeur et la première condition qu'elle en exige est une avance sur son salaire futur. La guerre arrêtant la vie normale, supprimant l'activité productrice, mit les paysans pauvres dans une situation désespérée.' (Croizat, op. cit., p. 3).
84 Achard, op. cit., p. 111.
85 Croizat, op. cit., p. 3.
86 Bériel, op. cit., p. 121.
87 Geuneau, op. cit., p. 177.
88 Clerget, op. cit., p. 179.
89 Huvelin, op. cit., p. 26.
90 Latron, 'La production et le commerce de la soie', p. 80.

3

Reflections on a Subsistence Economy: Production and Trade of the Mahdist Sudan, 1881–1898

Yitzhak Nakash

In 1881 a revolt broke out in the Sudan against Egyptian rule. It was led by Muhammad Ahmad ibn Abdallah who assumed the title of Mahdi.[1] In the following years, the supporters of the Mahdi (*al-ansar*) succeeded in gaining control over large parts of the Egyptian Sudan; this culminated in the occupation of the capital Khartoum in January 1885. Until 1898, when the country was occupied by the Anglo-Egyptian forces, an independent Mahdist state existed in the Sudan. After the Mahdi's sudden death in June 1885, the state came under the rule of the Khalifa Abdallah ibn Muhammad.

The discussion of the history of the Mahdist Sudan is significant for several reasons: the separation from the previous (Egyptian) political, social, and economic system, the attempts of the Mahdist rulers to attain self-assertion, the embroilment of the state in continuous warfare with its neighbours, and the assumption of a declared fundamentalist Muslim ideology. These conditions undoubtedly had their impact on the development of the local economy.

The present article deals with the agriculture, manufacture, and trade of the Mahdist state. The discussion of agriculture focuses on the increased importance of slaves in the total labour force, and on the changes in the size of the cultivated area. We shall, further, examine the reasons for the increase in local manufacture during the Mahdiyya. The causes for the decrease in trade as well as the manner in which it took place will also be discussed in detail. Finally, we shall address ourselves to another important aspect: that of a fundamentalist Muslim ideology coping with reality and economic needs.

AGRICULTURE

(a) Labour

Before the Egyptian occupation (1820–21) the presence of slaves in the Sultanate of Sinnar was prominent mainly in the households of the rich.[2] In the regions north of Khartoum slaves constituted about 4 per cent of the total population and formed but a small fraction of agricultural labour.[3]

The first 20 years of Egypt's rule in the Sudan saw the development of a substantial slave-trade in the country. As a result all groups of the local population could own slaves.[4] This and the Egyptian tax system which forced entire regions to meet their tax payment annually in advance according to fixed rates, compelled the inhabitants to adopt a new system of land tenure based on slaves. Agricultural slavery soon prevailed along the Nile banks, especially in the fertile regions of the north which were in close proximity to towns, whereas the less fertile regions were still cultivated by independent fellahin.[5]

The most important and sincere efforts to reduce slavery took place during the period of Khedive Ismail (1863–79). In August 1877 Ismail concluded with Great Britain the Slave-Trade Convention which immediately ended the trade within Egyptian territory while providing for its termination in the Sudan by 1889.[6] As a result the inhabitants of the north could no longer pay part of their taxes in the form of slaves, while the shortage created in the supply of slaves hindered local agriculture and caused a severe crisis in the economy of the Sudan.[7]

The first years of the establishment of the Mahdist state saw the recapturing of many slaves who had been released during the Egyptian period.[8] Father Ohrwalder (an Austrian priest and a missionary, captured in 1882 by the Mahdists and held captive for ten years at Omdurman until his escape to Egypt) indicates that 'Omdurman is full of slaves; even in the poorest houses one female slave at least will be found'.[9] According to McLoughlin, the average rate of slaves among the local population during the Mahdiyya reached at least 20 per cent.[10] The percentage of slaves varied according to the region and nature of the society among which they lived.

In the north of Sudan, in agriculture and domestic work, slaves constituted 20, perhaps even 30 per cent of the total population.[11] It appears that among the Baqqara tribes the rate of slaves was as high as 40 per cent of the total population, while among the nomads their percentage barely ranged between eight and ten per cent. The proportion of slaves among the fellahin ranged from 17 to 25 per cent.[12] North of Khartoum, agricultural work was based on slaves, and the intensity of land tenure was often a function of a family's ability to keep slaves, the number of which would range between 20 and 200.[13] The proportion of slaves among the total labour force in the regions of the White and Blue Nile south to Khartoum, and near the Abyssinian border, was also considerable.[14] The regions of Darfur and Kordofan, i.e., central, west central, and western Sudan were characterized by the presence of two nomad groups: those whose economy was based on camel-breeding, and the Baqqara tribes. During the Mahdiyya many of the latter lost their herds because of wars and diseases and were forced to settle down and take up agriculture.[15] It is likely that this increased their need for slaves.

Moreover, slaves did not play a decisive factor in the army during the Mahdiyya. Data relating to the years 1891 and 1895 show that the number of black slaves in the Mahdist army reached some 7,000 out of a total of 40,000 to 46,000 warriors,[16] i.e., between 15 (15.2%) and 18 (17.5%) per cent. When called to war, the inhabitants responded personally, leaving their slaves to attend to their lands, herds, and domestic work. This obviously increased the dependence of the local population on slaves. The British attitude towards the problem of slavery in the country after the occupation in 1898 confirms this situation. H. Jackson, who served in the Condominium Government at that time, wrote that

> The Government had to choose between almost equally distasteful alternatives: the temporary sanction of slavery or the immediate liberation of the slaves, the latter a course which might bring economic ruin upon the country. Liberation would have resulted in the abandonment of most of the cultivation along the river banks, the loss of many of the flocks and herds of the nomad-Arabs and the consequent death of thousands of innocent individuals who, through no fault of their own, had been brought up under a social system that was repugnant to Western ideas, but accepted as an indispensable condition of their everyday lives. More than this, to have freed all the slaves would have meant letting loose upon society thousands of men and women with no sense of social responsibility, who would have been a menace to public security and morals.[17]

The question arises whether it is possible to determine the number of slaves among the total agricultural labour force during the Mahdiyya. Neither the Egyptian Administration before the Mahdiyya nor the Condominium Government afterwards made a census. The British Consul-General in Egypt estimated in 1903 that the population of the

Sudan during the Mahdiyya shrank from 8.5 to 1.9 million.[18] Although this by all accounts seems to be a rough estimate,[19] and should therefore be treated with caution, it may serve as a basis. As indicated above, slaves constituted an average of at least 20 per cent of the total population during the Mahdiyya, i.e., about 400,000 out of approximately 2 million; assuming that only half (viz., 800,000) of the free population was engaged in agriculture, it would appear that slaves formed about half of the total labour force. It would therefore be reasonable to suggest that the importance of slaves in the total labour force of the Sudan during the Mahdiyya was decisive, and that they constituted the bulk of labour in agriculture, herding, and domestic work.[20]

(b) Land

Before the Egyptian occupation an individual was not allowed to increase his property rights over lands outside the confined territory of his community. Egyptian rule, in contrast, encouraged private ownership, and thus even an individual of moderate means could purchase a piece of land located several hundred miles from his residence. As a result considerable private landed property was accumulated in the northern Sudan on the eve of the Mahdiyya.[21] This was paralleled by an overall increase in the size of the cultivated area of the Sudan owing to the introduction of new crops, the investment of capital and technology, the increase in the size of the local population and in the proportion of the agricultural labour force, and the settling of immigrants in the almost empty lands between the Blue Nile and the Setit.[22]

The Mahdi expressed flexibility with regard to the captured lands. His approach was pragmatic and changed according to circumstances of time and region. The Mahdist occupation of the northern Sudan on the one hand and the western on the other (the latter a region many vast areas of which were under the rule of the Sultanate of Darfur until the Egyptian occupation in 1874) brought about the accumulation of lands with different systems of land tenure. While the northern regions were characterized by private ownership, this system did not prevail in western Sudan.

The Sultan in the Sultanate of Darfur, as the sovereign owner of land, used to grant estates for cultivation to holders of important military posts, members of the aristocracy, local *jallaba*,[23] and holy families. The great officers of state dominated the estate system and their estates generally retained a military character. As the Sultanate became less warlike and more centralized, the military estate declined (although it never completely disappeared), while the charitable estate became the standard form of grant. Some of the characteristics of this land tenure remind one of the *iqta'* and *sadaqa* systems that existed in different parts of the Middle East.[24] We have no indication regarding changes either in the status or the ownership system of these lands between 1874, when the region was occupied by Egypt, and 1883, when it came under the rule of the Mahdiyya. It is reasonable to assume that owing to the lax control of the Egyptian administration over this region, no considerable change took place in this system, and only part of these lands were declared state property. No indication of the Mahdi's attitude towards lands in the western Sudan is available from his writings (*al-Manshurat*), which include a volume of his decisions and ruling in matters of law (*al-Ahkam*). It is likely that the owners of these lands who accepted the Mahdiyya were allowed to continue to possess them after the Mahdist occupation. The status of lands granted by the Fur Sultans as *sadaqa* or *waqf* to holy families is more difficult to estimate, for some of them did not recognize the Mahdiyya.

The Mahdi's attitude with regard to the northern lands is more fully documented. In September 1884, Muhammad al-Khayr Abdallah Khujali, the *amir* (military governor) of Berber asked for clarifications regarding the manner in which he should treat the lands in his province. He wrote that the poor used to lease their lands to others who had the means to cultivate them. Khujali also indicated that he himself was inclined to permit this practice while levying a tithe on the transaction, and added that the lands in his domain, unlike lands in other regions ruled by the Mahdist state, were characterized by a different ownership system. Although he did not specify, we may assume that he was referring to private ownership. In his reply the Mahdi indicated that 'the poor who cannot use his land and finds someone to use it in lieu of the agreed [payment] according to the transaction, can do it'. In this dispatch the Mahdi permitted the leasing of lands, and empowered Khujali to determine the status of lands in his province in the light of circumstances of time and place.[25] One may assume that the Mahdi acted thus since he realized that this would increase the size of the cultivated area of the state.[26]

The Khalifa's policy towards landed property and agriculture in the first four years of his rule remains unclear. It is likely that the wars and the measures he took for consolidating his rule drew his attention away from agriculture, and that regulations fixed by the Mahdi with regard to real estate transactions remained valid. It may be said that until 1890 Abdallah actually ignored agriculture.[27] In that year, however, he adopted a definite policy aiming at an increase of the cultivated area and the encouragement of agriculture. For his change of attitude several causes may be adduced. In 1889 the Sudan suffered from a great famine caused by a severe drought and further aggravated by swarms of locusts that spread over the country. The famine broke out at a rather unfortunate time, almost simultaneously with the forced immigration of the Baqqara tribes from their lands in the west to the capital and the Gezira (a move that was part of Abdallah's attempts to assert his rule). The removal of the Baqqara from their lands necessitated providing them with food at whatever price. Some of these tribes were removed to Omdurman, where they were supplied with subsidized grain, while others were given lands in the Gezira requisitioned from their owners without compensation. The situation became acute following the influx of desperate people from the provinces to the capital in search of food.[28] This and the accompanying high rate of mortality encouraged the Khalifa to dedicate greater attention to the improvement of agriculture, and to urge his governors and the population to devote all their attention to it.[29]

An expression of Abdallah's change of attitude can be found in his granting permission to a certain proportion of the people of Dongola to continue cultivating their lands even in case of war.[30] This change was probably also an indication of the new policy he had adopted aiming at defending and consolidating the existing state boundaries. In August 1890, addressing his officials, the Khalifa claimed that he sought peace and intended to follow a policy of non-belligerence unless attacked from outside. He ordered all the commanders (*umara*) to return to their fields and give their full attention to the improvement of soil and cultivation.[31] At the same time Abdallah tried to conciliate those tribes still hostile to his rule, again by encouraging them to engage in agriculture.[32] This policy was not confined to the vicinity of the capital only. Between August 1890 and July 1892 Muhammad Ahmad, the governor of Darfur, reported several times that the province was quiet, its roads safe, and that its people were once more busily cultivating their fields. In order to encourage the economic recovery of this province the Khalifa decided to remit all taxes for the year 1309 (August 1891 – August 1892) in the whole of Darfur.[33] The Khalifa's change of attitude is confirmed in the British report on the Sudan for 1895:

> In the early days of Mahdiism, the entire country being under arms, agriculture was abandoned, but the great famine had the effect of dispersing the large central camps and gradually the population are reverting to their former ways, while the Khalifa himself now encourages agriculture.[34]

Abdallah's efforts were rewarded: as early as 1890, owing to considerable rainfall and hard work that included the repairing and rebuilding of water canals damaged during the wars, excellent crops could be reported.[35] In 1895 it was reported that there was plenty of grain at cheap prices in the Sudan, and that the inhabitants did not suffer from hunger. This continued also during the last years of the Khalifa's rule.[36]

The report on the Sudan for 1891 estimated that during the Egyptian Administration more than two-thirds of the Sudan's cultivated area became waste and wild. In 1895 it was reported that during the Egyptian period only half of the cultivable area was under cultivation.[37] Although these reports are based only upon estimates and guesswork and should therefore be treated with caution, it would be correct to say that, as a whole, a significant decrease occurred in the cultivated area of the Sudan during the Mahdiyya as the inevitable result of the frequent wars, the decrease in the population, the severe drought of 1889, and of the inability and/or unwillingness to invest fresh capital and technology in agriculture.

MANUFACTURE

By the mid-1850s the official monopoly in the Sudan was entirely abolished. This was followed by the introduction of *laissez-faire*[38] which enabled a free penetration of goods into the country. What limited local manufacture existed, on the eve of the Mahdiyya, was consequently exposed to the competition of cheap imported articles. The table below lists a number of selected articles, the import of which specifically hampered local manufacture.

TABLE 1
IMPORTS INTO THE SUDAN, 1879, 1880, 1881

Article	1879	1880	1881
Clothing (pc.)	24,781	26,687	21,765
Cotton goods (tons)	8,578	7,204	7,683
Sewing cotton (tons)	67	256	151
Shoes (tons)	19	10	4
Sandalwood (tons)	589	116	280
Soap (tons)	205	205	135

Source: D.H. Stewart, *Report on the Sudan*, Cd. 3670, 1883, pp. 34–5.

The British officer, D.H. Stewart, when referring in his report to manufactures, simply stated that there were 'none except a kind of light cotton made at Dongola, and called tamur [*dammur*]'.[39] To this, however, may perhaps be added carpentry, and production of boats, all on a limited scale.

In contrast to the Egyptian period, a lively manufacture developed in the Sudan during the Mahdiyya since the local economy had to provide almost unaided for its own needs. In the early years of the establishment of the state, works of embroidery incorporating gold and silver threads were freely exported to Egypt, but in a later period, owing to regulations of the Mahdi against the wearing of jewellery, this kind of manufacture almost stopped. Gold and silver were also used for the production of coins. One of the important characteristics of the independent Mahdist state was the minting of coins, and both the Mahdi and the Khalifa established workshops in Khartoum and Omdurman for this purpose. In 1891, the monthly production rate reached one thousand coins.[40] Long and short lances were also manufactured for both private and military use, as well as iron stirrups, different kinds of knives, and agricultural tools.[41] There existed a certain amount of leather work, mainly the manufacture of shoes, sandals, different bridles for horses and donkeys, harnesses, saddles, and boxes for carrying clothes. Also, a factory for soap was established in Omdurman with the encouragement of the Khalifa. The manufacture of boats, which was halted for a short period owing to the official monopoly established by the Khalifa on all boats, was renewed in 1896 by the encouragement of Abdallah. Naʻum Shuqayr (a Syrian official in the service of the Egyptian Government, who later joined the intelligence department, and made an outstanding contribution to the historiography of the Mahdiyya in his book) related that a dockyard was functioning near Omdurman, mainly for repairing and maintaining the state steamships.[42]

There was also an intensive production of cotton goods. R.C. Slatin (an Austrian officer in the service of the Egyptian Administration who was nominated in 1881 governor of Darfur, and captured in 1884 by the Mahdists) related that all women used to weave either for private use or for selling. There were also several weavers in each village who worked the cotton into various goods. Cloth in considerable quantities was manufactured in the Gezira and sold in the local market. The best threads were spun in the province of Berber. Cotton materials were also manufactured in the province of Dongola; this province was quite famous for the production of materials used for boat sails. Kordofan's goods too were known for their durability rather than their beauty. In addition to cotton weaving, women produced mats of various shapes and sizes which were sold all over the Sudan. The quality of some of these was so high that they were exported to Egypt. Darfur in particular specialized in this field.[43]

The Mahdist state, being surrounded by hostile neighbours, faced severe difficulties in obtaining arms and ammunition. This problem became worse during the Khalifa's rule. It stemmed from the depletion of the ammunition reserves that had been accumulated during the period of occupation, the deterioration of arms, and the limitations imposed by the British on the export to the Sudan of materials used for the production of ammunition. Abdallah therefore urged the Sudanese merchants to smuggle lead, sulphur, and files from Egypt and the Hijaz via Suakin, Aswan, and Massawa. The problem of supply became acute when the Mahdist state lost Tukar in 1891.[44] The difficulties in obtaining these materials from external sources encouraged Abdallah to invest capital and to mobilize the knowledge of some of his captives in order to produce ammunition in the Sudan. For this purpose he needed sulphur, nitre, lead, copper, files, gunpowder, cups for Remington rifle bullets, and detonators. Lead was produced from Kafod and Jabal al-Kutum in Darfur, but mining was difficult and therefore the total annual product did not exceed 2¼ tons at the most.[45]

Difficulties occurred as well in the production of ammunition: several people offered the Khalifa their services, but since most of them were swindlers, these attempts led to little.[46] Only after a long period did a Greek named Yusif Pertrachi succeed in producing ammunition of a reasonable quality. He was killed, however, in an explosion that took place in the workshop where he worked, after which the manufacture was removed from Omdurman to the island of Toti. There, Abdallah used the services of F.M. Lupton, who was the governor of Bahr al-Ghazal until his captivity in 1884. When Lupton died in 1888, Abdallah used the services of Hasan Zaki and Karl (Charles) Neufeld. The former was a physician in the Egyptian army who was captured by the Mahdists. The latter was a German merchant who came to Egypt for business and set out for the Sudan in order to make easy money. He was captured by the Mahdists and sent to Omdurman. Abdallah also ordered the gathering of all copper pots in the Sudan for the production of cartridges by the goldsmiths he had mobilized. In addition, his governors sent to the capital empty cartridges collected in the field, to re-use them. This was carried out in a factory for bullets established in Omdurman by the Khalifa. In 1891 it was reported that the daily production rate of gun-powder reached 356 kg., and that there was plenty of it.[47] Shuqayr, on the contrary, related that the monthly rate reached only

445 kg.[48] Also between 80 and 100 boxes of bullets, each containing 44 bullets, were produced every month.[49]

While it is true that the substantial decrease in the import of cotton goods, leather work, and soap encouraged local manufacture, the nature of the Mahdist state drew Abdallah's attention mainly to the military sector. Hence, what increase there was in private production was a consequence of the decrease in import, rather than the result of investment of capital and technology.

TRADE AND COMMERCE

(a) Domestic Trade

The decrease in domestic trade started in the mid-1870s when Khedive Ismail ordered the closing of the White Nile for trade in order to put an end to the intensive slave trade that was carried on along the river.[50] This was further intensified during the Mahdiyya for several reasons: the frequent wars until 1889, the decrease in population, the great famine of 1889, and the overall lack of security on the roads.[51] In the 1890s, it is likely that the increase in the security on roads, the improvement of agriculture, and the development of local manufacture, were paralleled by a relative increase in the scale of domestic trade. The system of trade was centred around Omdurman which operated both as a wholesale and retail centre. Dongola and Dar Shaiqiyya supplied dates, Berber sent salt, mats and baskets woven from palm leaves. Sesame and millet were sent from Kordofan, the Gezira sent corn, cotton and resin, and Karkuj supplied sesame and small quantities of gold. Al-Fashir sent consignments of salt, lead from the mines at al-Kutum and Kafod, cloths for flags, ostrich feathers, and slaves. Omdurman in return supplied ammunition (the empty cartridges were often sent back to be refilled), firearms, clothing and perfumes.[52] Several reasons may be adduced for the development of this system. First, the necessity to provide for the needs of the capital, which was relatively more populated and where most of the ruling elite resided. Second, the specialization of crops for each region (e.g., the growing of dates in Dongola), which made the exchange of goods from other regions in the Sudan necessary; this was carried on through the capital. Third, the unique location of Omdurman near the confluence of the White and Blue Nile, the relative distance between the different provinces, the existence of only a few direct routes connecting them with one another, and the provinces' relative proximity to the capital.

Domestic trade in slaves, which was hampered in the 1870s, gained momentum during the Mahdiyya. Ohrwalder related that:

During the early days of Mahdiism the slave trade received an enormous impetus, more especially subsequent to the capture of Bahr el-Ghazal and the occupation of Darfur. After Gessi Pasha's victory over Zubeir Pasha's son and the dispersion of the slave-dealers, several of the latter fled into the interior, where pursuit was impossible; then came the era of liberty under the Mahdi's banner, the slave-dealers emerged from their hiding places, and with quantities of slaves, proceeded to Omdurman.[53]

It appears that there were at least four main collecting centres of slaves: in al-Qallabat, Beni Shangul, al-Fashir, and the most important in Omdurman. The slaves captured in al-Qallabat were mostly Abyssinians whereas those brought to al-Fashir were taken during the raids waged on the neighbouring tribes. The slaves gathered in the centre of Beni Shangul were removed to Dar Birtat, Rusari, and Fazughli and from there sent in groups to all parts of the Sudan.[54] There was apparently a slave market in every place where a treasury existed. The largest was in Omdurman near the central treasury. The male market was probably separated from that of females, as was the case in Omdurman.[55] During Abdallah's period it was forbidden to sell adult males, who were declared the monopoly of the Khalifa.[56] It was permitted, however, to trade freely in male children, youths and middle-aged adults as well as in girls and women. Prices ranged between five rials for a young male to one hundred for a young female.[57] The owner of a slave was obliged to possess a permit verifying that the slave had been bought legally. It had to be signed by two witnesses, one of whom should preferably be a *qadi*. This procedure was instituted because slaves who ran away from their owners were often recaptured and sold by others as if they were their own property.[58]

The decrease in the exportation of slaves during the Mahdiyya[59] was not accompanied by a similar decrease in the domestic trade in them. This assumption is supported by the fact that the price level of slaves during the Mahdiyya remained stable.[60] On the whole, it seems that there was a balance between the local demand for slaves and the existing supply. As we have no indication of any excessive demand, we do not know of any surplus; the local market was thus able to absorb most of the supply of slaves.[61]

(b) Foreign trade
By the beginning of Khedive Said's rule (1854–1863) the monopoly on goods exported from the Sudan was abolished and Europeans traded in the country either directly or through local agents. Trade, which

until 1820 had been carried out through two main routes — the first from Darfur and Kordofan to Asyut, and the second from Berber to Suakin[62] — developed substantively during Egyptian rule, when the number of trade routes was expanded, and the Nile became a vital path of communication for Egypt carrying the bulk of its imports from the Sudan. New impetus was given to Berber, located on a crossroads leading both to Egypt and the Red Sea while, by the end of Egyptian rule, Suakin became the main gateway for both export and import of goods.[63]

The decrease in the intensity of foreign trade which had begun in the 1870s continued during the Mahdist period. The siege of Suakin in 1885–86[64] no doubt hindered foreign trade through the major coastal town of the Sudan. Hostilities on the Abyssinian frontier had occurred frequently throughout the Egyptian period. War began early in 1887 and in March 1889 the Ethiopian army was defeated by the Mahdists. Abyssinia fell into anarchy from which the Italians profited by establishing control over Eritrea. These events hampered trade between Kassala and Massawa. As for the Egyptian frontier, a *jihad* against Egypt had been planned during the Mahdi's period but was not carried out. Additional delays arose during Abdallah's rule, and thus for almost two and a half years (between November 1886 and May 1889) the expeditionary force remained at its advanced base in Dongola. The two armies met on August 1889 and the Mahdist force was defeated.[65] One may assume that at least until the end of 1889 Sudan's foreign trade was severely hampered mainly along the roads from Berber and Dongola to Wadi Halfa and Aswan.

Another cause for the disturbance in trade with Suakin, Wadi Halfa, and Aswan was the prohibition declared now and again by the Anglo-Egyptian authorities on trade with the Mahdist state in order to prevent the smuggling of arms and ammunition into the Sudan.[66] The high rate of taxes occasionally imposed on imported goods during the Khalifa's period, and the absence of an acceptable Sudanese currency, also hindered foreign trade.[67] The scale of trade was also affected by the attitude of the Mahdi and the Khalifa. Determined to isolate the Sudan from outside influence, they attempted to create a distinct barrier between *dar al-Islam* (the region over which the Mahdist state spread) and *dar al-harb* (the area inhabited by unbelievers, which was bound to come one day under the government of the Mahdiyya). In a despatch sent in July 1884 from the Mahdi to the inhabitants of Suakin, he indicated that they would be allowed to trade in the Sudan provided they accepted the Mahdiyya. Should they refuse, trade with them would be forbidden.[68] The Khalifa also expressed a similar attitude in a letter he sent in 1304 (1886/7) to Egyptian merchants who came to the Sudan:

The region from which you now come is under the government of the unbelievers and it is not right that there should be a connection between its people and the people of a country under the government of the Mahdia. Your coming is for the sake of trade, so in the best interests of the Faith. We have thought it most expedient that there should be no sale in the Sudan of the goods you have brought ... If God Most High wills, after your country has entered under the government of the Mahdia and been snatched out of the hands of the infidels, there shall be a complete connection between you and the people of the Sudan.[69]

Abdallah, being a member of the Ta'aisha, one of the Baqqara tribes, was not entirely aware of the importance of foreign trade. He objected to it, fearing any connection with foreign countries that would expose the Sudan to foreign influence and to the possibility of their obtaining intelligence. For some time he even sought to erect a wall between Egypt and the Sudan to prevent the penetration of foreigners into the country.[70]

Yet, trade with the neighbouring countries was carried on throughout the Khalifa's period. Recognizing that it would be a waste to keep the country's main products (gum, ivory, and ostrich feathers) in the Sudan, and in order to provide for his private needs and those of his favourites, Abdallah for a while entrusted the bartering of Sudan's produce for Egyptian luxury goods into the hands of a Jew called Ben Zion Koshti (Basiyuni).[71] Moreover, the Khalifa realized eventually that a certain amount of trade was vital for the state, and that it would increase his private income. With the relaxation of wars, and owing to the severe famine of 1889, Abdallah not only permitted trade but even encouraged it.[72] Trade received impetus and was generally stable.[73]

This new approach showed itself in sending a special representative in 1889 to northern Sudan to encourage the local inhabitants to trade in Wadi Halfa. They were furnished for this purpose with funds from the local treasury to purchase grain, spices and clothes. The information which these people brought back with them also proved to be of value. Early in 1890 Muhammad Khalid Zuqal, a merchant himself, was sent to Abu Hamad and Dongola for the purpose of promoting trade there. The beneficial influence of his presence was soon felt, and in April 1890 he was appointed governor of Dongola.[74] About the same time Ali Sa'd Farah, also a merchant, was nominated governor of Berber, but died on his way to the town. These nominations indicate a change not only in Abdallah's attitude towards foreign trade, but also in his willingness to foster it. In a letter sent by Muhammad Khalid Zuqal to a merchant in Upper Egypt he assured all merchants of his protection, together with permission to dispose of their goods as they pleased, and a safe conduct for their return to Egypt. The Egyptian merchants availed themselves of the opportunities and, in August 1890, after paying the tithe to the Mahdist authorities, made profits of 100 per cent on clothes, 250 per cent on oil, and 300 per cent on sugar. The attempt of al-Nur Ibrahim al-Jirayfawi, who was at that time head of the treasury (*amin bayt al-mal*), to force the Egyptian merchants to come with their goods directly to Omdurman did not succeed because of their objection and that of the markets of Abu Hamad and Berber, who feared a decrease in their profits.[75] On the renewal of foreign trade in this period Ohrwalder wrote:

> A lively trade ... sprang up between Berber, Sawakin, Assuan, and Korosko; and Omdurman merchants were allowed to come to Sawakin and purchase goods; the Beit el-mal made considerable profits, and the people were less oppressed than before.[76]

There were five customs houses for the collection of tithes imposed on imported goods. They operated in Kukrayb, Berber, Dongola, Kassala, al-Qadarif, al-Fashir, and Omdurman. It is likely therefore that during Abdallah's period at least five trade routes were in use: Berber–Aswan, Berber–Suakin, Dongola–Wadi Halfa, Kassala–Massawa, and al-Qadarif–Massawa.[77] Slatin indicated that trade almost ceased on the roads of Kassala–Massawa, al-Qadarif–Massawa, and Suakin–Kassala when the Italians occupied Kassala and Eastern Sudan in February 1894.[78]

The trade of the Sudan was carried out by the Mugharaba on the road between Binban and Dongola, and by the 'Ababda who used to trade on the roads of Kurusku–Abu Hamad, Wadi Halfa–Dongola, and Aswan. The latter were also the main suppliers of information and newspapers from Egypt to Omdurman. The import of goods from Suakin was usually carried out by the Hadanduwa and the Ja'aliyin. As a whole the Sudanese merchants imported from Suakin, and mainly from Egypt, cotton goods, perfumes, sugar, rice, jams, sweetmeats, dried fruits, medicines, spices, coffee, honey, butter, cheese, oil, flour, and occasionally corn. Because of laws set by the Mahdi which prohibited the smoking of tobacco, hashish and opium, these were secretly smuggled into the Sudan.[79]

The central treasury imposed a monopoly on the export of gum, ivory, ostrich feathers, senna-leaves, and tamarinds.[80] Gum was purchased by the treasury at a price ranging from 5 to 30 rials for each *cwt* (50,848 kg.) and sold at auction to merchants at a price ranging from

20 to 40 rials.[81] The rate of profit was not fixed and could range from 33 to 300 per cent. The purchaser of gum was usually permitted to export it to Egypt. In Berber, where the receipt was compared with the weight of his luggage, he had to pay a rial for each *cwt*. If he wished to take the gum either to Suakin or Aswan, he was compelled to pay an additional tax: a Maria Theresa gulden for each *cwt*.[82] Considering the fact that this coin was equal to five *'umla jadida* rials (a coin which was current in the Sudan at that time), it appears that he had to pay additional taxes ranging from 15 to 30 per cent of the price he paid to the treasury in Omdurman.

As early as 1886 the Khalifa expressed his interest in ivory. In a letter he sent in July the same year to Abu 'Anja, the Commander-in-Chief (*amir al-umara*), who was at that time in southern Sudan, Abdallah wrote that 'in the past we did not allow to sell or use it without our permission, and now we want to store it in the treasury to decide what should be done with it. Protect and confiscate it wherever you find it and send [us] all you have and do not sell a thing from it. Enquire about what is brought from the regions of Shaka and Tulu, confiscate and send it to us.'[83] In the winter of 1892 Abdallah sent an expedition led by Haj Zubayr al-Fadl to the equatorial regions. One of its missions was to collect ivory. For this purpose entire villages in the region were looted.[84] Ivory was brought to the capital about once a year, but owing to the gradual loss of Mahdist territories in the equatorial regions the scale of this trade was small.[85] From figures quoted by Collins from British intelligence reports in 1892–98, we learn that the export of ivory from the Sudan to Suakin and Aswan reached some £14,194, i.e., only 4.4 per cent of the total export.[86] Ostrich feathers were also brought in small quantities and the treasury paid for them 5 rials per *cwt*.[87]

The exportation of slaves during the Mahdiyya was not renewed on a large scale. We only know of barter existing in the coastal towns of the Red Sea; slaves were exchanged in Suakin and the Hijaz for materials used for the manufacturing of gun powder.[88] Slatin indicated that although this trade still continued the caravans of slaves sent from the Sudan in former days had all but stopped.[89] The Khalifa prohibited the export of males above seven years old fearing that they might be recruited into the Egyptian army,[90] and at the same time attempted to increase the *jihadiyya* force, which was mainly manned by blacks. Also it appears that the Mahdist state was unable to obtain new slaves easily, since raids on tribal concentrations for this purpose were not waged frequently enough. Abdallah on the one hand avoided sending expeditions to remote regions, fearing that they might rebel and endanger his regime. On the other hand, after 1889, access to the South, the equatorial regions, and Bahr al-Ghazal became especially difficult following H.M. Stanley's expedition and the Belgian presence in the Congo.[91] Other factors hindering the export of slaves were the measures taken by the British in order to prevent the exportation of slaves to Egypt and the Hijaz, the Mahdist loss of Tukar (situated in the region through which the trade route leading to the Red Sea used to pass),[92] and the existence of a stable domestic slave trade in the Sudan.[93]

We have only partial figures on the scale of foreign trade during the Mahdiyya. The data we possess relate to the years 1892–98 and exclude Massawa. Shuqayr indicated that the value of goods imported to the Sudan in these years via Aswan and Suakin reached 477,869 Egyptian pounds while export to these towns reached 397,451 Egyptian pounds.[94] Although Sudan's foreign trade witnessed positive changes in the years after 1890, it can be assumed that as a whole there was a remarkable decrease in its scale in comparison to the Egyptian period.

CONCLUSION

We may conclude that, as a whole, the fundamentalist Muslim ideology could not stand up to reality for more than a short period. Trade with Egypt existed as early as the Mahdi's period despite his objection to it. Moreover, in the Khalifa's decisions ideology hardly played any role at all. Aware that a certain amount of trade was vital for the local economy and that it would increase his private income, he allowed, even encouraged, its existence. Thus, in the 1890s, when the state became less warlike in nature and as Abdallah turned his attention to defending the state's existing boundaries, his decision-making became by definition a function of the economic needs of the state and of his personal considerations.

The attempts of the Mahdi and the Khalifa to isolate the Sudan and the limited scale of foreign trade led to the development of a subsistence economy. Unable to promote economic growth, its value lay in its ability to provide the minimal economic conditions necessary for the independence of the state. It is likely then that economically the Mahdist state could have survived longer than it did, and that the cause of its fall in 1898 was not internal or economic in nature, but external, namely the British occupation of the Sudan.

REFLECTIONS ON A SUBSISTENCE ECONOMY

NOTES

This article is a revised version of a more comprehensive study of the economy of the Sudan during the Mahdiyya. The study in its original form was submitted to the University of Haifa in September 1984 as an M.A. thesis entitled 'Changes in the Economy of the Sudan During the Mahdiyya, 1881–1898.' My appreciation goes to my supervisors Professors Gabriel Warburg and Gad Gilbar for their assistance and encouragement. I alone, however, am responsible for any error.

1. For details on the decline of Egypt's hold over the Sudan during the 1870s, and on the causes for the Mahdist revolt see: N. Shuqayr, *Jughrafiyat wa-Ta'rikh al-Sudan* (Beirut, 1967), pp. 540–620 (hereafter: Shuqayr, *Ta'rikh*), R. Hill, *Egypt in the Sudan 1820–1881* (London, 1959), pp. 134–42 (hereafter: Hill, *Egypt*), P.M. Holt, *The Mahdist State in the Sudan 1881–1898* (London, 1970), pp. 32–44 (hereafter: Holt, *Mahdist State*), P.M. Holt and M.W. Daly, *The History of the Sudan* (London, 1979), pp. 74–80 (hereafter: Holt and Daly, *History*).
2. R. Hill, *On the Frontiers of Islam* (London, 1970), pp. 29–30.
3. J. Spaulding, 'Slavery, Land Tenure and Class in the Northern Turkish Sudan', *IJAHS*, Vol. 15, no. 1 (1982), p. 9 (hereafter: Spaulding, 'Slavery').
4. Ibid., p. 10.
5. Ibid., pp. 2, 14–15.
6. Holt, *Mahdist State*, p. 37.
7. Hill, *Egypt*, p. 146.
8. G. Warburg, 'Ideological and Practical Considerations Regarding Slavery in the Mahdist State and the Anglo-Egyptian Sudan: 1881–1918', in P.E. Lovejoy (ed.), *The Ideology of Slavery in Africa* (Beverly Hills and London, 1981), p. 255 (hereafter: Warburg, 'Ideological').
9. F.R. Wingate, *Ten Years' Captivity in the Mahdi's Camp 1882–1892* (London, 1893), p. 386 (hereafter: Wingate, *Ten Years*).
10. P.F.M. McLoughlin, 'Economic Development and the Heritage of Slavery in the Sudan Republic', *Africa*, Vol. 32 (1962), p. 361 (hereafter: McLoughlin, 'Economic').
11. Ibid.; Spaulding, 'Slavery', p. 11.
12. McLoughlin, 'Economic', p. 361.
13. Ibid., p. 367.
14. Ibid., p. 369.
15. Ibid., p. 364.
16. *General Military Report on the Egyptian Sudan 1891*, p. 7 (hereafter: *GMRES, 1891*), *General Report on the Egyptian Sudan 1895*, pp. 5–6 (hereafter: *GRES, 1895*).
17. H.C. Jackson, *Behind the Modern Sudan* (London, 1955), pp. 93–94.
18. McLoughlin, 'Economic', pp. 361, 367.
19. Holt, *Mahdist State*, p. 254.
20. G. Warburg, 'Slavery and Labor in the Anglo-Egyptian Sudan', *AAS*, Vol. 12, no. 2 (1978), p. 221 (hereafter: Warburg, 'Slavery').
21. Spaulding, 'Slavery', pp. 2–3.
22. Hill, *Egypt*, p. 153.
23. The *Jallaba* were small-scale Muslim traders coming from the North to the South, and to the regions of Darfur and Kordofan where they found favourable opportunities for trade. Some of them remained petty traders, others acted as agents for wealthy operators in Kordofan and Darfur, and some even occupied important administrative posts in the absence of skilled clerks there.
24. For details see R.S. O'Fahey and M.I. Abu Salim, *Land in Dar Fur. Charters and Related Documents from the Dar Fur Sultanate* (N.Y., 1983), pp. 12–21.
25. From the Mahdi to Muhammad al-Khayr Khujali, 7 Sep. 1884, *Manshurat al-Imam al-Mahdi, al-Ahkam*, pp. 39–42 (hereafter: *al-Ahkam*).
26. M.I. Abu Salim, *al-Ard fil-Mahdiyya* (Khartoum, 1970), p. 64 (hereafter: Abu Salim, *al-Ard*).

27 Shuqayr, *Ta'rikh*, p. 1260.
28 Holt, *Mahdist State*, p. 193.
29 Shuqayr, *Ta'rikh*, p. 1260.
30 Abu Salim, *al-Ard*, p. 64.
31 Holt, *Mahdist State*, p. 197.
32 *GMRES, 1891*, p. 5.
33 L. Kapteijns, *The Mahdist Faith and Sudanic Tradition. The History of the Masalit Sultanate 1870–1930* (London, 1985), pp. 99–100 (hereafter: Kapteijns, *Masalit Sultanate*).
34 *GRES, 1895*, p. 9.
35 Wingate, *Ten Years*, pp. 377–8.
36 *GRES, 1895*, p. 9, A. B. Theobald, *The Mahdia* (London, 1967), p. 183.
37 *GMRES, 1891*, p. 4, *GRES, 1895*, p. 9.
38 For details see: Hill, *Egypt*, pp. 49, 53, 73–4, 97–8.
39 D. H. Stewart, *Report on the Sudan*, Cd. 3670, 1883, p. 23.
40 *GMRES, 1891*, p. 15. For details on the monetary system in the Mahdist state see: Y. Nakash, 'Fiscal and Monetary Systems in the Mahdist Sudan 1881–1898', *IJMES*, Vol. 20, no. 3 (1988), (forthcoming).
41 R. C. Slatin, *Fire and Sword in the Sudan* (London, 1922), p. 341 (hereafter: Slatin, *Fire*).
42 Shuqayr, *Ta'rikh*, p. 1260.
43 Slatin, *Fire*, pp. 341–43, *GRES, 1895*, p. 9.
44 Shuqayr, *Ta'rikh*, p. 1254, *GRES, 1895*, p. 7.
45 Shuqayr, *Ta'rikh*, p. 1254.
46 For details see: Wingate, *Ten Years*, pp. 367–75.
47 *GMRES, 1891*, p. 8.
48 Shuqayr, *Ta'rikh*, p. 1254.
49 Ibid.; *GRES, 1895*, p. 7.
50 Stewart, *Report*, p. 22.
51 *GMRES, 1891*, p. 14.
52 Wingate, *Ten Years*, p. 380, Kapteijns, *Masalit Sultanate*, p. 108.
53 Wingate, *Ten Years*, p. 383.
54 F. R. Wingate, *Mahdiism and the Egyptian Sudan* (London, Cass, 1968), p. 478 (hereafter: Wingate, *Mahdiism*).
55 Ibid.; Wingate, *Ten Years*, p. 383.
56 Slatin, *Fire*, p. 339.
57 Wingate, *Mahdiism*, p. 479, *Ten Years*, p. 382, *GMRES, 1891*, p. 15.
58 *GMRES, 1891*, p. 15, Slatin, *Fire*, p. 339.
59 See pp. 65–6.
60 Compare for example Slatin's and Wingate's figures that relate to different periods of the Khalifa's rule: Slatin, *Fire*, p. 341, Wingate, *Mahdiism*, p. 479.
61 Holt, *Mahdist State*, p. 196.
62 Wingate, *Mahdiism*, p. 51.
63 Hill, *Egypt*, pp. 60, 156–7. On the development of Suakin during Egyptian rule see: G. H. Talhami, *Suakin and Massawa Under Egyptian Rule 1865–1885* (Washington D.C., 1979).
64 Wingate, *Mahdiism*, p. 298.
65 Holt and Daly, *History*, pp. 101–5.
66 Holt, *Mahdist State*, p. 256.
67 See note 40.
68 M. I. Abu Salim, *al-Murshid ila Watha'iq al-Mahdi* (Khartoum, 1969), p. 175.
69 Holt, *Mahdist State*, pp. 255–6.
70 *GMRES, 1891*, p. 6, Shuqayr, *Ta'rikh*, p. 1261, Wingate, *Ten Years*, p. 323.
71 R. Hill, *A Biographical Dictionary of the Sudan* (London, 1967), p. 78.
72 *GMRES, 1891*, p. 6, *GRES, 1895*, p. 10, Shuqayr, *Ta'rikh*, p. 1261.
73 Trade with Massawa was disturbed from 1894 as a result of the Italian presence in Eastern Sudan. Disturbances in the trade with Suakin also occurred, due to the policy of the Anglo-Egyptian authorities there. See Y. Bedri and G. Scott, *The Memoirs of Babikr Bedri*, Vol. I (London, 1969), pp. 194–5.

74 The biographical details on Zuqal in Hill's *Biographical Dictionary of the Sudan* (261–62) are incomplete. It is known that Zuqal was arrested in April 1886 by Hamdan Abu 'Anja for six months. He was then sent to Omdurman where he stayed under house arrest until 1889. He was released in the same year as part of Abdallah's attempts to conciliate the *awlad al-balad* (a designation of the riverain tribesmen). As indicated, he was sent in 1890 to Hamad to promote trade there and in April of the same year nominated governor of Dongola. In March 1891 he was dismissed from his post and sent to prison from which he was released only in 1897 by the Belgians. For further details see Holt, *Mahdist State*, pp. 76, 143–5, 188, 195, 198, 199.
75 Holt, ibid., pp. 195–6.
76 Wingate, *Ten Years*, p. 323.
77 *GMRES, 1891*, p. 14.
78 Slatin, *Fire*, p. 336.
79 Ibid., pp. 335–6, Wingate, *Mahdiism*, p. 478, Holt, *Mahdist State*, p. 256.
80 Slatin, *Fire*, p. 335, *GMRES, 1891*, p. 14, Holt, *Mahdist State*, p. 256.
81 Slatin, *Fire*, p. 335, Wingate, *Ten Years*, p. 323, *GMRES, 1891*, p. 15.
82 Slatin, *Fire*, p. 335.
83 Shuqayr, *Ta'rikh*, p. 1261.
84 R. O. Collins, *The Southern Sudan 1883–1898. A Struggle for Control* (New Haven & London, 1964), pp. 140, 177 (hereafter: Collins, *Southern Sudan*).
85 Slatin, *Fire*, pp. 335–6, *GMRES, 1891*, p. 15.
86 Collins, *Southern Sudan*, 57[n].
87 *GMRES, 1891*, p. 15.
88 Wingate, *Mahdiism*, p. 479.
89 Slatin, *Fire*, p. 337.
90 *GMRES, 1891*, p. 7, *GRES, 1895*, p. 10, Wingate, *Ten Years*, p. 384.
91 Wingate, *Ten Years*, p. 384, Warburg, 'Ideological', p. 251.
92 Ibid.; *GMRES, 1891*, p. 15.
93 Warburg, 'Ideological', p. 25.
94 Shuqayr, *Ta'rikh*, p. 1261. Collins (57) cites only the export figures of the Sudan to Suakin and Aswan which reached a total of £317,080.

4

Land Tenure and Taxation in Iran, 1800−1906

Ahmad Seyf

Documentation for Iranian land tenure and taxation is scarce − even more so than for other economies in the Middle East. There was no land register during the nineteenth century, and in the absence of national archives similar documents have not survived, or are so scattered that they are not easily accessible. As a result, it is difficult to measure the exact rate of taxation on land. Similarly, it is not possible to determine the size of the land-holding and its probable changes over time. We know, however, that private property in land increased at the expense of lands owned by the state towards the end of the nineteenth century.[1]

Broadly speaking, the tenure systems may be classified as follows:

(i) *Shahee* lands, literally meaning lands owned by the Shah, also referred to as *Khaleseh* lands;

(ii) *arbabi* lands, owned by individual landowners;

(iii) *vaqf* lands, owned by religious institutions. There were occasions where powerful *mullahs* appropriated the surplus from this kind of land on their own private account;

(iv) peasant properties, lands owned by the direct producers.

Given the absence of a land register, itself a reflection of the absence of legal institutions concerning property rights, it is almost impossible to determine the actual distribution of land ownership between these categories. It can, however, be argued that the *Shahee* lands were in turn divided into:

(a) Those in which the peasants were directly liable for the payments of taxes normally via the headman of the village, *kadkhuda*.

(b) Those where revenue was farmed by individuals on the payment of certain sums of money to the Shah. The amount these farmers would exact was usually no concern of the Shah and was entirely dependent upon their own power of extraction.

(c) Those where the revenue was granted to state officials in lieu of their salaries.

The common feature of (b) and (c), often referred to as *tuyul* holding, was their inherent insecurity of tenure which in turn contributed to bring about a situation in which 'make what you can while you can'[2] became the guiding rule. This was translated into an arithmetical progression of plunder, from the sovereign to the subject, each unit in the descending scale renumerating himself from the unit next in rank below him, and helpless peasants being the ultimate victims.

The *arbabi* lands were owned either by an individual, *malek*, or group of individuals, *khurdeh malek*. The difference between a *khurdeh malek* and a peasant proprietor was that the former was not directly engaged in production and was usually a city dweller like most of the *maleks*. In other words, *khurdeh maleks* did not perform labour on land. In *arbabi* lands, it was *malek* or *khurdeh malek* who were responsible for the payment of the taxes. We do not consider peasant properties as *arbabi* lands, because no rent was paid to any individual and the headman of the village performed the duty of collecting taxes. It sometimes happened that the government's share of the surplus from the *arbabi* lands was granted to a third party, in which case the *malek* or *khurdeh malek* would be responsible to him.

The *vaqf* lands belonged primarily to the religious institutions, such as holy shrines and mosques. In addition, there were numerous cases where individual proprietors willingly transferred part of their revenue to a shrine or mosque hoping to escape paying too much in taxes and possible confiscation. It was a relatively safe way of protecting one's property from confiscation by the state and its powerful officials, but it sometimes happened that the lands were confiscated by powerful *mullahs*.

As far as surplus appropriation was concerned, in each case lands were also divided, on the basis of the mode of irrigation, into (i) *abi* – lands artificially irrigated, and (ii) *daimi* – those depending upon rainfall.

Another differentiation must also be made. With the exception of the peasant proprietors, the rate of surplus being appropriated was correlated to the number of factors, i.e. land, water, labour, seed and plough animals supplied by each party. The greater the number of these factors supplied by the proprietor, the greater was his share of the total output.

Last but not least, there were lands occupied by the tribes, where both the methods of land-use and modes of taxation differed from the rest of the country. Generally speaking, it may be said that pastoral nomads were tribal, though not all tribes were nomadic, and this distinction complicated the issue even further. However, information on the lands under tribal use and on the mode of taxation is scanty.

On the subject of the rate of surplus appropriation in Iranian agriculture, there is a constant tendency among scholars to generalize from a particular rate or a given mode of collection, which, despite being valid for certain localities, was certainly not applicable to the entire kingdom. For example, it has been asserted that the rate was one-fifth of the harvest in the *daimi* cultivation and one-third in the irrigated areas.[3] This approach can be criticized on a number of grounds.

(a) It tends to undermine the salient feature of Iranian agriculture in the nineteenth century, that is, the absence of legal and economic institutions concerning individual possession, which in turn led to arbitrary modes of surplus appropriation. In other words, this approach presupposes the legality of individual possession, which as will be subsequently shown did not exist.

It is, however, argued that uncertainty about the rate of tax (the proportion of the output that went to the State) contributed also to the imprudence and lack of intelligent projection for the future by the landowners as indicated by their unwillingness to invest in agriculture.

(b) This approach also does not distinguish between tax and rent (the proportion of the output that was taken away by the owners of land or water) and tax–rent combination (when the State was the owner of the means of production, in this case, land and water).

(c) To assess the mechanism of surplus appropriation in Iranian agriculture it is important not only to distinguish between tax and rent and the tax–rent combination; but also to emphasize the role of the State. This approach, however, tends to overlook this important issue.

As will be shown later, tax and the tax–rent combination constituted a major part of the surplus and involved the State in the process of production as well as surplus appropriation. Consequently its fiscal policy, that is the ways in which this surplus was spent by the State, was bound to have a considerable impact on the development of agriculture on the one hand, and on the well-being of the mass of the peasantry on the other. The available evidence indicates that in the nineteenth century, unlike the situation between 1550 and 1650,[4] not only did the State spend the surplus unproductively and fail to invest to maintain and expand the public works (especially irrigation systems and roads which were essential for the development of agriculture), but also its failure to maintain internal security on the one hand, and its oppressive measures against the peasantry and private landowners on the other, contributed effectively to the perpetuation of backwardness in agriculture. Its oppressive measures and destructive fiscal policies left the peasantry with little incentive to improve productivity, while fear of confiscation in the case of landowners meant that they often preferred to hoard the surplus appropriated as rent rather than to invest part of it to improve productivity. It further follows that not only was the surplus relatively small − owing to the backwardness of agriculture − but the fiscal policies of the State constrained the transformation of this surplus into capital. This surplus, therefore, failed to enter into the process of production to 'expand' itself.

This paper sets itself the objective of demonstrating that no uniform rate of taxation − or for that matter, surplus appropriation − existed in Iran during the nineteenth century. This is, in fact, believed to be an indication of the absence of a legal framework concerning property rights. For this purpose, it is appropriate to examine each locality separately.

The Caspian Provinces

There is overwhelming evidence indicating that these provinces were relatively more prosperous than the rest of the country. It is also true that these provinces had the highest population density in Iran. An estimate made in the early 1840s suggested a density of 112.6 persons per square mile for Mazandaran and 53.7 for Gilan as compared with 9.1 persons for Kerman, 13.4 for Fars, and 20.9 for Khorasan.[5] The major crop of Mazandaran was rice and that of Gilan, raw silk during the first half of the nineteenth century. Following the collapse of silk production in the mid-1860s in Gilan,[6] rice culture was encouraged there too.

Consul K. E. Abbott, writing in 1843, suggested that in Mazandaran the division of the harvest from the lands owned by the Shah, 'with or without irrigation', was one-fifth and four-fifths of produce respectively. In this system, the peasant had to bear all the necessary expenses. When the Shah provided the seed, oxen and ploughs, the produce was equally divided. In addition

> There are also taxes on horned cattle, sheep, goats, asses, mares (horses generally and oxen are not taxed) and on fruit trees and fruit grounds, and a capitation tax is levied which the adult

population of villages but not the inhabitants of towns pay, it varies in different parts.⁷

On *arbabi* lands, when the peasant worked and sowed the ground at his own expense, the proprietor took 30 per cent and the remainder went to the cultivator. Out of the 30 per cent, four-sevenths or about 17 per cent was paid to the State (tax), and the proprietor kept the remaining 13 per cent (rent). In his view, the peasants 'are not in the condition of serfs although they become the subjects or servants of the lord of land'. Abbott added, 'they are tenants of the proprietor'.⁸ It is interesting to note that even in a relatively small province like Mazandaran, there were places where the distribution of the output was different from the above. Abbott asserted in the same document that in the rice-fields the following system prevailed:

(i) When expenses were paid by the peasant on *arbabi* lands:
50 per cent to the peasant.
25 per cent to the government (tax).
25 per cent to the proprietor (rent).

(ii) When the proprietor furnished the expenses:
37.5 per cent to the peasant.
25 per cent to the government (tax).
37.5 per cent to the proprietor (rent and profit).⁹

Furthermore, it is also reported that

> When the property belongs to the peasants, the governor of the district exacts almost what he pleases or is able to get from him ... He [the peasant] therefore often finds it more advantageous to be without than with landed property of his own.¹⁰

A few years later, in 1848, in another document Abbott maintained that in the *Shahee* rice-fields the government's share (tax–rent combination) was between one-sixth and one-third of the produce, and added that 'most of the villages in Mazandaran come under the denomination of *khaleseh* [*Shahee*]'.¹¹ On *arbabi* lands, however, he expressed the opinion that 'the rate is very uncertain', but 'the owner of a village usually claims from his peasantry ... one-fifth to one-third, and he levies also a tax of one toman per family'.¹² It is not clear what proportion went to the government, but it was said that these rates applied when there was no shortage of labour, because when there was a shortage

> Strangers are invited to do the work on more favourable terms to themselves; sometimes an equal division of the produce between the labourers and land-owner is made.¹³

It was further asserted that 'the tribes [in Mazandaran and Gorgan] are exempt from all taxation in consideration of their performing military service'.[14]

In the adjoining province of Gilan, the system was different. In a document written in 1865, it was suggested that 'the price of the peasant's labour is in most cases one-half of the produce, be it rice or silk'.[15] The peasantry working on silk had to furnish the silkworm eggs, while in the rice-field the seed was provided by the proprietor.

There was yet another mode of surplus appropriation in Gilan, by which the landlord let his mulberry or rice plantation to the peasant, receiving from the latter, in lieu of rent, a share in the produce of his labour. In silk production, the landlord's share was as high as three-fourths and, in the rice-fields, one-third of the produce. The government's share was not specified nor the rate given for *khaleseh* lands, but it was alleged that the State's fiscal policy acted as a major obstacle in the development of agriculture because all lands, irrespective of their qualities, were assessed alike and the same amount was exacted in good years and in drought.[16] It appears, however, that the proprietor took the lion's share in most cases and the peasantry were left in a miserable condition.

Nevertheless, Consul Churchill, writing on the same subject in 1877, expressed the opinion that the peasantry in Gilan were better off than the Indian peasants, and estimated the annual money incomes of the former at between £5 and £9 compared with the latter's £2.[17] It will be subsequently shown what these estimates implied in real terms, but let us recall that the severe plague of 1877 in Gilan may have created a situation in which the peasantry appeared to have an enhanced bargaining position in their relationship with the landlords. Consequently, the argument that the peasants of Gilan had 'no reason to be unhappy'[18] probably referred to a short-term phenomenon, brought about primarily as a result of the plague. This point is reinforced by the fact that 'in many districts of Gilan the peasantry are heavily in debt to their landlords, who exact a usurious rate of interest, from 25 to 40 per cent being the lowest figure upon such loans'.[19] This view was expressed in 1865, the year of silkworm disease,[20] when silk production was considerably higher than in 1877. Unless it is assumed that the plague of 1877 resulted in a considerable loss of life among the peasantry, Churchill's optimistic assessment of the situation seems improbable.

Still, his report – despite his optimistic assessment – shed some light on the arbitrariness of surplus appropriation in Gilan. He estimated that the tax-collectors contrived to extract from the peasants 10 to 20 per cent more than they were nominally entitled, and added that 'so long as they do not exceed these limits everybody feels satisfied'.[21] Despite this alleged all-round satisfaction, the following passage from the same document shows the actual mechanism and indicates the damaging impact of the prevailing fiscal system on the transformation of the surplus into capital, i.e. into productive use: 'when the tax-gatherer grows rich he is pounced upon by the governor, who makes him disgorge'.[22]

Had the practice stopped here, the surplus might have remained in the province and somehow circulated there, but 'in his turn the governor is called upon by the Shah either to pay large presents on his appointment or heavy fines for reported malversations'.[23] So long as the Shah or his powerful ministers received their shares of the surplus, malversations continued, but, as British Consul at Rasht noted in the mid-1860s, the peasantry was

> reduced to great straits [as a result], deserts the village to elude the pursuit of his creditors. In a thinly populated province like Gilan, where the supply of labour is already far below the demand, the practice alluded to must necessarily operate as a serious check on agriculture.[24]

Despite the apparent excess demand for labour, it was very poorly paid, and this tends to imply that labour productivity was perhaps low. More importantly, it indicates the deep-rooted oppression which, regardless of the market forces, regulated the levels of earnings. The estimated annual income of an individual peasant gives a broad indication of the poverty of the mass of the peasantry in the 'most propserous' province of Iran, i.e. Gilan. By comparison the living standards in the rest of the country must have been worse. Although it is not clear whether these estimates were per capita or per household yearly income (most likely it was the latter), the lower estimate gives a daily income of about 3¼d. (old pence) and the higher, 6d. Table 1 shows the quantities of some of the basic items of consumption that could be purchased, provided that all the daily income was spent on a single item.

There is no doubt that the single-commodity consumption pattern is most unrealistic; still, these estimates show that the total daily purchasing power at the disposal of a peasant, with or without a family, was equal to 1lb. of soap, or 4lbs. of flour. Allowing for non-food expenditure, the money available for food consumption was even lower. Had there been estimates of per capita consumption of these items available, it would have become possible to measure the poverty of the peasantry more realistically, but information of this nature is non-existent.

LAND TENURE AND TAXATION IN IRAN

TABLE 1
QUANTITIES OF BASIC NECESSARIES OF LIFE IN lbs A GILANESE PEASANT COULD AFFORD TO BUY, SPENDING ALL HIS DAILY INCOME ON A SINGLE ITEM, IN 1876

Commodity	Lower limit Annual income £5	Higher limit Annual income £9
Rice	6	12
Wheat	7	13
Barley	6	12
Flour	4	7
Mutton (1877)	1	2
Beef (1877)	2	4
Soap	1	2

Source: Churchill, 'Trade of Gilan', in *P.P.* 1878, lxxiv

It is interesting to note that the rate of surplus appropriation in the province of Asterabad, on the Caspian shore, was different from those operating either in Gilan or Mazandaran. In Asterabad, the mode of division of the product in rice-fields was equal division, whereas on corn- and barley-growing lands the proprietor took only one-tenth. It is not clear which party was responsible for the payment of the State's share, nor is any information available as to its magnitude. Irrigation works, like *qanats*, or subsurface waterducts, were maintained by the landlords, but repairs to open ducts or canals had to be effected by the cultivators themselves. In money terms the produce of each acre under rice cultivation (irrigated) was said to be worth £8. 16s. whereas that of corn and barley (*daimi* or rain-fed) was valued at 16s. in 1881.[25] Higher yields in the rice-fields as compared with wheat and barley lands may also explain the relatively much higher rate of surplus appropriation. No estimate of the yearly income of the peasantry is available, but it can be alleged that the peasantry in the province of Asterabad, despite being relatively better off than their fellow peasants in many parts of the country, were by no means prosperous. Consul Lovett remarked that

> all their meals the adults get through 10 oz. of rice for breakfast, 22 oz. for the midday meal, and at supper they consume another 22 oz.; actual dry rice consumed is about 27 oz.[26]

Furthermore, 'usually the peasants do not have more than two wives – one old and the other young'.[27] If a peasant household is assumed to consist of three adults, or two adults and two children, this means that a peasant household earning £9 per annum (the upper limit of estimated income for Gilan) could not afford to buy sufficient rice to feed itself. Households earning as much as £12 had about 1d. extra per day to spend on other basic necessities of life.[28] It can be asserted that as prices were higher in Asterabad as compared with Gilan, the peasants in the latter province were in a relatively better financial position. The daily earning of a Gilanese peasant with an annual income of £9 was equal to 12lbs. of rice or 4lbs. of mutton, whereas the same level of income could procure 4.7lbs. of rice and only 2lbs. of mutton in Asterabad.

The Province of Azarbaijan

Azarbaijan was the largest and most populous province of Iran. Its agricultural production consisted of *daimi* and *abi* cultivation. Food as well as cash crops (wheat, barley, tobacco and cotton) were produced. During the 1860s, mainly as a result of 'cotton famine' in Europe, the cultivation of cotton was encouraged in this province; but the expansion was short-lived. Evidence also indicated that its tobacco production suffered a set back in the 1890s as the Ottoman administration prohibited the import of Persian tobacco into Turkey.[29]

Concerning land taxation in Azarbaijan, there was no uniform mode or rate of surplus appropriation. Not only did it vary in different types of land use, *daimi* or *abi*, but different localities seem to have had different rates.

Documents on the first half of the nineteenth century are scanty, but Consul Dickson, writing in 1859, noted that in Azarbaijan taxes annually levied represented one third of the grain produce, collected mostly in kind, and one-third of the straw, the value of which was normally paid in cash. In addition, every family paid a 'house-tax' of 11 *kran* 5 *shahi* (about 10s. 2d.), every mare, mule, and female buffalo was taxed at 2½ *kran* (about 2s. 3d.) and every sheep and goat at 7½ *shahi*, or 4d. He added that

> two-thirds of the above taxes, being the share belonging to the State, are paid to the *'Teeool'* [*tuyul*] holder, and the remainder to the proprietor of the village.[30]

Two points call for further comment. First, *tuyul* holding, which is often referred to as 'feudal' land ownership, was a kind of revenue assignment where its holder collected a given proportion of the produce as tax and not as rent. In the above case, the amount of tax exceeds the rent (the share of the proprietor of the land) by one-third. Second, this kind of land-holding was different from feudal conditional ownership, i.e. fief. This argument must be examined in the framework of an opinion already expressed that 'every government officer holds one or more villages in what is called *"Teeool"'*, the taxes of which were 'supposed to correspond to the amount of his salary'.[31] It further follows that the 'right' to claim a share of the produce was dependent upon holding an official function.

Some years later, however, in 1864, Consul Abbott differentiated *khaleseh* from *arbabi* lands and suggested that the modes and rates of surplus appropriation were different too. On *khaleseh* lands, under irrigated farming, the produce of grain was divided into ten shares, three of which went to the government and the rest to the cultivator. In fact, 'an abuse of power' made them, Abbott commented, one-third and two-thirds respectively. But when the land was *daimi* (rain-fed), the government's share was only one-tenth.

On *arbabi* lands no distinction was made between irrigated and *daimi* cultivation, but generally speaking the proprietor received one-tenth (rent), two-tenths going to the government (tax) and the remainder to the cultivator. In this category, peasants engaged in *daimi* cultivation were clearly worse off than those working on government *daimi* lands, because they paid 20 per cent more of the output in taxes. Mules were no longer taxed unless owned by muleteers, for which the amount was as before i.e. 2½ *kran*, whereas taxes on sheep and goats rose by 33 per cent, to 10 *shahi* (5½d.) per head.

In the same report, Abbott also distinguished taxation on cash crops, such as cotton, tobacco, melon etc. which had to be paid in cash to the extent of two-tenths of the produce 'at the price of the day'. Capitation taxes were also different. Instead of 11 *kran* 5 *shahi* per family, it was 10 *kran* for each male above 15 years of age if married, whereas unmarried males of this age group paid only 5 *kran* per head. The inhabitants of towns were exempted from this payment.[32]

A different picture emerges from a report written in 1888 on Azarbaijan. It may indicate a change in the revenue system of the province since 1864 when the previous report was prepared. As to the possible causes of this change, one can mention a short-lived expansion of cotton production in the mid-1860s and the great famine of the early 1870s. However, in the second report, W. G. Abbott, the younger brother of K. E. Abbott, divided the landlords of the province into 'just' and 'unjust' ones. Leaving aside Abbott's moral approach, the former, Abbott maintained, entered into agreements with their peasants according to a system called '*mus'edeh*'. Accordingly he lent the peasants 10 *kharwar* of seed (a *kharwar* was 650lbs.), which had to be returned plus five *kharwar* interest after harvest, i.e. 50 per cent interest. The peasant also added another 10 *kharwar* as seed. A total seed of 20 *kharwar* would normally yield, according to Abbott, 200 *kharwar*. One-tenth rent to the government, as against two-tenths in 1864, and the landlord's share was another tithe, plus 15 *kharwar* for the repayment of the initial seed loan. Altogether, 35 *kharwar* went to the landlord, 20 to the government, leaving the peasant with 145 *kharwar*, or more than 70 per cent of the produce.

The second group of landlords did not lend any seed and took away two-tenths in addition to the numerous imposts,[33] for example, poll-tax, cattle-tax, tax on ploughs, and *gur al* (literally meaning 'see and take'). The capitation tax was significantly different from that of 1864. Male adults paid 5 *kran*, half as much as in 1864, but in 1888 'married women ... and young girls' were also taxed at 2½ *kran* per head. Taxes on sheep and goats were reduced to 5 *shahi* per head, while a yoke of oxen for the plough paid 2 *toman* (20 *kran*).[34] While praising the 'just' landlords, who 'have the prosperity of their tenants at heart', Abbott concluded:

> Many of the evils from which the villagers suffer have their origin in the careless and unequal distribution of the fiscal burdens, rather than in systematic oppression on the part of their masters.[35]

Whether there was 'an unequal distribution of the fiscal burden' or 'arbitrary oppression', Durand, the British ambassador at Tehran, asserted in 1895 that Azarbaijan was 'dangerously misruled',[36] and ten years later the British Consul at Tabriz (the provincial capital), Wratislaw, pointed out:

> There seems little doubt that the population is becoming more and more impoverished and has less money to spend on foreign-made goods. This is particularly the case in the town of Tabriz itself, where poverty is daily increasing and is driving many of the inhabitants to emigrate to other parts of Persia where the cost of living is supposed to be less.[37]

In addition, there were also a large number of Azarbaijanis who went to the southern provinces of Russia in search of employment and more tolerable living conditions.[38]

The Province of Khorasan

Agricultural production in Khorasan consisted of *daimi* as well as *abi* cultivation of wheat, barley, cotton and opium. On the one hand, an average annual rainfall of less than 10 inches and, on the other, continued decay of *qanats* implied that agricultural production could develop only to a limited extent in this province. Had there been investment to provide a regular supply of water, land under cultivation could have increased considerably, but in its absence, as Elias reported in 1897, 'millions of acres of rich virgin soil lie fallow for want of necessary water'.[39] The question of water shortage was so vital that it appears to have affected land ownership in Khorasan. The same Consul asserted that whenever there was sufficient rain:

> The cultivator becomes for the time being the proud possessor of as many acres as he cares to monopolize, and there is besides no formality to be gone through, and no reference necessary to any authority for permission.[40]

Small wonder that little improvement was made in the production techniques in agriculture. To give an example of the stagnant rural technology, a simple comparison between the following remarks made on cotton cultivation in Khorasan in 1862 and 1897 respectively clarifies the point. In 1862, Consul Eastwick reported that 'the method of cultivating cotton in Khorasan, of picking and cleaning it, is the worst possible. In fact, no pains whatever are bestowed on the plant, or its product.'[41] Some 35 years later, Consul Yate, reporting from the same province which by then was producing a large quantity of cotton, remarked: 'No improved agricultural implements of modern European manufacture have as yet been brought into use in Khorasan. At present the most primitive tools are used.'[42] It should be mentioned, however, that the expansion of cotton was partly at the expense of opium and partly of wheat and barley.[43]

As to the taxation system of Khorasan, none of the reports written in the nineteenth century dealt with this subject. Nevertheless, a report prepared by Sykes in the early years of the twentieth century gives some useful information on the revenue system of the province. The fact that Sykes served as British Consul at Mashhad for several years in the 1890s gives a particular importance to his report as it is based on first-hand information. In his report, Sykes examined two different types of villages, *arbabi* and what he called *rayati* (owned by the peasants). Two typical villages were chosen, and it was found that in the *arbabi* village 50 per cent of the inhabitants were landless labourers, and only ten out of 20 adult males were tenants owing eight yoke of oxen.[44] In the latter group, only one-third were land-owners, and of the rest, one-third ordinary landless labourers, one-sixth shawl-weavers, and the rest shopkeepers and carpenters.[45] About 40 per cent of the land in the *arbabi* village was irrigated by a *qanat* owned and maintained by the landlord, and the rest was said to be *daimi* cultivation. For any repair work on the *qanat*, the villagers received 'a small wage for their labour' from the landlord.⁴⁶ In the peasant-owned village, however, the source of water was not specified. In the former village, the tenants bore all the expenses of cultivation and provided their own seed grain. The water was provided *prima facie* free of charge by the proprietor who, on both irrigated and unirrigated land, took away half of the crop, out of which he paid the government's share of 13 per cent, leaving 37 per cent for the proprietor.⁴⁷

In the peasant-owned village the situation was different. One-third of the inhabitants, about 500, paid no taxes at all in view of their poverty; it is most likely that they represented the landless labourers. Another third – shawl-weavers, shopkeepers and carpenters – paid a poll-tax of 4 *kran* per family, while the land-owning peasants, in total 100 families, paid 350 *tomans* in cash, and 10 *kharwar* in grain. In addition, 25 *toman* and one *kharwar* of grain were paid to the village elders, altogether about 6 per cent of the inhabitants, and another 25 *toman* were paid for the food and other expenses of visiting government officials.⁴⁸ Compared with the shawl-weavers and shopkeepers, the agriculturalists paid a family tax of more than ten-fold. It is difficult to determine how representative these villages were, but there is no doubt that the living standards of the peasantry were low, and for various reasons it could hardly improve.

The Province of Kermanshah

The province of Kermanshah, on the western frontier, appeared to be an exception to the rule in terms of cultivation and water provision. For many years it was a major grain-producing area, but lack of proper means of communication meant that more often than not the surplus grain could not be transported to the regions in need. For example, Napier found that about 80,000 tons of wheat which were stored in the province in the early 1870s were of little value to anyone on account of the impossibility of removal. This was against the background that a *kharwar* of grain valued at 7 *kran* in Kermanshah could easily sell for 30 and 40 *kran* elsewhere.⁴⁹

There is no evidence indicating any improvement in the next three to four decades. As late as 1903, Consul Rabino noted: 'It is usually impossible to export to the interior of Persia the Kermanshah's grain, the cost of transport being so very high.'⁵⁰ Table 2 shows the rates of transport cost to various parts of the country and to Baghdad for a *kharwar* of wheat, normally valued at 10 to 18 *kran* in Kermanshah.

An examination of the underlying causes of the backward transport system goes beyond the scope of this paper, but the fact remains that in these conditions the producer is unlikely to produce a surplus,

TABLE 2
THE RATE OF TRANSPORT PER KHARWAR (650 lbs) FROM KERMANSHAH, IN 1902–1903 (Krans)

To:	Min.		Max.
Rasht	110		180
Qazvin	100		170
Isfahan	100		150
Qom	70		100
Tehran	140		200
Kashan	70		100
Baghdad (1901–02)		40	
Tabriz (1901–02)		120	

Source: Rabino, Consular Report on Kermanshah, in P.P. 1903 lxxviii, p. 9.
Rabino, 'Trade and General Condition of the city and province of Kermanshah', in, P.P. 1903 lxxvi, p. 24.

as its value can hardly be realized. It is difficult to say whether it was because of this or other factors that, as Consul Herbert claimed in the late 1880s, there appeared to be a decline in the extent of land under cultivation in the province. He wrote: 'There is much less corn grown in the neighbourhood of Kermanshah than there was formerly, and not more than one-third of the land formerly cultivated is now under the plough.'[51] In contrast, however, in a report prepared in the early years of the twentieth century, it was said: 'The soil being fertile, and water plentiful in all seasons, the greater part of the province is either under cultivation or forms natural pasture grounds of large extent.'[52] Nevertheless, judging by the following data (Table 3) on the export of grain from Kermanshah to Baghdad, its main market, one may be led to believe that the greater part of the province was in fact pasture grounds, which in turn implies widespread nomadism.

In the cultivation-based areas, however, irrigation was performed 'without great outlay of capital' and *qanats* were 'very scarce in this part of Persia'.[53] The water to irrigate the lands came mainly from rivers, being plentiful in the province, but part of the cultivation had to rely on rain. As expected, *daimi* and *abi* cultivation were taxed differently. When the landowners supplied only land and water, they took away one-fourth to one-third of the produce from the irrigated lands, whereas from the *daimi* lands their share was one-fifth. When the landowner supplied seed and oxen in addition to land and water, his share was three-fourths.[54] Over and above a number of irregular

TABLE 3

THE QUANTITY OF GRAIN (IN CWT) EXPORTED TO BAGHDAD FROM KERMANSHAH, 1900–1906

Year	Quantity
1900	101
1901	25739
1902	47265
1903	14102
1904	1074
1905	71
1906	6

Source: Compiled from Consular Reports on Kermanshah, in P.P., various volumes.

dues, 'villagers have to supply labour free of charge when their masters are building',[55] whereas, as was seen earlier, in part of Khorasan, even when a *qanat* needed repair, the owner of the village employed the villagers, who received 'a small wage for their labour'.

Towards the end of the nineteenth century, the main cash crop produced in the province was opium, for which the landowner provided seed and implements and furnished all the expenses; in return he received about two-fifths of the produce. The initial expense represented about 15 per cent and the rest, about 45 per cent, went to the cultivators. Initially, the landlord took away two-thirds of the produce, but for each *man* (6½ lbs.) of the opium produced he had to pay 10 *kran* in cash to the cultivators.[56]

It is not clear what proportion of the total produce went to the government, but with an estimated total population of between 300,000 and 350,000, the land revenue of the province for 1902 was fixed at 72,000 *toman*.[57] Even this relatively small sum could not be collected easily. As Consul Rabino noted: 'I have been assured that for some years past a claim of 30,000 *toman* has been made yearly by the Governor *pro tem.* on the treasury in Tehran in order to balance account.'[58] But 'with a proper system of taxation and of collection of revenues' the province of Kermanshah could, Rabino asserted, 'have a large surplus revenue to remit to the Capital'.[59]

As to one of the likely causes of this depressed state of revenue, it is possible to argue that a large proportion of the inhabitants of the province appeared to be tribal; these were very lightly taxed and in some places, here as elsewhere, paid no taxes at all. As an attempt to illustrate this point, let us recall that Rabino estimated the total amount of taxes paid by 17 large and small tribes of Kurdistan (west of Kermanshah). According to this source, per capita tax of these tribes varied between 18 *shahi* (one kran = 20 *shahi*) for the Ketki tribe to 6 *kran* 2 *shahi* paid by the Duradji tribe. The overall average tax per head, however, was about 3 *kran*.[60] For the sake of comparison we have estimated the per capita tax paid by the peasants of the central provinces of Iran. On the basis of estimates provided by Consul Preece for 25 villages, with a total population of 68,000, the per capita tax paid by these peasants varied from 1 *kran* 6 *shahi* in one of the poor villages to 87 *kran* 10 *shahi* (improbably high figure) by the village of Surmak which was peasant property. The overall average per capita tax paid by these peasants was about four and a half times higher than the average paid by the Kurdish tribes, being 13 *kran* 6 *shahi* as compared with 3 *kran* for the latter. More than 82 per cent of these peasants, that is 55,300, paid a per capita tax at least twice as much as the former, whereas only 5 per cent, about 3,600 in number, paid less than that average.[61]

The Southern Provinces
Our examination of the modes and scales of surplus appropriation in various provinces seems to indicate quite clearly that no uniform pattern was in existence. As will be subsequently shown, an absence of uniformity was predominant in the rest of the country, thus giving further support to this point.

Ross, the British Consul at Bushire, indicated in his trade report for 1879 that the unevenly distributed and arbitrary fiscal burdens had led to 'the gradual depopulation of once flourishing districts', because

> When office is systematically given to the highest bidder, without reference to any fixed and well grounded assessment, and where taxes of districts are gradually being raised without corresponding increase of production[62]

disturbances ensue, and production declines. This was bound to be the consequence, as 'in return for his contribution to the revenue, it is difficult to point to the benefits conferred by the government to the husbandman', especially since 'no roads are constructed, no courts of justice constituted, no personal protection provided'.[63] The lawlessness appears to have become quite serious. The peasant, Ross continued, 'ordinarily prepares himself for his night's repose by arming himself to the teeth'.[64]

> A military force is certainly maintained, but the most frequent active employment of the soldiers is operating against the peasantry to enforce payment of revenue.[65]

On the revenue system of the province of Fars, he referred to the district of Kazeroon where land was said to be by and large 'private property'. The first factor influencing the rate of surplus appropriation was whether cultivation was undertaken by the owner of the land himself or whether it was done by others. In the former case, 11 per cent went to the government (tax), 20 per cent to the reapers and 2 to 4 per cent to threshing and treading the corn. In addition to seed and implements, the landowner also furnished 14 *kran* for each *gao* of cultivation (the space of land cultivated with one ox) for the labour of ploughing and sowing. In the latter category, the government received 14 per cent (tax) while the share of the proprietor was about 9 per cent (rent).

The second major division appears to have been between food and cash crops, such as cotton, sesame-seed, tobacco and so forth. As these crops were summer cultivation, these were always undertaken by proprietors of water and 'agriculturalists' conjointly. The landlord provided the water and the peasant furnished seeds and implements and the harvest was divided as follows:

20 per cent to the government (tax).
38 per cent to the proprietor (rent).
42 per cent to the peasant.

It was not made clear why the government share was relatively higher, from 11 per cent to 14 and subsequently to 20 per cent, but the above division seems to signify the importance of water in Iranian agriculture. Compared with *daimi* cultivation where the share of the landowner was only 9 per cent, the owner of water received a little less than two-fifths of the produce. Gardens and opium cultivation paid no taxes to the government and the landowner's share was half of the output.

Finally, Ross divided the 'agriculturalists of Kazeroon' into two groups: *ryot-i-Padishah* (literally meaning 'King's subject') and the non-*ryot* (either peasant proprietor or one working on a plot of land owned by individual landowners). The *ryot* cultivator not only paid more taxes to the government, but had to pay his taxes in cash and 'at 30 per cent above market value'. Those *ryots* who owned their lands, Ross maintained, paid 15½ per cent of the harvest in cash, which at the above enhanced valuation worked out to be over 20 per cent. Broadly speaking, a poor *ryot* paid annually about 60 *kran* while a wealthy *ryot* was squeezed for as much as 1000 *kran*. It is to be noted that Ross's account of the *ryot* and non-*ryot* cultivation is somehow vague and it is not clear why those who owned their own lands were still considered as *ryot-i-Padishah*.

In some parts of Fars, however, rice was also produced and had its own system of division. If the cultivator was a *ryot-i-Padishah*, he paid three-fifths to the government whereas the non-*ryot* paid half. The only possible explanation for this high rate of surplus appropriation seems to be that the government provided the water for irrigation.

It would be wrong to assume that the above system was universal in the province of Fars, let alone in other southern provinces. Around Shiraz (the provincial capital), a short distance from Kazeroon, the outturn was divided into three parts — one-third for the cultivator and two-thirds for the proprietor. A *motesaddee* (overseer) was employed by the proprietor, receiving as his salary 3 per cent of the produce. A *kadkhuda* (village headman) was also appointed, taking 5 per cent, thus leaving the peasant with about one-quarter of the produce.[66]

Stack, who travelled through the central and southern provinces, gave an altogether different picture. According to his assessment, 'in the vast majority of cases' of *daimi* cultivation nothing was paid to the government, i.e. no taxes, nor were these lands owned privately, that is no rent. Stack claimed:

> In a country like Persia, where land without water is of comparatively little value, dry land may be brought into cultivation by anybody who will take the trouble and risk of breaking it up and throwing seed into it on the chance of timely rain.[67]

If the cultivator got a crop, he paid a fixed proportion of it to the State as a tax upon agriculture; if he did not get a crop, he had nothing to pay. It was, Stack remarked, 'a matter of private speculation' by the cultivator. In parts of Fars, this fixed rate was one-tenth and in the plain west of Ahwaz (in Khuzistan) the rate was said to be as low as one-hundredth.[68]

Around Shiraz, the rate of taxation of irrigated lands was, according to Ross, two-thirds of the produce. This high rate of surplus appropriation marks out the very important role that water tended to play in Iranian agriculture. In addition, it appears to have given the landlords, or the owners of water, an extra element of power to undermine the tenancy rights of the peasants. According to Stack 'wet lands are annually distributed among the plough-owning cultivators'.[69] It is interesting to note that 'in most villages the area to be divided is not very great, nor are the ploughs very numerous'.[70] Given the shortage of ploughs, the absence of long-term arrangements between the landowners and plough-owners can only be attributed to an even shorter supply of irrigated lands, thus giving the landowners the power to distribute it annually and demand higher rent. Although in his view 'a Persian village is less populous than the average village of India, and nothing strikes one more than the smallness of its arable area as compared with the broad fields around an Indian village', yet, Stack asserted, the revenue assessment of the former 'certainly seem heavy'.[71] He cited examples in which the cultivators received only two-fifteenths of the produce.[72] The only place where the revenue assessment appeared to be relatively rational was in the Yazd plain, where it was based upon a calculation of a village's water supply, whereas in the rest of the country 'the quality of land seems to be left out of account in Persian assessment'.[73]

Information on the ways in which agricultural produce was distributed in other provinces in the southern part of Iran is scarce, but the following selection of evidence provides a broad indication of the problem.

Generally speaking, these provinces, namely Kerman, Khuzistan and Baluchistan, appear to have been less heavily taxed than Gilan and Azarbaijan, the main reason being that on the one hand, population density in these provinces was extremely low, and on the other, cultivation-based settlements were less numerous. In Khuzistan, for example, where population density was low and the supply of cultivable land inadequate, 'the land tax is light, and every encouragement appears to be given to cultivators'.[74] On Kerman, Sykes, writing in 1896, noticed that 'the fact is no landlord can grind his tenants too hard or they would desert his village in a body and so ruin his property, population being very difficult to replace'.[75] According to his estimate, in Kerman and Baluchistan about 60 per cent of the total population were 'tent-dwellers', whereas in Khorasan these numbered only 60,000 out of an estimated total population of 427,500 in the 1870s, i.e. 14 per cent. The main reason for such a high rate of nomadism in Kerman and Baluchistan was that in these provinces 'no crops can depend upon the natural water supply'.[76] On the other hand, little or nothing was done to maintain and expand the irrigation systems which had been badly neglected for decades. Sykes also claimed:

> In Baluchistan there are several hamlets inhabited by slaves, who till the government property around Bampour. Their condition is extremely pitiable, as having no rights, they are kept on the verge of starvation and in rags. Nominally they receive one-third of the produce of the soil, but even this meagre percentage is subject to considerable official reductions.[77]

What exactly this passage seems to imply is unclear, but it does confirm the poor condition of the peasantry working on the State-owned lands. As a matter of fact, Stack also found that State-owned villages were more heavily taxed, sometimes two and a half times higher,[78] but strangely enough he went on to say that '[there is] a constant tendency of *arbabi* lands to become *divani* [State-owned] ... by confiscation, and by escheat'.[79] Given the frequently expressed opinion that the desolation of State-owned lands was greater than that of lands owned privately, the above trend can hardly be considered as a positive factor in the development of Iranian agriculture during this period. It should be mentioned, however, that towards the end of the nineteenth century this trend was to some extent reversed. As an attempt to counter the fiscal crisis of the State, State-owned lands were sold out and private landownership increased.[80]

CONCLUSION

A broad indication has been given of the revenue system of Iran in the nineteenth century. It has been shown that no uniform rate or mode of surplus extraction existed in Iran during this period. It would be fair to argue that the mode of surplus appropriation, especially its inherent arbitrariness, tended to diminish the revenue base and the supply of future income. As under any other form of surplus extraction relationship, the Iranian peasant was to the ruling class mainly a producer of revenue, but there was no *fixed assessment on the land*, enabling energetic peasants to keep a surplus. On the contrary, it appeared to be a *fixed proportion of the crop*; thus in Iran the more the peasant grew, the more he had to turn over to the tax-collector (State officials or individual landowners). It is most likely that this was an important factor making it difficult to achieve technical improvement.

Furthermore, the Iranian system of tax-farming contained a built-in temptation to squeeze the peasants heavily. If the Shah left an assignee in charge of a single area for a substantial period of time, he ran the risk of losing control over his subordinates as the latter developed an independent source of revenue and basis for his power. On the other hand, if the assignees were changed frequently from one province to another, the subordinates would be tempted to get as much out of the peasants as possible in the time available. Cultivation would then decline and, ultimately, the revenue of the State. As a matter of fact, the latter course was the one taken by the Iranian despots in the nineteenth century. Fard-Saidi suggested that in 1848–96 the governorship of Fars changed hands more than 15 times, of Khorasan more than 20 times, and that of Khuzistan at least 15 times. During the same period, at least 13 governors ruled over Kerman.[81]

At the same time, however, absence of a legal framework concerning property rights meant that there was no landed aristocracy that had succeeded in achieving independence and privilege against the supreme despot, the Shah, while retaining political unity. Instead their independence, if it can be called that, had brought anarchy in its train, as was the case in Iran in the eighteenth century.

We have no statistical data to demonstrate the effects of the revenue system on agricultural production, but there appears to be reasonable ground for conjecture that it had a detrimental impact on the development of agriculture in Iran, to the extent that it was no longer capable of supporting a stagnant, if not declining, population. The frequency of food scarcity, in extreme cases of famine – as in 1810–11, 1816–17, 1860–61, and 1870–72 – and of bread riots in Iranian towns may be an indication of this deteriorating situation. On numerous occasions, it developed into rebellion against the local governors.[82]

Although the official historians referred to these instances as 'agitation by the bandits and trouble-makers', the underlying cause of disorder was the fact that the poorer classes found subsistence more and more difficult and tried to safeguard their existence. Saiid Khan, a rebel leader in the province of Baluchistan, proposed in 1881 to place 1,000 well-armed soldiers at the disposal of the government in return for '100 pickaxes and shovels for the purpose of cultivation, 10 pairs of draught oxen, and 150 sacks of grain for seed ... [besides] some old privileges in the field of taxation'.[83] What this set of demands manifested in simple economic terms was the provision of an initial capital plus a guarantee for a safe and reasonable reward for labour i.e. the obvious preconditions for production and the creation of wealth vis-à-vis the development of agriculture. Preconditions that, as we have shown in this article, appear to have often been lacking in Iran during the nineteenth century.

NOTES

1 A. Seyf, 'Some Aspects of Economic Development in Iran, 1800–1906', Ph.D. thesis, Reading University, 1982, pp. 232–4 (hereafter, Thesis).
2 G. N. Curzon, *Persia and the Persian Question*, London, 1892 (reprinted Cass, 1966), 2 vols., vol. 2, p. 443.
3 See for example, M. R. Fashahi, *Tahavvolat e Fekri va Ijtema'i dar Jame'a Feodali e Iran*, Tehran, 1975, p. 199.
4 Seyf, Thesis, pp. 68–74.
5 J. R. MacCulloch, *A Dictionary, Geographical, Statistical and Historical of Various Countries*, 2 vols., London, 1841, vol. 2, pp. 492–3.
6 Seyf, Thesis, pp. 256–66.
7 K. E. Abbott, 'Narrative of a Journey from Tabriz Along the Shores of the Caspian Sea to Tehran, 1843/4', in FO 251/40, p. 22.
8 Ibid., pp. 22–5.
9 Ibid., p. 190.
10 Ibid., pp. 102–3.
11 K. E. Abbott, 'Report of a Journey to the Coast of the Caspian Sea During 1847/8', in FO Confidential Prints, No. 136, p. 8.

12 Ibid., p. 9.
13 Ibid., p. 9.
14 Ibid., p. 9.
15 K. E. Abbott, Consular Report (CR) on Gilan, in *Parliamentary Accounts and Papers* (hereafter, PP), 1867, lxvii.
16 Ibid., in PP 1867, lxvii.
17 H. L. Churchill, CR 'Trade of Gilan', in PP 1878, lxxiv.
18 Ibid.
19 Abbott, CR Gilan, in PP 1865, lxvii.
20 See Seyf, Thesis, pp. 261–6.
21 Churchill, CR 'Trade of Gilan', in PP 1878, lxxiv.
22 Ibid.
23 Ibid.
24 Abbott, CR Gilan, in PP 1865, lxvii.
25 B. Lovett, CR 'Trade and Commerce of the Province of Asterabad', in PP 1882, lxxi.
26 Ibid.
27 Ibid.
28 Based on prices given in ibid., PP 1882, lxxi.
29 See Seyf, Thesis, pp. 514.
30 W. J. Dickson, 'Trade of Azarbijan', in PP 1861, lxiii.
31 Ibid.
32 W. G. Abbott, CR 'Some Accounts of the Province of Azarbijan', in FO 60/286.
33 W. G. Abbott, CR 'The Agricultural Resources of Azarbijan', in PP 1888, cii.
34 Ibid.
35 Ibid.
36 M. Durand, 'Memorandum on the Situation in Persia', in FO Confidential Prints, No. 6704, p. 2.
37 A. Wratislaw, CR 'Trade of Azarbijan', in PP 1906, cxxvii.
38 See M. H. Hakimian, 'Wage Labor and Migration: Persian Workers in Southern Russia 1880–1914', *Int. J. Middle East Stud.*, 17, 1985. See also Seyf, Thesis, pp. 161–3.
39 N. Elias, CR 'Trade of Khorasan', in PP 1897, xcii.
40 Ibid.
41 E. B. Eastwick, CR 'Trade of Khorasan', in PP 1863, lxx.
42 C. E. Yate, CR 'Trade of Khorasan', in PP 1898, xcvii.
43 See for example, Yate, CR 'Trade of Khorasan', in PP 1894, lxxxvii and P. M. Sykes, CR 'Trade of Khorasan', in PP 1906, cxxvii.
44 P. M. Sykes, *Report on the Agriculture of Khorasan*, Calcutta, 1910, reprinted in C. Issawi (ed.), *The Economic History of Iran, 1800–1914*, Chicago 1971, p. 253.
45 Ibid., p. 254.
46 Ibid., p. 255.
47 Ibid., pp. 253–4.
48 Ibid., pp. 254–5.
49 Quoted in J. U. Bateman-Champain, 'On the Various Means of Communication between Central Persia and the Sea', in *Royal Geographical Society Proceedings*, 1883, p. 127.
50 H. L. Rabino, CR 'Trade of the Province of Kermanshah', in PP 1903, lxxviii.
51 A. Herbert, CR 'Trade and Industries of Persia', in PP 1887, lxxxv.
52 Rabino, CR 'Trade and General Condition of the City and Province of Kermanshah', in PP 1903, lxxvi, p. 15.
53 Ibid., p. 33.
54 Ibid., p. 33.
55 Ibid., p. 33.
56 Rabino, CR 'Trade of Kermanshah', in PP 1905, ci.
57 Rabino, CR 'Trade and General Condition ...', p. 65.
58 Ibid., p. 65.
59 Ibid., p. 65.

60 Ibid., p. 62.
61 J. R. Preece, CR 'Journey to Yazd, Kerman, Shiraz ... and on the Trade of Isfahan', in PP 1894, lxxxvii.
62 E. C. Ross, CR 'Trade of Bushire', in PP 1880, lxxiii.
63 Ross, CR 'Trade of Bushire', in PP 1880, lxxiii.
64 Ibid.
65 Ibid.
66 Ibid.
67 E. Stack, *Six Months in Persia*, 2 vols., London, 1882, vol. 2, p. 251.
68 Ibid., p. 252.
69 Ibid., p. 253.
70 Ibid., p. 253.
71 Ibid., p. 257.
72 Ibid., p. 258.
73 Ibid., pp. 271, 275.
74 T. E. Gordon, 'Report on a Journey from Tehran to Karun and Mohammareh via Qom... Dizful and Ahwaz', in PP 1890/1, lxxxiv, p. 10.
75 P. M. Sykes, CR 'Trade of Kerman and Baluchistan', in PP 1896, lxxxviii.
76 Ibid. See also G. C. Napier, *Collection of Journal and Reports on Special Duty in Persia, 1874, Strictly Confidential*, London, 1876, pp. 204–94.
77 Sykes, CR 'Trade of Kerman ...', in PP 1896, lxxxviii.
78 Stack, *Six Months ...*, vol. 2, pp. 271–2.
79 Ibid., p. 248.
80 Seyf, Thesis, pp. 232–4.
81 M. Fard-Saidi, 'The Early Phases of Political Modernization in Iran, 1870–1925', Ph.D. Disst. (unpublished) Pennsylvania University, 1974, p. 90.
82 See Seyf, Thesis, pp. 101–3, 116–37.
83 A. Gasteiger, *From Tehran to Baluchistan – Narrative of a Journey in 1881*, n.p. 1884, p. 37.

5

Recent Trends in Agricultural Development in the Near East

A. A. El-Sherbini

INTRODUCTION

The Near East has been at the centre of world attention for more than thirty years. Its strategic importance stems from its geographic location between East and West, and from its huge oil reserves which constitute more than 57 per cent of the known world crude oil reserves. It is also a region characterized by rapid change, social upheavals and political conflicts which constitute a constant source of concern to many developed and developing countries. At present, four wars have been underway for many years in the region. The causes of instability are many, and food riots have erupted suddenly in Egypt, Morocco, Tunisia, and Sudan consecutively with such violence that they have threatened to destabilize existing regimes. The Sudan food riots led in 1985 to the fall of the Government. This has seldom occurred in other regions of the world. In essence, food politics have become an important new dimension of food security in this vital region, as will be demonstrated later in this paper.

DEMANDS ON THE AGRICULTURAL SECTOR

The scope of the region covered herein encompasses all Arab countries (including Somalia and Sudan), in addition to Turkey. This differs from the coverage adopted by some agencies, research institutions, and writers who often include Iran, Pakistan, and Afghanistan as part of the region.

In portraying the recent trends of agricultural development in the region, the focus will be on the performance of the agricultural sector with respect to the demands put on that sector by the national economies of the countries in the region. These demands are numerous and multifaceted, but may be succinctly summarized as follows:

- Provision of adequate food supplies for the country's population.
- Contribution to national wealth and capital formation.
- Earnings of scarce foreign exchange.
- Provision of sufficient employment opportunities, particularly for the rural population.
- Supply of necessary raw materials for domestic industry.

It is not possible within the scope of this paper to present empirical evidence concerning the assessment of sectoral performance with respect to these various demands. However, there is ample evidence in available literature to document the deteriorating trend of sectoral performance in meeting these critical demands. For instance, the import gap of basic cereals has risen from about 12 million tons in 1975 to about 28 million tons in 1983, which reflects an increase of about 133 per cent in only eight years.[1] Apart from basic staples, the region is currently a large net importer of other important foodstuffs such as vegetable oils, sugar, fats, dairy products, and meat.

The agricultural sector, which was a major source of capital formation and foreign exchange earnings until the late 1960s, has now been superseded by other sectors and sources in several countries of the region. It presently occupies third or fourth place after such sources as workers' remittances, oil, mining, tourism and foreign aid. In most countries of the region, the share of agriculture in the aggregate GDP has shown a declining trend, particularly giving way to a relative expansion of the services sector. This is, of course, partly a factor of the vigour of other sectors in some of these countries, but is also a sign of stagnating investment and development of the agricultural sector itself.

Agriculture's failure to generate sufficient employment opportunities in the region is worth special consideration. In effect, the sector has not even been successful in retaining its historical share of total population and labour force. This has been essentially a result of lower productivity in the agricultural sector in comparison with other sectors, leading to income disparities which triggered a massive rural exodus. Low labour productivity could be attributed to two factors. The first is stagnating or declining yields per hectare, which is the result of a combination of poor incentives, inadequate institutional support, and the lack of appropriate technological development particularly in the vast dryfarming areas of the region. The second factor accounting for low labour productivity is the continuous decline in cultivated area per labour unit due to land fragmentation and population pressure on limited arable land. This explains why even in countries with relatively high yields, such as Egypt, labour productivity (and consequently per caput real farm income) has been stagnating or declining.

This particular weakness in the sector's performance has led to serious imbalances stemming from rural migration, such as overburdening the urban centres, and the speculative investment of migrant remittances in land acquisition which has driven land prices to astronomical levels. Ironically, in labour exporting countries, this has given rise to a situation of serious labour shortages in the agricultural sector.

As a source of raw materials for domestic industries, the sector also faces certain difficulties in some countries of the region. One problem is the shift from industrial crops to other crops such as forage, fruits and vegetables. This has limited the supply of raw materials for domestic industry. Another problem has been the continuous rise in the farmgate prices of agricultural raw materials in the face of inflexible price structure for processed products administered by the government. Some public sector processing industries are already sustaining heavy losses which constitutes a drain on government budgets. Vegetable oils, sugar, fruit and vegetable canning and processing industries are examples of these adverse developments.

NEW DIMENSIONS IN FOOD SECURITY

Of all the shortfalls in the performance of the agricultural sector in the region, the problem of food availability merits special attention. The Middle East is not normally identified with hunger and mass starvation. Nonetheless, periodically poor rainfalls and runoff, fragile food distribution systems and limited foreign exchange bring some countries in the region precariously close to famine conditions. A very good example is the present situation in the Sudan, where almost seven million people are threatened with starvation as a result of severe drought and lack of access to food, which in effect reflects a potentially more serious situation than the recent Ethiopian disaster.

However, by and large the region has not suffered from severe shortages in food availability (i.e., domestic production plus imports). In fact, dietary energy supplies in the region have been rising in recent decades, especially in relation to other regions. The problem, however, concerns *food security* and the increasing over-dependence on foreign sources for the supply of food, particularly cereals, which constitute the main elements in the provision of per caput calorie and protein intake in many countries of the region. The region's food security is threatened by exogenous forces such as the world food crisis of 1972–4 when grain prices increased by 250 per cent.

It is important to explore the factors which have led to the explosion in the region's cereals demand since the early 1970s. Some planners assert that population growth in the region is the main culprit for the rapid growth in cereal demand. But population is not a homogeneous variable; it consists of rich and poor people. The same increase in population would have one effect on the demand for food if it occurred among the poor and a different effect among the rich. Thus, we must recognize the *graduation* of the population into socio-economic classes, which in the Middle East region was essentially a result of income growth, both in the oil-rich countries and the middle-income countries through remittances and other sources of income growth.

The sudden rise in the income of oil-rich countries and the emergence of a sizeable middle class in other countries of the region (with the exception of the LDCs) has resulted in a significant shift from direct to indirect cereal consumption (in the form of animal feed) which represents a move up the food chain and changes in the composition of the food basket from plant to animal protein. As a consequence, the weight that feed use assumes in total cereal demand has increased rapidly. This explains the significant rise in the region's imports of coarse grains since the early 1970s, particularly earmarked to livestock and poultry feeding. For instance, Egypt's imports of maize increased from less than half a million tons four years ago to around two million tons in 1985, out of which only 300,000 tons were earmarked to direct human consumption.

The above analysis is in line with the findings of a study published by the International Food Policy Research Institute (IFPRI)[2] which forecasts that surge in demand for coarse grains as animal feed is expected to alter the mix of crops that make up the cereal gap in the region. As a result, regional coarse grain deficits are projected to increase substantially by the end of the century. Already some countries in the region are suffering from coarse grain shortages. A recent article in a leading Egyptian newspaper showed that 4,155 poultry farms are in a predicament to the extent that 4.5 million chicks had to be exterminated by a parastatal distributor due to lack of feed.

The food–feed competition in the region also has socio-political implications. Historically, that competition was only indirect and localized. It has been essentially competition for the land on which to grow food or feed, such as the competition between Berseem clover and winter wheat in the Nile delta of Egypt. Today, there is also direct competition for the final disposition of grain production between feed and food. Thus another dimension has been added: people who compete with people for the indirect versus direct consumption of cereals.

As a result, any increase in the demand for feed grains would be reflected in the grain market by driving prices of cereals up. In the extreme case, the animals for the consumption of the rich would be crowding out the direct demand for the subsistence of the poor.

Greater emphasis on basic food self-reliance at both the national and regional levels should become an effective strategy for coping with the food–feed competition in the region. The argument of self-reliance rests partly on the political and economic irreversibility of trade in cereals, the cost of which can become very large if food security is threatened by a world crisis. Some countries in the region that have let agriculture go and rely on imports of basic food staples cannot easily reverse policies to count on domestic supplies when international prices rise. Similarly, countries that have filled the middle-class demand for meat with cheap feed imports may be under domestic political pressure to continue doing so despite rising costs of such imports.[3]

PRODUCTION AND INSTITUTIONAL CONSTRAINTS

It is important at this juncture to consider some major constraints on agricultural production in the region and its failure to cope with the various demands put on that sector. These constraints are many and reflect significant diversities among the countries of the region. Any fruitful analysis should be carried out on a country-by-country basis. Nonetheless, it is possible to delineate certain structural developments which have been at work in almost all countries of the region, albeit with varying impact. These can be summarized as follows:

1. The environmental impact

The region has a slender agricultural resource base which has been subjected to adverse long-term environmental changes affecting the entire life-supporting system of the region. Desertification, resource degradation, soil erosion, water-logging and salinity are examples of environmental developments at work in the Middle East region. Some of these developments are of a natural origin, but many changes are man-made. They are the result of over-grazing, poor range management, the increasing conflict between livestock and crop production, and population pressures on marginal land. As an example, much of the vast gum arabic area in western Sudan has been gradually converted into acacia trees, reflecting an acute case of desertification. In Egypt, around 20,000 hectares of good irreplaceable fertile land are lost annually to urban sprawl.

Although there are no accurate data about the size of land overtaken by desertification or that of reduced productivity, all indications point at the gravity of the problem in a region which is not generally hospitable to agricultural development. The difficulty of arresting the deterioration of the life-support system in the region is that it is rather imperceptible in the short run and, consequently, has not received the necessary government attention and external donors' interest and assistance.

2. Production instability

The bulk of the arable land in the region is earmarked to dry farming. Adequate rainfall is crucial to profitable farming. But rainfall variability in the large arid and semi-arid areas of this region has often given rise to considerable production instability, particularly in the case of wheat and coarse grains. So far, not much has been done to solve this problem. The annual variations in rainfall have not even been carefully studied and analyzed. An attempt was made in this respect in my book entitled *Food Security Issues in the Arab Near East* (Pergamon Press, 1979), which yielded useful results in constructing probability distributions of variations in crop yields in response to the intensity and distribution of annual rainfall.

However, some recent developments are encouraging. For instance, Syria has established a 'green belt' of fruit trees such as olives, almonds, pistachios, and vineyards which can resist rainfall fluctuations in dryfarming areas. The area covered by this green belt grew from 352,033 hectares in 1975 to 524,897 hectares in 1985. Subsequently, fruit production in these areas has increased by about 60 per cent in the ensuing period.

3. Power relations

Although agrarian reform has been introduced in several countries of the region, there exists a chasm between those in the rural areas who are able to profit from the increased productivity of the land and others without the means to extract a decent living from their land and labour. In some countries, the relative prosperity of the regions' surplus farmers is frequently the result of their differential claims on the state's resources. Where modernization, mobilization, and commercialization have had their heaviest impact on rural life, there have emerged two agricultural societies, one commercially oriented and favoured, the other composed of neglected small farmers. The distinction between the so-called 'secteur moderne' and 'secteur traditionnel' in some Maghreb countries of the region reflects this striking duality.

In other countries of the region, long after the breakdown of feudal systems and large estates, a shift of power relations has recently taken place to the advantage of medium-size farmers in rural areas. This new class has allied itself with local authorities to the detriment of small farmers. As a result of many privileges, the medium-size farmers have been able to specialize in the production of highly profitable uncontrolled crops such as forage crops, fruits, and vegetables. In contrast, the underprivileged small farmers were forced to grow government-controlled crops which are comparatively much less remunerative, such as basic cereals and cotton.

To the foregoing structural constraints, should be added the limited agricultural resource endowments of the region where cultivated areas constitute only 6 per cent of total land area. Other factors include the low technological base of production, and the lack of adequate physical and institutional infrastructure such as transportation and communication, research, marketing and distribution systems in many countries of the region. Although several countries are expanding irrigation facilities, irrigated farming as a proportion of total cultivated area remains very low. Other factors which militate against faster growth of farm output include inadequate input delivery networks, insufficient and poorly motivated extension systems, and inappropriate government pricing and subsidy policies.

As a result of this combination of natural, institutional and policy constraints, Near East food production grew at a rate of about 2.2 per cent per year in the last decade. Such a rate is lower than that achieved in Latin America or Asia; however, it is higher than that of Sub-Saharan Africa. Slightly more than half of the growth was 'intensive' or attributable to increased output per unit of land; the remainder came from bringing additional (and increasingly marginal) land under cultivation.

Since the rate of expansion of the cultivated area in the region is unlikely to be maintained, it is evident that further growth of food production in the region must increasingly come from more intensive land use. Thus, currently the region is clearly in the process of shifting from extensive to intensive agricultural growth. This process will be difficult and expensive. It will certainly deeply involve the state and it will both require and stimulate considerable rural social change.

REGIONAL SEGMENTATION

It is clear that such aggregate data conceal wide differences among countries or groups of countries in the region. A strategy of regional segmentation has the merit of delineating differences between groups of countries in the region, with the objective of assessing their food potential and vulnerability. For practical purposes, the region may be segmented into five groups of countries in relation to their capacity to ensure food availability (either through domestic production or imports) in a descending order as follows:

1. Very rich oil-producing countries with a very limited agricultural potential
This segment includes the small gulf states, Saudi Arabia, and Libya. Both Libya and Saudi Arabia have poured billions of dollars into highly capital-intensive and costly food production projects. Although less than 2 per cent of the country's land area is arable, Libya authorized more than US$ 10 billion for agricultural development in the five-year plan beginning in 1981. Saudi Arabia increased its planned investment in agriculture for the period 1980–85 to US$ 21,669 million. In a recent speech at FAO, the Saudi Minister of Agriculture claimed that his country has become nearly self-sufficient in wheat production, which increased from negligible levels to 1.3 million tons at present. The government policy of subsidizing wheat production (at a farmer's price of US$ 600 per ton) is costing the country US$780 million per annum. The issue is whether this production process can be maintained at reduced budgetary cost, now that major investments can be treated as sunk costs.

2. Rich oil-producing countries with underutilized food production potential
This segment includes Algeria and Iraq. Until the mid-1970s, both countries lavished the bulk of their abundant resources on prestigious industrial projects, infrastructures, and urban development. As a result, their average indices of per caput food production in 1980–82 (1969–71 = 100) dropped to 75 and 87 respectively.[4] These alarming developments prompted the two countries to rechannel significant resources to agriculture. Thus, Algeria gave new emphasis in its 1980–84 Plan to agricultural development and raised its allocation for agriculture to US$ 12,274 million with particular focus on developing dryfarming areas. Similarly, Iraq set aside US$ 10.5 billion in its 1976–80 Plan for agricultural development, 60 per cent of which was earmarked to irrigation development. However, this momentum has been thwarted in recent years by the war with Iran.

3. Middle-income countries with adequate food production potential
This group includes Turkey and Syria. The two countries have significant agricultural potential, particularly in comparison with other countries

in the region. Their arable land/man ratios are relatively high and their average per caput food production in 1980–82 stood at 115 and 168 respectively.[5] The latter index reflects the highest achievement in the region. Turkey in particularly is reliant on its own grain production in meeting domestic demand. Its cereal imports as a percentage of total domestic requirements declined from 2.5 per cent in 1975 to barely 0.74 per cent in 1983. Because of the instability of its cereal production, Syria has not enjoyed the same advantage and in 1983 had to import 1,560,880 tons of cereals compared with 369,408 in 1975. However, Syria has a significant food production potential through the expansion and intensification of irrigated agriculture, as well as in increasing dryfarming production in relatively high rainfall areas through the improvement of technology and extension.

4. Middle-income countries with fragile foreign exchange resources
This is the group in which most of the food riots have occurred in recent years. It includes Egypt, Morocco, Tunisia and Jordan. Although the four countries have relatively important agricultural sectors, they also tend to be those who have given high priority to industrialization in the 1960s and early 1970s to the detriment, in part at least, of agriculture. As a result, their reliance on foreign sources for meeting their food demand requirements has significantly increased in recent years. At present, the four countries rely on foreign sources of supply to meet about 50 per cent of their cereal requirements. So far, however, these countries have been able to meet their food import bills by foreign exchange generated from volatile and unpredictable sources such as workers' remittances, tourism, and foreign aid. As consumer prices of basic food staples are heavily subsidized in these countries, rising food demand constitutes an increasing drain on government budgets. All attempts to reduce subsidies and increase prices have been thwarted by urban violence. In essence, the governments of these countries have become 'hostages' to their own food subsidy systems. At present, new efforts to invigorate food production are underway, but long-term prospects of food availability, particularly for the poor classes in these countries, are difficult and uncertain.

5. The least developed countries of the region
This segment includes Sudan, Somalia, South Yemen, and North Yemen. Apart from their relatively low per caput GNP, all four countries have very limited import capacities. Their indices of per caput food production in 1980–82 have all fallen below 100, with Somalia registering the most dramatic drop in the region (its index stands at 60). The problem of

food security in this group is not only one of food availability, but also one of *access* to food supplies by the rural poor. This is essentially the result of poor infrastructures and the existence of clusters of extreme poverty, particularly in remote areas of these countries. The recent famine in southern and western Sudan is a vivid example of food inaccessibility, ironically in a country which is endowed with abundant agricultural resources.

REGIONAL COOPERATION

In conclusion, something should be said about the prospects of food self-sufficiency at the regional or sub-regional levels. So far, intra-regional trade at present accounts for less than 15 per cent of the region's overall trade with the rest of the world.

The first major attempt at regional cooperation was the preparation of the 'Major Programme for Agricultural Development in the Sudan', which was undertaken by the Arab Fund for Agricultural and Social Development of Kuwait in 1975. The programme aimed at the realization of large food surpluses and agricultural raw materials in Sudan for export to food-deficit Arab countries. Subsequently, an Arab Authority for Agricultural Development was established in Khartoum to carry out the programme with initial funding of US$ 500 million. Unfortunately, the programme was beset by poor management and leadership, in addition to serious obstacles resulting from the instability and erratic performance of the macro-environment.

Very recently, regional cooperation was given a new hope by the establishment of a 'Project Promotion Agency for Arab Food Security' based in Saudi Arabia. It is presently underwriting joint ventures encompassing four major projects in Sudan with an estimated capital of US$ 430 million and covering such food products as rice, cereals and pulses, livestock and meat products, and food processing industries. The above-mentioned Arab Authority for Agricultural Development will be one of the major subscribers in the capital of these projects.

The private sector has also taken a recent initiative by establishing in 1984 an 'Arab Company for Agricultural Investment' with an authorized capital of one billion dollars. The founders include 300 leading Arab businessmen and the company's capital will be offered for subscription in all Arab countries. The company's headquarters will be in Bahrain. The company intends to implement several agricultural projects in Arab countries such as flowers and vegetables in glass houses in Saudi Arabia and Kuwait; rice, cereals, and pulses in Sudan; dairy products in Egypt and Tunisia; cereals in Algeria and Jordan; green

RECENT TRENDS IN AGRICULTURAL DEVELOPMENT

fodder in Syria; poultry farms in Qatar; honey in South Yemen; and date production in United Arab Emirates.

Undoubtedly these are positive developments in which the capital-surplus countries of the region are playing the major part. However, the attainment of regional self-reliance in food production remains a distant goal at best. It is challenged not only by the spiralling growth rates of food demand, but also by political conflicts among various groups of countries in the region, social unrest, and continuing instability.

NOTES

1 FAO Computer Printouts, Supply Utilization Accounts for 18 countries in the region. The data cover all cereals, wheat flour converted to grain equivalent, and milled rice converted to paddy.
2 N. Khaldi, 'Evolving Food Gaps in the Middle East/North Africa Region', International Food Policy Research Institute, Dec. 1984.
3 I am indebted to Professor P. Yotopoulos of Stanford University for valuable insights into the food–feed controversy.
4 *World Bank Development Report*, 1984.
5 *World Bank Development Report*, 1984.

6

The Oil Nationalization Movement, the British Boycott and the Iranian Economy 1951–1953

Kamran M. Dadkhah

1. INTRODUCTION

The Oil Nationalization Movement of 1951–53 was a most significant episode in modern Iranian history. Although nationalization of a foreign oil company was not without precedent (Mexico had nationalized its oil concerns in 1938), Iran's takeover of the Anglo-Iranian Oil Company immediately precipitated an international crisis. Subsequent events — tacit approval of this nationalization by the International Court in the Hague, Britain's economic boycott of Iran, and the eventual downfall of Iranian Premier Mossadegh — profoundly affected future developments both in Iran and in the international oil market.[1]

Justifiably enough, the movement has attracted critical examination[2] and occupies a prominent position in general studies of contemporary Iranian history.[3] Yet all of these studies lack a detailed and quantitative analysis of economic factors bearing on the Nationalist Movement.[4] Consequently, historical analyses of the Mossadegh era suffer from two deficiencies. While some scholars acknowledge the severe economic crisis during this period,[5] they underemphasize the role played by economic factors in hastening the Movement's demise, choosing instead to concentrate on the political process and the role played by foreign powers and Iranian political parties. Others overemphasize Mossadegh's economic acumen; indeed, a national mythology has developed which erroneously credits him with remarkable economic improvements.[6]

This study will attempt to provide a more balanced view of this tumultuous period through a realistic assessment of economic conditions during Mossadegh's tenure. Such a study could hold important implications for policy formation in many LDCs, especially in those facing a sudden drop in foreign earnings. This study will present a quantitative analysis of the Iranian economy during the Mossadegh era. It will show that while oil revenue was a vital component of Iran's economy, the government neither anticipated nor planned for the repercussions attendant upon its long-term cutoff. The study will also show that the Iranian government adopted unsuccessful short-run policies to counter the effects of the British boycott; as a result, Iranian economic conditions deteriorated rapidly in all aspects.

To what extent the economic failure of Mossadegh's regime was responsible for the demise of the nationalist movement can only be surmised at present. Its investigation requires a study of all aspects of Iranian society during the movement, and it is, therefore, well beyond the limited scope of the present paper.

Section 2 of this paper provides a review of the role of oil revenues in the Iranian economy, together with a discussion of Mossadegh's view of the crisis. Section 3 studies the boycott's effect on the balance of trade and foreign exchange earnings in Iran, then elaborates on Mossadegh's import–export policies. The issues of governmental budgetary practices, deficit financing, and monetary policy are found in Section 4; while the relationship between money and inflation is discussed in Section 5. Section 6 takes up the problems of investment and growth and, finally, Section 7 contains the concluding remarks.

2. OIL REVENUE AND THE IRANIAN ECONOMY

In Iran, oil revenue has traditionally been the main source for foreign exchange earnings, government revenues, and saving and investment. In fact, the situation today is not very different from what it was in Mossadegh's time. Since the government received its oil revenue in the form of foreign exchange, its decisions concerning the allocation of resources affected both domestic aggregate demand and the supply of foreign exchange, imports, and import prices. Iran received less than 10 per cent of the Anglo-Iranian Oil Company's yearly oil exports revenues valued at approximately half a billion dollars. In order to finance its domestic expenditures, the oil company sold foreign exchange to the Iranian government which, in 1950, amounted to about $50 million. The Iranian government, in turn, allocated part of its foreign earnings to finance direct imports by government agencies (notably Plan Organization in 1950) and sold another part to private importers. (See Table 1 below for details of Iran's sources and uses of foreign exchange.) A 1952 report to Majlis by Mossadegh's finance minister Mahmoud Nariman showed that about 25 per cent of government outlays was

TABLE 1
FOREIGN EXCHANGE RECEIPTS AND OUTLAYS OF IRAN 1950–54
(in million dollars)

RECEIPTS

Year	Purchase of Foreign Exchange from:			Foreign Aid and Loans	Total
	Exporters	Others	Oil Company	Oil Revenues		
1950	61.8	4.3	56.1	58.9	—	180.9
1951	53.7	6.0	21.5	8.4	8.8	98.4
1952	59.5	4.0	—	—	—	63.5
1953	78.1	5.4	—	—	42.9	126.4
1954	94.9	11.9	11.9	22.5	81.4	222.6

OUTLAYS

Year	Sale of Foreign Exchange for:		Repayment of Principal and Interests on Loans	Government Foreign Exchange Outlays[1]	Total
	Imports	Non-Commercial Purposes			
1950	145.2	7.4	1.8	21.2	175.6
1951	145.7	7.6	2.0	11.9	167.2
1952	71.7	4.9	2.4	5.3	84.3
1953	94.4	2.2	—	9.1	105.7
1954	173.1	17.3	13.2	30.3	233.9

[1] The foreign exchange expenditures of Plan and Budget Organization, National Iranian Oil company and other government agencies.

Source: H. Shajari, *Bank-i Markazi Va Tajrobiat-i Pouli Iran* (Bank Markazi and Monetary Experience of Iran), Tehran: Markaz-i Nashr-i Sepehr, 1972, pp. 166 and 170–1.

financed prior to the cutoff of oil revenues through the sale of foreign exchange to businessmen and importers, who collectively conducted at least 75 per cent of the nation's foreign trade. When oil revenue ceased, the government's income was reduced by 37 per cent.[7] Only a portion of this oil revenue, after being exchanged for Rials, entered the government's general budget. Until 1941 (when the allied forces occupied Iran and Reza Shah abdicated) oil revenue was excluded from the ordinary government budget and kept in a special account for arms purchases and development expenditures.[8] From 1941 onward, government revenues in the ordinary budget included a part of oil income used to cover current expenditures.

Oil revenue furthered investment in the economy in two ways. As a source of saving, it provided necessary funds for investment. It also provided the necessary foreign exchange with which to purchase machinery and plants from abroad. If oil revenue were excluded, Iran ran a huge balance of trade deficit. Thus, her ability to import machinery and to establish modern industries was dependent on oil revenues. Oil revenues also assisted saving in two distinct ways. On the one hand, oil revenue was the source of government saving and investment. Indeed, a portion of the oil revenue was earmarked for the First Seven Year Development Plan approved by Parliament in 1949.[9] On the other hand, oil revenue provided the government with a ready source of income which in turn decreased the burden of taxation on the private sector. Lower tax rates left the private sector with more money to be saved and invested.

From the foregoing discussion it is clear that oil revenue played a vital and integral part in the economy, and that its cutoff would have generated severe economic hardship. Given these facts, it seems reasonable to ask why Mossadegh insisted on interpreting the Oil Nationalization Law[10] literally, and rejected all proposals for compromise with AIOC. If he had decided to continue the struggle through to ultimate victory, then why did he fail to develop a viable plan to sustain the economy during the crisis?

The contradictions between reality, ideals, and strategy derive from four factors:

(i) Historians have documented that Mossadegh and other National Front leaders misjudged the international oil markets, believing the world too dependent on Iranian oil to forgo its use for any lengthy period. This point has already been discussed extensively in the literature.[11]

(ii) Despite his education and intelligence, Mossadegh's governmental experience was anachronistic. When he was minister of finance, during the early 1920s, oil revenue was not substantial and neither the government nor the economy was oil revenue dependent.[12]

(iii) Mossadegh had correctly assessed both the rivalry between industrial countries and the American interest in Iranian oil. Rohani, in his invaluable book,[13] argues that the American government and oil companies fully supported both the AIOC and the British government in their dispute with Iran. Yet even a cursory reading of the same book will convince the reader that it was the U.S. oil companies' interest in Iranian oil that ultimately forced the British to capitulate and relinquish half their share in Iranian oil. Mossadegh had misjudged American foreign policy, which he expected to be as isolationist as it had been in the early twentieth century. At the end of his days as premier, when the more sympathetic Truman administration was replaced by Eisenhower's conservative government, Mossadegh rejected the final U.S.–British proposal which was closest to the Iranian demands, and made the grave error of invoking the threat of a communist takeover in order to obtain American support and financial aid.[14]

(iv) To understand the Mossadegh government's lack of a long-term economic plan, one has to reflect on Mossadegh's own economic doctrine. As adduced from his numerous public speeches, he was neither a socialist nor even a Keynesian, believing rather in a balanced budget, sound money, and a limited government role in the economy. In a speech at the fourteenth Majlis on the question of issuing notes, he pointed out:

> For your information, it is well known that when notes are issued beyond the need [of the economy], even with a hundred percent gold coverage, its value will decline and as a result there will be an increase in the cost [of living] ... some have thought of a solution in the form of taxing people to get [the notes] back from them. This is a cure worse than the disease.[15]

On another occasion, he criticized the government's monopoly of foreign trade, arguing that it had caused shortages and high prices during the Second World War. By contrast, Mossadegh noted that during World War I, merchants provided the country with all required goods and there was no inflation. (The accuracy of his statement is not at issue here.) Furthermore, he praised the British owned Imperial Bank of Persia, which held a monopoly on issuing notes in Iran, for its sound monetary policy.[16]

It is worth mentioning that as prime minister, Mossadegh intended 'to make a drastic cut in public expenditures, which, in postwar years, had been menacing the national economy with inflation and bankruptcy'.[17] A good portion of these expenditures was allotted to armed forces which were protected by the Shah. It is not clear if Mossadegh succeeded in cutting the armed forces budget.[18]

Mossadegh believed that oil revenue could further develop and haul Iran out of its cycle of poverty. But he intended to accomplish this within the bounds of the existing economic system and the principles of sound finance. Mossadegh may have doubted whether the economy, if left to itself, could make the necessary adjustments to an oil-less economy. But he definitely was no believer in planning or a government-directed economy. Toward the end of his days as premier, the Plan Organization was directed to draw up plans for an oil-less economy. Yet, despite the gravity of economic conditions, these plans remained strictly at the drawing board stage and Mossadegh made no serious strategic decision to change the long-run course of the economy. As one sympathetic observer noted:

> Iran's Plan Organization, which was responsible for economic and social planning, had a devoted and high-caliber staff under the direction of Ahmad Zanganeh. But the Plan Organization lacked the financial means for executing any program it might have devised, a deficiency which could only have been removed by the concluding of an oil agreement, and of even greater importance, it did not have the full support and interest of Mossadegh and his chief lieutenants that was necessary for success. The Plan Organization failed to receive the attention due it for the same reason that all other aspects of the positive program were neglected ...[19]

Recently, Makki[20] has argued that the aim of the National Front was to secure the political and economic independence of Iran and that its leaders harboured no illusions about the dependence of international oil markets on Iranian oil. There is no question about the first assertion. The second, however, fits neither facts nor logic. First, both the National Front and the government had promised the public that the nationalization of oil would bring higher income and better living conditions. Second, the government's failure to prepare the economy for a loss of oil revenue is clear evidence that Iranian leaders anticipated an early settlement of the dispute and resumption of oil revenue. Such expectations could be fulfilled only through compromise or unmitigated dependence of the world on Iranian oil. Compromise had already been eschewed. Consequently, with no presumption of world dependence on Iranian oil, the whole movement would be reduced to mere political adventurism, unworthy to be sure of Dr. Mossadegh.

It should be emphasized that the foregoing argument is not intended as a condemnation of Mossadegh or his intentions. Mossadegh exercised the right of a sovereign nation to its natural resources and stood ready to compensate the British company for its losses. At issue, however, are his expectations from AIOC and the British government. He could not have expected them to stand aside and watch Iran enter the international oil market to the detriment of their interests. In fact, if they had done so, Mossadegh and the National Front would have looked irrational and ungrateful to have expelled such benevolent and good-natured partners. The same goes for the American oil companies. They were in the oil business to make a profit; Mossadegh was naive to expect anything else.

Thus, the actions of the oil companies and the British and American governments were predictable because they were in accordance with their interests. Mossadegh's fatal mistake was to misjudge the reality of the oil market and the Iranian economy.

3. BALANCE OF TRADE, DEVALUATION AND FOREIGN AID

The first and most immediate impact of the oil revenue cutoff was a sharp decline of foreign exchange earnings. In 1950, Iran received about $59 million in oil revenue and purchased $56 million from AIOC. This amounted to about 64 per cent of Iran's total foreign exchange receipts. In 1951, oil revenue dwindled to only $8.4 million and the AIOC sale of foreign exchange to the Iranian government was limited to $21.5 million. In 1952 and 1953 both items were nil (see Table 1). On the assumption that the crisis would be transitory, Mossadegh first turned to foreign exchange reserves. He transferred 14 million pounds (1,264 million rials) from reserves which covered notes issued, and used them for immediate and necessary expenditures of the government.[21] This transfer was a reasonable action under the circumstances and had no adverse effect on the economy.[22] Still, it could be only a temporary remedy. Partly by design and partly because of market reaction to the shortage of foreign exchange, the government soon resorted to devaluation of Rial.

The devaluation reduced imports and stimulated exports. Although the volume of exports increased dramatically, foreign exchange earnings did not increase. Nonetheless, a myth has developed that Mossadegh was somehow able to balance Iran's exports and imports during this trying period. For example, Nirumand states that

> Exports and imports were brought into balance during the fiscal year 1952–1953, with exports growing rapidly during the succeeding years, almost doubling within two years. Imports remained at about the same level during this period, totalling no more than two-thirds of exports in Mossadegh's last year in office.[23]

TABLE 2
INTERNATIONAL TRANSACTIONS OF IRAN 1950–54

Year	Data from Iranian Customs in Billion Rials								Data from IMF in Million Dollars				
	Exports			Import Total	Exports			Import Total	Exports			Import Total
	Oil	Non-Oil	Total		Oil	Non-Oil	Total		Oil	Non-Oil	Total	
1950	22.2	3.5	25.7	7.1	20.00	2.61	22.61	11.42	620	60	680	258
1951	6.8	4.4	11.2	7.4	14.00	5.00	19.00	12.90	435	95	530	243
1952	—	5.8	5.8	5.2	—	5.33	5.33	12.10	—	70	70	158
1953	.3	8.4	8.7	5.8	.10	7.54	7.64	15.36	3	87	90	166
1954	2.0	10.3	12.3	8.0	1.13	8.78	9.91	20.75	35	105	140	221

Sources: Ministry of Economic and Financial Affairs, *Annual Bulletin of Iran's Foreign Trade* different years. IMF, *International Financial Statistics*, Supplement to 1966/67 issues.

This and similar claims are based on Iranian customs data which show that, between 1950 and 1953, Iran's non-oil exports rose by 129 per cent in volume and 136 per cent in value.[24] Table 2 shows Iran's international transactions from 1950 to 1954, according to both Iranian customs and IMF data. The IMF data describe the Gregorian year, while Iranian customs data are for the Iranian year. Note that for 1953, the IMF data coincide with eight months of Mossadegh's premiership while the Iranian data coincide with only five months.[25] According to the Iranian customs data, total exports surpassed total imports (which had remained at the 1950 level) from 1951 to 1953, despite the loss of oil exports. But the exports appear vigorous only because the exchange rate applied to imports is the lower official rate, while that applied to exports is the market rate.[26] This becomes evident when one considers IMF data, where the same exchange rate is applied to both exports and imports. As can be seen in 1952, imports exceeded exports by about 7 billion Rials. But, more important, if one looks at the figures in dollars, it is evident that exports increased slightly, while imports dropped drastically, from $258 million in 1950 to $158 million in 1952.

There still remains the fact that the volume of non-oil exports doubled from 194 metric tons in 1950 to 444 metric tons in 1953. The customs data on volume of trade are more reliable than those on the value of trade. Therefore, the issue cannot be dismissed as merely caused by error or inflated reporting. The increase in the volume of exports together with IMF data on the value of trade (neglecting the three months' difference in reporting periods) show that the unit price of non-oil exports increased from $309 per ton in 1950 to $331 in 1951 and then declined to $198 in 1952 and $196 in 1953. In other words, in 1952 the unit price of Iran's exports dropped by about 40 per cent.

There are four possible reasons, not mutually exclusive, for such decline: (a) Iranian merchants lowered their prices (in terms of dollars) to increase the amount of exports; (b) there was a shift to bulkier items in Iran's exports; (c) the exporters did not repatriate the proceeds of exports; and (d) there was a decline in international prices. Although it is not possible to determine the precise role of individual factors, it is unlikely that a single factor could be solely responsible for the 40 per cent decline in export prices. Furthermore, the effect of the first two factors may well be marginal. The third factor was a result of the general environment of uncertainty prevalent during Mossadegh's term in office. The fourth factor requires elaboration.

A National Bureau of Economic Research study[27] shows that the business cycle in the U.S. (and to a great extent, by virtue of international transmission of economic conditions, for developed countries) that corresponds to our period of study had its trough in October 1949 and its peak in July 1953. Indeed, America was engaged in the Korean War during 1950–1953. Yet, export and import prices almost universally increased and then declined relative to the peak year of 1951. In particular, export prices (including petroleum) of Middle Eastern countries increased by 17 per cent in 1951 and then dropped 6 per cent in 1952 and another 9 per cent in 1953.[28] Thus, Mossadegh's efforts to promote exports were frustrated by a number of factors, most notably a decline in international prices and the flight of capital from Iran. The latter was due to the general uncertainty and insecurity felt by the public in general and monied classes in particular.

It is noteworthy that in those days, Iranian exports mainly comprised rugs and agricultural products, whose short-run supply was not highly elastic. Therefore, even if Mossadegh's efforts had been successful, it would have been very difficult to sustain even a moderate rate of increase in exports. It is also worth noting that all $600 million of oil income (see Table 2) did not accrue to the government of Iran. The largest part went to AIOC. Iran's oil revenue, as mentioned above, was only one-tenth of this figure (see Table 1).

During the oil crisis, especially when Mossadegh had lost hope of Britain coming to terms with oil nationalization, the National Oil Company tried to sell oil directly to international customers. Despite this company's efforts and the Iranian government's flexibility in granting substantial discounts to buyers, the total amount of oil loaded for the international market was only 118,600 tons. This included the ill-fated 600 tons carried by the detained tanker *Rose Mary*, whose cargo was turned over to AIOC by order of the Colonial Court in Aden. At the official price of $12 per ton — assuming that discounts and production costs amount to 50 per cent of the price — the export of 118,000 tons of oil brought Iran less than $1 million. Thus the British boycott, which included pressuring the potential buyers of Iranian oil, was completely successful.

Mossadegh, for a time, entertained the possibility of selling oil to socialist countries. But it does not seem that he was serious in this respect. He wanted American support and, as will be discussed below, had hoped for American financial assistance. The sale of oil, which the U.S. considered a strategic item, to the Soviet bloc would have dashed such hopes. Most probably, Mossadegh considered negotiations with Poland and Hungary as a bargaining chip to soften the British position and a warning sign to the United States that in the absence of American support Iran might develop close ties with the Soviet bloc.[29] However, other forms of trade with the Soviet Union did expand during

Mossadegh's premiership. As Table 3 shows, imports from the Soviet Union increased from merely 4.63 per cent of total imports in 1950 to almost 14 per cent of total imports in 1952, though it declined in 1953. In the same manner, exports to the Soviet Union increased from 2.61 per cent in 1950 to over 13 per cent in 1952 and 1953. During the same time, imports from Britain dropped from 24.6 per cent in 1950 to 9.87 per cent in 1953, while exports to Britain declined from 18.78 per cent to 5.03 per cent. Trade with the U.S., except for some fluctuations, kept its share. It was trade with the rest of the world that expanded considerably (see Table 3).

The overall picture, however, shows that current accounts of Iran's international transactions were in deficit, Mossadegh's policies had only narrowed the gap by reducing imports. Thus, Mossadegh had to attempt to improve the capital account of Iran's balance of payments and this involved both the U.S. and USSR.

Mossadegh had expected foreign exchange relief through U.S. foreign aid. On 19 October 1950, the United States signed the first Point Four agreement with Iran.[30] The amount of aid allocated for each year was $23 million, to be used for special projects. However, the actual amount of foreign aid received during Mossadegh's premiership was only $8.8 million (see Table 1). Indeed, between 1949 and 1952, Iran received only $16.5 million in economic aid and $16.6 million in military aid.[31]

On the other hand, the Soviet Union had owed Iran a substantial amount of gold since World War II. Mossadegh's government continued negotiations with the Soviet Union to settle accounts between the two countries and obtain a source of badly needed international currency. But the Soviet Union extended the discussions, finally reaching an agreement with General Zahedi's government and delivering the gold in two instalments to Ala's government.[32]

All in all, Mossadegh's foreign trade policies met with defeat. The main source of foreign exchange was cut off. No substantial foreign aid became available and no means of increasing non-oil exports suggested itself. The reduction of imports adversely affected consumption – for example, sugar had to be rationed in 1952 – and investment (see Section 5 below).

4. BUDGET DEFICIT AND ITS FINANCING

The loss of oil revenue meant the loss of government income. As pointed out above, only part of the total oil revenue entered the government's general budget. However, the total amount of oil revenue kept the machinery of government running. Table 4 shows that total oil revenue

TABLE 3
IRAN'S DIRECTION OF TRADE (EXCLUDING OIL) 1950–54[1]

Year	US		USSR		UK		Rest of the World	
	Imports	Exports	Imports	Exports	Imports	Exports	Imports	Exports
1950	22.37	10.92	4.63	2.61	24.60	18.78	48.40	67.70
1951	22.26	6.22	10.90	22.16	17.88	11.73	48.97	59.90
1952	20.50	10.96	13.87	13.20	11.10	4.37	54.53	71.47
1953	17.30	11.83	5.33	13.13	9.87	5.03	67.49	70.01
1954	22.20	10.04	6.75	16.64	7.75	7.44	63.30	65.88

[1] Figures are percentages of total. Imports (exports) refer to Imports to (exports from) Iran.
Source: Plan Organization, Statistical Center of Iran, *Bayan Amari Tahavolat-i Eqtesadi va Ejtemai Iran* (Statistical Outlook of Economic and Social Evolution of Iran), Tehran, 1976.

in 1950 was over 2.8 billion Rials, which constituted 35 per cent of general budget expenditures. In 1950 the government faced a general budget deficit of 134 million Rials. In the first year of Mossadegh's government, expenditures increased while the loss of oil revenue reduced government revenues. The budget deficit also increased, to over 1.6 billion Rials. In addition, development expenditures not included in the general budget almost ceased (see Section 5 below). The government transferred over a billion Rials from reserves covering notes (see Section 3 above) to pay for the current outlays, and tried to hold down expenditures. Although the government did succeed in reducing the expenditures, in 1952, despite its efforts to raise income, the deficit remained almost at the previous year's level. Note that customs revenue dwindled because imports had decreased. Oil revenue had totally ceased and therefore other revenues declined as well. To cover the deficit, the government could increase taxes, sell bonds to the public, or expand the money supply. Mossadegh tried all three options.

Mossadegh used his legislative power, granted by Parliament, to ratify a land tax, an automobile and radio tax, a fixed tax of tradesmen and artisans, a tax on income from agricultural land and stamp fee, and revisions of the income tax and property tax laws.[33] These new taxes were intended to increase government revenues while simultaneously reforming an inequitable tax system administered by an inefficient tax collection machinery. Because they were to be collected at a time of recession,[34] these measures for increasing government revenues bred taxpayer discontent.

Mossadegh also tried to sell bonds to the public. Even at the best of times, Iranian governments have experienced difficulty in selling such bonds. A simple economic logic explains the difficulty. Government bonds pay the same interest rate as that prevalent in the official money market, which consists of banks and their customers. In this market, the rates are controlled by the government. At the same time, the interest rate prevailing in the unofficial market, which consists of private money lenders and their customers, is much higher; interest rates of 30 per cent and 40 per cent in this market are not unusual.[35] Thus, the explicit cost in buying government bonds turns the public away. Bonds issued by Mossadegh's government carried an interest rate (called a prize) of 6 per cent over a two-year period. With the inflation rate prevailing at the time of Mossadegh (see Table 6), the real rate of interest (i.e., nominal rate of interest less inflation rate) was negative. Mossadegh had to appeal to nationalistic sentiments in order to collect money through bond sales. Some responded to his appeal, but these were mostly people with limited resources who could not continue their bond purchases.[36]

TABLE 4
IRANIAN GOVERNMENT REVENUES AND EXPENDITURES 1950–54

Year	Oil Income[1]	Revenues[2]			Expenditures[3]	Million Rials Surplus (+) Deficit (−)
		Customs	Others (Including Oil)	Total		
1950	2871	3178	4974	8152	8286	−134
1951	544	3423	4487	7910	9674	−1664
1952	—	2774	4548	7322	8882	−1560
1953	—	3796	6363	10159	10543	−384
1954	1901	4900	7369	12269	12306	−37

[1] Oil income received by the Iranian government (Table 1) converted into Rial using official selling rate of exchange for dollar. Not all oil income entered the general budget.
[2] Includes the portion of oil income that entered the general budget.
[3] Does not inlcude Plan Organization expenditures.

Sources: Iran's Ministry of Finance, as reported in *Bayan Amari ... op. cit.*; IMF, *International Financial Statistics*, Supplement to 1966/67 issues.

The government issued 500 million Rials worth of bonds in the autumn of 1951. Although the bulk of these were sold, Mossadegh soon abandoned the idea as a way to raise revenues.

Being unable to raise enough money by other means, the government resorted to printing money. In 1952, currency in circulation increased by 1.72 billion Rials and, in the next year, by 1.7 billion Rials (see Table 5). Not all of the latter increase can be attributed to Mossadegh, since he was in office for only five months during that (Iranian) year.

TABLE 5
CURRENCY IN CIRCULATION AND MONEY SUPPLY IN IRAN 1950-54

Year	Currency in Circulation	Demand Deposits (Billion Rials)	Money Supply	Rate of Growth of Money Supply (percent)
1950	7.27	6.80	14.07	12.38
1951	7.07	7.34	14.41	2.42
1952	8.79	9.18	17.97	24.71
1953	10.49	11.79	22.28	23.98
1954	11.29	12.54	23.83	6.96

Sources: *Bayan Amari ..., op. cit.*; and Bharier, J. *Economic Development in Iran 1900–1970*, Oxford University Press, London, 1971.

The increase in currency in circulation caused an increase in money supply (currency in circulation plus demand deposits) of 3.56 billion Rials in 1952 and 4.31 billion Rials in 1953. Thus, the money supply increased by about 24 per cent in both 1952 and 1953, compared to a mere 2.4 per cent increase in 1951. Part of this increase was due to the credit extended by Bank Melli to government agencies and municipalities.

Thus, the cutoff of oil revenue caused a substantial budget deficit. True to his convictions, Mossadegh attempted to avoid deficit financing through monetary expansion; but the crisis endured, and he had to relent. The increase in money supply was bound to create inflation.

5. MONETARY POLICY AND INFLATION

Mossadegh's term in office was characterized by high rates of inflation (see Table 6), although the figures may not fully depict the inflationary situation in that shortages are not reflected in the consumer price index (CPI). Inflation started immediately after he took office, but this early

THE OIL NATIONALIZATION MOVEMENT

TABLE 6
RATE OF GROWTH OF MONEY AND INFLATION IN IRAN, 1950-54

	1950		1951		1952		1953		1954	
					Rate of Growth of:[2]					
Month[1]	Money	CPI	Money	CPI	Money	CPI	Money	CPI	Money	CPI
January	− 2.1	− 9.7	11.1	−12.2	1.4	12.4	22.6	4.6	28.9	14.9
February	− 3.9	−11.5	13.8	− 5.6	1.1	6.2	23.1	3.7	27.5	15.0
March	− 1.2	−14.6	12.6	− 1.8	2.3	5.9	25.7	3.4	29.4	17.5
April	− 1.9	−20.4	12.9	3.5	2.6	9.5	28.9	0.2	22.1	24.8
May	1.3	−20.7	8.8	5.8	5.7	10.0	28.6	1.0	18.9	25.3
June	2.7	−19.1	10.7	5.0	8.3	9.8	35.7	3.8	7.9	21.5
July	0.2	−20.2	11.5	6.6	8.6	9.4	34.3	5.5	5.4	18.6
August	5.4	−23.2	5.2	10.3	10.8	7.7	36.7	7.0	− 1.9	16.6
September	2.9	−23.2	4.3	9.8	12.4	5.7	38.6	11.5	− 5.0	14.6
October	4.3	−22.1	4.7	11.8	18.0	6.3	34.2	9.3	− 5.5	16.2
November	5.9	−18.7	2.2	12.5	19.5	6.9	30.9	11.2	− 1.1	14.4
December	12.0	−13.7	1.8	10.7	20.5	7.9	30.6	12.7	0.0	12.3

[1] Data is for the Iranian months; therefore, May, for example, coincides with the Iranian month Ordibehesht (i.e., from April 21 to May 21).

[2] Rates of growth of money supply and consumer price index (CPI) are computed over the same month of the previous year, to avoid seasonal fluctuations. Therefore, both are annual rates.

Sources: *Bayan Amari... op. cit.* for CPI and *International Financial Statistics* supplement on Money, 1964. Since monthly data from Bank Melli was not available, the IMF series were utilized. Due to definitional differences, the value of money supply reported by IMF is below the annual figures of Bank Melli. However, the rate of growth of annual figures for both series are almost identical.

inflation cannot be attributed to his policies. As the data on the rate of growth of money supply show (see Table 6), the inflation that started in early 1951 was due to a gradual increase in money supply that had started one year earlier. After almost five years of stable money supply in the period immediately after World War II, the money supply increased by 1.55 billion Rials (12 per cent) in 1950. The effect of this increase in money supply was delayed about a year. In the same manner, although early in 1953 inflation showed signs of subsiding due to a stable money supply in 1951, the inflation of late 1953 and early 1954 can at least partially be attributed to Mossadegh's policies.

Regarding the inflation during the Mossadegh era, three questions need to be answered. First, to what extent was the government's resort to monetary expansion responsible for inflation? Second, were there other factors at work that exacerbated the situation? Finally, how were the economy and the populace affected by this inflation?

Inflation is a central issue in macroeconomic theory and policy. Therefore, it is not surprising that a number of theories, including quantity theory, cost push and structuralist theories, have been proposed to explain this phenomenon.[37] These theories generally agree with the empirical evidence that an increase in money supply and inflation occur together. Theories disagree, however, over the relationship between money and prices. Proponents of cost push and structuralist theories believe that money is a passive (or endogenous) variable,[38] an accommodating factor that increases in response to an already existing inflation. The adherents of quantity theory (including the New Classical[39] economists) argue that money is an exogenous variable and its increase is the cause of inflation. In order to determine which of the above views gain empirical support, one may resort to the tests of statistical (or Granger) causality.[40] These tests, details of which are available from the author, show that in Iran the direction of causality runs from money to prices. These results confirm that during the period under study, inflation was a monetary phenomenon. Therefore, the expansion of money supply inevitably led to inflation.

As to the other sources contributing to inflation, two factors are deemed to be important. The first is the struggle by labourers to increase their share of national income (cost push theory), and the second is the international trade factors, namely the price of imported goods and devaluation. In cost push theory the sequence of events leading to inflation begins when labourers, dissatisfied with their share in the national income, demand and receive higher wages. The capitalists, in order not to lose their share, increase their prices and thus reduce real wages (i.e., the purchasing power of wages). The government ratifies this state of affairs by increasing money supply. Indeed, if the government fails to do so, recession will ensue.

In the modern history of Iran, 1941–53 is the only extended period where labour unions had freedom of action. Ervand Abrahamian has compiled the data on the number of national strikes in this period. A graph of the number of strikes superimposed on a graph of CPI during this period shows at least a weak correlation between the two series.[41] For instance, while few strikes occurred between 1947 and 1950, the CPI kept rising; when the number of strikes showed an increase in 1950, the CPI decreased. Abrahamian believes that the strikes were not the cause of inflation, but a response to it, noting that 'wage earners often had little choice but to join unions and strike for higher wages, since the cost-of-living index rose from

472 in 1942–43 to 1030 in 1944–45' (p.351). However, since Mossadegh's period is characterized by a substantial increase in the number of national strikes, it is reasonable to assume that labour's struggle to increase (or maintain) its standard of living was a contributing factor to inflation.

The second contributing factor was import price increases, especially in view of the amplifying effect of devaluation. In countries like Iran, devaluation contributes to inflation through two different channels. First, an increase in import prices causes the general price level to go up. This is usually offset by lower prices of domestically produced goods, if the aggregate demand remains unchanged. Yet in the face of such price increases, certain rigidities, such as domestic industries' need to import intermediate goods, may necessitate an increase in demand by the government. Second, devaluation increases the value, in domestic currency, of international reserves held by the central (or national) bank, raising the credit side of its balance sheet. This increase is often balanced by increasing money in circulation on the debit side. During Mossadegh's reign, because Bank Melli's reserves were reduced drastically, the second effect was in all likelihood negligible.

To summarize, the Iranian government's policy of monetary expansion to finance the budget deficit was the prime cause of inflation. Labour strikes and import price increases, resulting from international inflation and devaluation, intensified the inflation process.

Inflation disrupts an economy by creating uncertainty. The value of money, which is the basis of all economic decisions, becomes volatile and unpredictable; the relative value of different commodities and services changes drastically, while distribution of income is altered due to no apparent fault or decision of any group of people. The effects of this uncertainty on investment and growth are discussed in the next section. However, it should be emphasized here while a general rise in prices results in a gain in value on all types of property, inflation is anathema to the wealthy classes because of the uncertainty it creates.

The harm of the inflation was not limited to the well-to-do; the general populace suffered from the increase in prices as well. Moreover, Mossadegh's period was a time of shortage when some basic goods, such as sugar and cube sugar, were rationed. Some have argued that inflation during the Mossadegh era did not affect the masses and only made the well-to-do uneasy. The rural population was immune to the inflation, they argue, because of the barter nature of the rural economy. They also claim that the urban masses did not suffer from the inflation because only the price of imported luxury items increased. A breakdown of the cost of living index, however, shows that between 1950 and 1953, food prices rose by about 34 per cent, clothing by 33 per cent and rent by 13 per cent.[42] These are hardly imported luxury items. Furthermore, the prices are interdependent, where a rise in one group of prices pulls up the prices of other commodities. Thus, consumers had to suffer from shortages, rationing and inflation all at a time when the economy was experiencing stagnation and decline.

6. INVESTMENT AND GROWTH

Tables 2 and 4 show that between 1951 and 1953 net exports became negative. Current government expenditures declined sharply in 1952, but rebounded in 1953. However, in real terms (after adjustment for inflation) it did not reach the 1951 level. To complete the picture and determine what happened to national income and employment, which is related to income, we turn to the study of investment during the Mossadegh era. Investment is an important economic factor both as a component of national income and as an addition to the productive capital of any society. The latter role is especially important in developing countries, such as Iran, where limited capital is the major restriction on production. Investment can be undertaken by both the private sector and the government. Regarding private investment, the period under study was dominated by three elements: shortage of foreign exchange and therefore limited imports of machinery and equipment, uncertainty resulting mainly from the prominence of the Tudeh Party, and relative democracy.

Not all Mossadegh actions were in conformity with even relative democracy. For a considerable period of time he governed with martial law in effect. He also conducted an unconstitutional referendum. In this referendum the ballot boxes for pro-government and opposition voters were put in separate places. The voters opposing the government not only risked being beaten up by the thugs, but their fingers were dipped in an ink that did not wash and its colour (green) was different from the colour of ink used for pro-government voters (black). Thus, Mossadegh in power was far less democratically minded than Mossadegh the ordinary citizen or parliamentary deputy. Still, compared to other governments that have ruled Iran, his was probably the most democratically inclined.

Although the Mossadegh era provides an opportunity for empirical study of the effects of these elements on private investment, such a study will be incomplete for three reasons. First, the three factors occurred together, and therefore it is not possible to determine their relative weights in the outcome. Second, Mossadegh lasted in office for slightly more than two years, which is not a long enough period to assess the impact of the aforementioned forces. In particular, it is difficult to evaluate the threat of the Tudeh Party which became imminent only in the last few months of his regime. Finally, estimation of Iranian national accounts began in 1959, long after Mossadegh's downfall. Thus, out of necessity, we have to rely on incomplete data for our investigation.

Table 7 shows the total number of companies in Iran and their capital, the number of newly formed companies and their investment, the number of dissolved companies and their capital, and also the value of imported machinery and equipment. The data show that after Mossadegh ascended to power in 1951 the amount of investment drastically decreased — by more than 50 per cent in real terms. At the same time, although the number of firms going out of business was smaller than in the previous year, apparently they were larger firms and their capital was more than three times that of all dissolved firms in the previous year. Thus, while gross investment was positive, the real addition to capital stock in operation was negative in 1951 for companies only. In 1952, the situation was reversed and the amount of real gross investment stood almost at its 1950 level. In 1953, however, there was a drastic drop in investment; and in 1954, despite the coup and the passing of the Tudeh threat, the amount of real investment remained at the 1953 level.

The last column of Table 7 clearly indicates the sensitive reaction of industrial investment to the oil revenue cutoff. Imports of machinery and equipment in 1953 were almost one third of the 1951 levels. Since Iran did not produce machinery and equipment, at least for modern industries, the decline in industrial investment is evident.[43]

Two conclusions can be drawn from the foregoing discussion: (1) private investment declined during the Mossadegh era, and (2) the shortage of foreign exchange caused the decline. Evidence supporting this latter conclusion are: (a) investment did not materially increase in 1953 and 1954 when uncertainty caused by the Tudeh Party threat and the general insecurity of the country was alleviated — the same argument applies to the influence of democracy; and (b) while imports of machinery and equipment, and therefore industrial investment, declined, 352 companies with a substantial amount of capital were formed in 1952. It was the lack of foreign exchange that limited investment, especially industrial investment, while uncertainty may have been an exacerbating factor. That conclusion is tentative, however, and more research on the subject is desirable.

The picture with respect to government investment was also bleak. In 1949 the Majlis had passed the First Development Plan Act which

TABLE 7
NUMBER AND CAPITAL OF COMPANIES IN IRAN, 1950–54

Year	Companies at the end of the year		New Companies Registered During the year		Companies Dissolved during the year		Imports of Machinery and Equipment
	Number	Capital (Million Rials)	Number	Capital (Million Rials)	Number	Capital (Million Rials)	(Million Rials)
1950	2431	17344	392	1486	236	828	824
1951	2552	14895	340	775	219	2961	956
1952	2640	18449	352	1680	264	596	545
1953	2836	21335	413	1531	217	455	345
1954	3169	23582	570	1809	237	399	499

Source: *Bayan Amari ... op. cit.*

allocated 21 billion Rials for development expenditures.[44] Because part of the resources for the plan had to come from oil income, the oil revenue cutoff prevented its implementation. Table 8 shows the sectoral allocation of plan funds and actual expenditures between the inception of the Plan Organization to September 1954. It is interesting that while Mossadegh's government was unable to meet the originally-planned expenditures, the allocation of funds for the plan was increased by over five billion Rials in August and November 1952. Apparently this step was taken to achieve economic self-sufficiency through further investments.

According to the figures in Table 8, in the five and a half years following passage of the Plan, the government spent only four billion Rials and obligated only nine billion. There is no record of these expenditures after Mossadegh's downfall, but a government report shows that 487 million Rials of the expenditures were made by the end of 1949.[45] What is clear is the low level of government investment and, therefore, of total investment during the oil nationalization movement.[46]

Thus, total income decreased during Mossadegh's regime, causing recession and an increase in unemployment. Furthermore, economic growth was hindered not only in those years but in years to come.

7. CONCLUDING REMARKS

In the preceding sections an attempt has been to depict the Iranian economy during the years of the nationalist movement. The cutoff of oil revenues overwhelmed the Iranian economy, and Mossadegh's short-run policies proved inadequate. The country suffered from many economic ills: lack of foreign exchange, low level of income, recession, inflation and shortages. The disastrous conditions in the Iranian economy during Mossadegh's era are attested to by many writers of different political and ideological persuasions.[47]

The extent to which economic factors contributed to the defeat of the nationalist movement is an important subject, deserving further attention. A satisfactory study of this subject requires an overall analysis of Iranian society in the post-World War II era. Although the present paper has a far more limited scope, certain observations are inescapable. While economic factors may not have caused the movement's failure, the disastrous economic conditions prevailing in the spring and summer of 1953 clearly set the stage for Mossadegh's overthrow.

The effortless and apparently inevitable overthrow of Mossadegh is a point observed by many writers, including some of his supporters.[48]

TABLE 8
PLANNED AND ACTUAL EXPENDITURES BY PLAN ORGANIZATION 1949 – SEPTEMBER 1954
(Million Rials)

Sectors	Allocation According to Plan Acts	Allocation According to Acts of 1952	Total	Expenditures	Obligations
Agriculture	5,250	2,090	7,340	1,010	4,740
Transport	5,000	1,971	6,971	1,533	1,988
Industries & Mines	3,000	1,288	4,288	1,180	1,702
Oil Develop.	1,000	–	1,000	213	–
Post & Telegraph	750	–	750	23	2
Social Welfare Works	6,000	–	6,000	220	579
TOTAL	21,000	5,349	26,349	4,179	9,011

Source: Motamen, H. 'Development Planning in Iran' *Middle East Economic Papers* 1956, p. 105

Jalal Al-i Ahmad goes so far as to implicate Mossadegh in his own downfall:

> But he [Mossadegh] had the competence not to let his inadequacy of preparations and cadres, as well as inappropriate conditions of leadership, be blamed for his defeat. With the dexterity of an experienced politician he found a culprit for his defeat; the coup initiated by the international oil trust and other events which are out of the reach of an ordinary mortal — even a prime minister.[49]

The question is, did the economic decline of the country facilitate Mossadegh's overthrow? The answer seems to be in the affirmative; and while it is not possible to establish the exact contribution of economic factors to the demise of the nationalist movement, one can make a persuasive case for a direct relationship between the two.

Mossadegh and the National Front had come to power with a simple, straightforward promise. They could take control of oil, end the meddling of Britain's oil company in the nation's internal affairs, and use the oil revenue for economic development. Prosperity and better living conditions would follow. A coalition of diverse political forces formed around this ideal, and the people gave Mossadegh a mandate to carry out his plan. But as time passed, economic hardship rather than the promised prosperity befell the nation. It became evident that Iran's economic problems could be solved only by cessation of the oil crisis. Yet, after his rejection of the second joint American–British proposal, it was clear that Mossadegh could not or would not solve the oil problem.

At the same time, deteriorating economic conditions deprived the government of its normal means of appeasing allies. Even worse, Mossadegh had to make tough economic decisions, thus alienating various groups of his supporters. In some instances government intentions directly opposed the ideology of some coalition members.[50] Tudeh's support of Mossadegh toward the end of the latter's premiership had two motives: Mossadegh had boxed himself into an opposition posture toward the West, and the economic disaster confronting his government and the country would provide the Tudeh Party with its best opportunity to attain power.

The fact that the nation did not defend Mossadegh[51] is a clear indication that his mandate was void. Mossadegh had failed in his own and in his nation's aspirations. It is true that Britain lost its power and position in Iran. It is equally true that many nations benefitted from the Iranian experience in their struggle for economic and political independence. But it is also true that, for Iran, Mossadegh's downfall was the sad end to a promising beginning. The Iranian poet, Mehdi Akhavan Salis, voiced Iran's disappointment in his poem dedicated to Peer Mohammad Ahmad Abadi (literally translated, 'old Mohammad of Ahmad Abad,' referring to Mossadegh's first name and the village near Tehran where he was under house arrest):

Did you see my heart that the beloved did not come?
The stallion arrived; but the rider did not come?

NOTES

1 In the words of Anthony Sampson, when oil-producing countries gathered to form OPEC, 'The lean specter of the fanatical doctor [Mossadegh] flitted over the first counterattack by the producing countries'. *The Seven Sisters*, 3rd ed., Bantam Books, New York, 1983, p. 163.
2 M. Fateh, *Panjah Sal Naft* ('Fifty Years of Oil'), 2nd printing, Kavesh Publications, Tehran, n.d. (first printing 1956) chs. 10–14; E. Elwell-Sutton, *Persian Oil, A Study in Power Politics*, Lawrence and Wishart, London, 1955; F. Rohani, *Tarikheh-i Melli Shodan San'at Naft-i Iran* ('History of the Nationalization of the Iranian Oil Industry'), Jibi Books, Tehran, 1974; S. Zabih, *The Mossadegh Era*, Lake View Press, Chicago, 1982; H. Makki, *Katab-i Syah* ('The Black Book'), Vol. 1, 2nd Printing, No Publications, Tehran, n.d.; Vol. 2, Amir Kabir, Tehran, 1985; Vol. 4, Nashreh Nasher, Tehran, 1983. See also, F. Fesharaki, *Development of the Iranian Oil Industry: International and Domestic Aspects*, Praeger, New York, 1976 and R. Ferrier, 'The Development of the Iranian Oil Industry', in *Twentieth Century Iran*, H. Amirsadeghi (ed.), Holmes and Meier Publishers, New York, 1977, pp. 93–128; S. H. Longrigg, *Oil in the Middle East*, Oxford University Press, London, 1954, ch. 10; B. Shwadran, *The Middle East, Oil and the Great Powers*, 3rd ed., Wiley, New York, 1973, ch. 5; *Asnad Naft* ('Oil Documents'), published by Iran's Ministry of Foreign Affairs, contains many documents on the oil issue up to the summer of 1951.
3 For example, R. W. Cottam, *Nationalism in Iran* (updated through 1978), University of Pittsburgh Press, Pittsburgh, 1979. ch. 13 and 15; N. R. Keddie, *Roots of Revolution, An Interpretive History of Modern Iran*, Yale University Press, New Haven, CT, 1981, pp. 132–41; E. Abrahamian, *Iran Between Two Revolutions*, Princeton University Press, Princeton, N.J., 1982, pp. 267–80; P. Avery, *Modern Iran*, Praeger, New York, 1965, ch. 26; M. Ivanov, *Tarikhi-i Noveen-i Iran* ('Modern History of Iran'), translated (from Russian to Persian) by H. Tizabi and H. Qaem-Paneh, Tudeh Publishing Center, Stockholm, Sweden, 1977, ch. 8; Anonymous, *Gozashteh Cheragh-i Rah-i Ayandeh Ast* ('The Past is the Light for the Future'), Front for the Liberation of the Iranian People Press, n.d., ch. 11; and H. Katouzian, *The Political Economy of Modern Iran, Despotism and Pseudo-Modernism, 1926–1979*, New York University Press, New York, 1981, ch. 9.
4 A partial exception is Chapter 27 of F. Rohani, where he discusses the economic conditions of Iran during Mossadegh's reign, which leaves a lot to be desired in the way of an economic analysis. Also, H. Katouzian has a very brief discussion of the subject in the Appendix to ch. 9, pp. 182–5.
5 H. Katouzian points out that 'the economy was in *decline*, and this reduced government revenues (from taxes and the like) even further; the government was so poor that it had to postpone salary payments to the state bureaucracy' (p. 180, emphasis in the original); E. Abrahamian observes, 'while promising extensive social reforms he [Mossadegh] was caught between dwindling oil revenues, increasing unemployment, and escalating consumer prices' (p. 274). M. Ivanov notes, 'Boycott of Iranian oil by imperialists and the resulting drop in the oil production, reduced government revenues; economic and financial conditions of the country deteriorated and unemployment rose' (p. 163). See also, S. Zabih, ch. 5.

THE OIL NATIONALIZATION MOVEMENT

6. B. Nirumand, *Iran, the New Imperialism in Action*, translated by L. Mins, Monthly Review Press, New York, 1969, ch. 5; see Section 3 of the chapter for further details on this point.
7. S. Zabih, p. 84.
8. M. Yektai, *Tarikh-i Darai Iran* ('The History of Iranian Public Finance'), 3rd ed. Dehkhoda, Tehran, 1973, p. 268.
9. According to the Plan, 7.8 billion Rials of the oil revenue was allocated for development purposes. This comprised 37.1 per cent of total revenues envisaged for the Plan; J. Bharier, *Economic Development in Iran 1900–1970*, Oxford University Press, London, 1971, p. 89.
10. For the text of the law and related documents, see F. Rohani, ch. 5.
11. For example, M. Fateh, F. Rohani and Ferrier.
12. Iran's revenue from oil in the ten years from 1919 to 1928 averaged less than £700,000 per year. Ferrier, Appendix A, p. 279; for a detailed account of the early history of Iranian Oil, see A. Lesani, *Talay-i Siah Ya Balay-i Iran* ('Black Gold or the Iranian Disaster'), 2nd printing, Amir Kabir, Tehran, 1978.
13. F. Rohani.
14. R. Cottam, pp. 215–16.
15. H. Key-Ostovan, *Syasat-i Movazeneh-i Manfi Dar Majlis Chahardahom* ('Policy of Negative Balance in the Fourteenth Majlis'), Vol. 1, Tehran, 1948, p. 114.
16. Ibid., p. 97.
17. S. Zabih, p. 71.
18. While Iran's defence expenditures for years 1929–49 and 1953 onward are available, the data for the 1950–52 period, which includes the major part of Mossadegh's reign, are not available.
19. R. Cottam, p. 272. For a history of planning in Iran, see G. B. Baldwin, *Planning and Development in Iran*, The Johns Hopkins University Press, Baltimore, MD, 1967; and F. Daftary, 'Development Planning in Iran: A Historical Survey', *Iranian Studies*, Autumn 1973, pp. 176–228.
20. H. Makki, pp. 1–11.
21. F. Rohani, p. 382.
22. Ibid., pp. 381–4; see also p. 389, where Rohani discusses the effect of government actions on the cover of notes issued as if this was an important economic question. Legally, the issue of notes cover is important, but, from an economic point of view, since Rial was never convertible, the question of cover is totally irrelevant.
23. B. Nirumand, p. 110. Although the falsehood of this point has been demonstrated before (see Rohani, p. 394), the myth persists; see, for instance, Katouzian, pp. 184–5.
24. J. Bharier, p. 112.
25. Mossadegh was prime minister from 29 April 1951 to 19 August 1953, excluding 18–21 July 1952. During those four days Ahmad Qavam replaced Mossadegh who had resigned because of a dispute with the Shah. The dispute was over the appointment of the defence minister which the Shah claimed as his prerogative. The popular uprising of Syeh Tir (July 21) forced Qavam out of office and restored Mossadegh as premier with authority over the defence ministry.
26. F. Rohani, p. 394.
27. G. H. Moore, *Business Cycles, Inflation, and Forecasting*, Ballinger, Cambridge, Mass., 1980, pp. 438–9.
28. IMF, *International Financial Statistics*, supplement to 1966/67 issues, pp. xiv–xv.
29. Ivanov criticizes Mossadegh for not selling the oil to socialist countries 'which would have solved the financial and economic problems of the country to a great extent and would have broken up the oil boycott' (p. 169). The anonymous author of *Gozashteh...*, op. cit. pp. 601–601b argues that the Soviet bloc turned down Mossadegh's overture.
30. The story of Point Four in Iran is recounted by its first director in Iran, W. Warne, *Mission for Peace, Point 4 in Iran*, The Bobbs-Merrill Company, Indianapolis, IN, 1956. The programme is evaluated by J. Amuzegar, *Technical Assistance in Theory and Practice, The Case of Iran*, Praeger, New York, 1966. According to Warne, 'One day in 1952 Dr. Mossadegh insisted to me that Iran needed $30,000,000 at once! It would be much cheaper, he said, "to give $30,000,000 now than for you Americans to have to fight your way back

to Tehran"' (p. 307). For the American government's attitude towards Mossadegh and the oil crisis, see, U.S. House of Representatives, Selected Executive Session Hearings of the Committee 1951–56, Vol. XVI, *The Middle East, Africa, and Inter-American Affairs*, U.S. Government Printing Office, Washington, D.C., 1980; and Y. Alexander, and A. Nanes (eds.), *The United States and Iran, A Documentary History*, University Publications of America, Frederick, MD, 1980, ch. 4 and D. Acheson, *Present at the Creation, My Years in the State Department*, Norton, New York, 1969, chs. 52 and 71.

31 M. Zonis, *The Political Elite of Iran*, Princeton University Press, Princeton, NJ, 1971, pp. 108–9.
32 *Gozashteh* ..., op. cit., p. 601.
33 M. Yektai, p. 206.
34 Since the end of World War II and the evacuation of the allied forces, the Iranian economy was in a depressed state. See Abrahamian, p. 367.
35 For a discussion of unorganized money markets in developing countries, see, for example, U. Wai, 'A Revisit to Interest Rates Outside the Organized Money Markets of Underdeveloped Countries', and A. Bhaduri, 'On the Formation of Usurious Interest Rates in Backward Agricultures', in W. Coats and D. Khatkhate (eds.), *Money and Monetary Policy in Less Developed Countries, A Survey of Issues and Evidence*, Pergamon Press, Oxford, 1980, pp. 531–48 and pp. 465–77; see also other papers in Part III-2(a) of the same book.
36 F. Rohani, p. 394.
37 Excellent surveys of the theories of inflation are D. E. W. Laidler and M. J. Parkin, 'Inflation – A Survey', *Economic Journal*, December 1975, Vol. 85, pp. 741–809; and H. Frisch, *Theories of Inflation*, Cambridge University Press, Cambridge, U.K., 1983.
38 The term is due to J. H. G. Olivera, 'On Passive Money', *Journal of Political Economy*, July/August 1970, Vol. 78, pp. 805–14.
39 New Classical economists refer to the adherents of the rational expectations cum natural rate models. See the excellent collection of articles, *Rational Expectations and Econometric Practice*, edited by R. E. Lucas, Jr. and T. S. Sargent, The University of Minnesota Press, Minneapolis, 1981, 2 vols.
40 See C. W. J. Granger, 'Investigating Causal Relations by Econometric Models and Cross-Spectral Methods', *Econometrica*, 1969, Vol. 37; and C. A. Sims, 'Money, Income, and Causality', *American Economic Review*, 1972, Vol. 62. Briefly, these are tests designed to find out which variable causes, or is exogenous relative to, another variable. The Granger test which is utilized in this study is based on the idea that if a variable, say x, is causing another variable, say y, then x should help to predict y above and beyond the prediction of y based on its own past values alone (i.e., an autoregressive model of order m of y). If x explains y but the reverse is not true, there is a unidirectional causality from x to y. If both help explain the other, bidirectional causality is involved.
41 E. Abrahamian, p. 351.
42 Plan Organization, Statistical Center of Iran, *Bayan Amari Tahavolat-i Eqtesadi va Ejtemai Iran* ('Statistical Outlook of the Economic and Social Evolution of Iran'), Tehran 1976, p. 286.
43 Nirumand, without referring to any data, asserts (pp. 109–10):

> But in order to be able to produce sufficient quantities of, say, sugar and textiles, which had previously been imported in large quantities, the necessary machinery and equipment first had to be imported. To achieve this, the country increased the output of export commodities, mostly agricultural products and carpets. That is why the balance of trade became positive under Mossadegh. He used the surplus to purchase the machinery required for industrial development and for increasing the productivity of agriculture.

But these are all unsubstantiated assertions; a story that Nirumand thought or probably hoped had happened.

44 For details, see H. Motamen, 'Development Planning in Iran', *Middle East Economic Papers*, 1956, pp. 98–111.

45 H. Mosharraf-i Nafici, *Gozaresh-i Aghay-i Doctor Mosharraf-i nafici Modeer-i Amel Sazeman-i Barnameh* ('The Report of Dr. Mosharraf Nafici Managing Director of Plan Organization'), Tehran, 1950. Later on a revised version of this report was submitted to Majlis by the government of Razmara (Summer of 1950).
46 Bharier estimates that gross domestic capital formation in constant prices (real gross investment) dropped by only a slight amount in 1951 and 1952, surpassing its pre-oil crisis level in 1953. He evaluates his estimates very poorly for these years; J. Bharier, pp. 50–1.
47 See note 5 above.
48 There is no shortage of accounts of Mossadegh's downfall. In addition to sources in note 3 above, see K. Roosevelt, *Countercoup, The Struggle for the Control of Iran*, McGraw-Hill, New York, 1979; also, the recollections of two officers who defended Mossadegh's residence in August 1953, I. Davarpanah, 'The 1953 Coup', *Ittila 'at*, 19 Aug. 1979 and M. Fesharaki, 'The 1953 Coup', *Ittila 'at*, 20 Aug. 1979.
49 J. Al-i Ahmand, *Dar Khadmat va Khianat Roshanfekran* ('On the Service and the Treason of the Intelligentsia'), 3rd printing, Ravagh Publications, Tehran, 1977, p. 368.
50 Abrahamian, pp. 275–6.
51 On that fateful day of 19 Aug. 1953, the National Front had only one martyr: Major (posthumously promoted to the rank of Colonel after the revolution of 1978–9) Mahmoud Sakhai, an infantry officer who was chief of police in Kerman (a city in southeastern Iran). But even Sakhai was murdered out of malice and not during resistance. Of course, later on Dr. Fatemi, Mossadegh's foreign minister, was executed and Lutfi, his justice minister, was murdered by government thugs.

7

The Costs of Foreign Investment: the Case of the Egyptian Free Zones

Leslie Sklair

While the *infitah* (open door economic policy) that President Sadat introduced to Egypt in 1973–4 has been widely discussed,[1] one of its key elements – the establishment of a number of Free Zones – has attracted very little attention. This is no doubt partly due to their relative lack of success in bringing in much real foreign investment. Nevertheless, the record of the Free Zones to date does repay study insofar as it reveals some of the major economic and non-economic difficulties of the *infitah* policy as a whole, and the particular social, political and cultural problems thrown up by the structure of exports and imports that it has created.

BACKGROUND

On 19 June 1974 President Sadat signed Law 43 concerning Arab and Foreign Investment and Free Zones into existence, and three years later (in Law 32 of 1977) it was amended to increase the incentives for foreign investors and remove obstacles that seemed to be discouraging them.[2] Law 43, as amended, is the cornerstone of the *infitah* – the open door economic policy. As Abdel-Khalek argues[3] the policy really represents an opening to the northwest rather than an opening as such, for the new Egyptian economic aspirations are directed *to* Western Europe and especially the United States and *away* from Eastern Europe and especially the Soviet Union. Therefore, although laws on foreign investment and even Free Zones had been passed under Nasser in the 1960s, they had not been part of a comprehensive and new economic policy.

The Arab–Israeli war of 1973 heralded both a geo-political and an economic transformation for Egypt. In geo-political terms, as the

Russian influence waned and the American interest waxed, it was not surprising that the respective economic models presented by the Superpowers would change in relative importance for Egyptian policy-makers. This did not mean that as U.S. influence increased from the mid-1970s the overwhelmingly-dominant public sector was disbanded, despite the continuing efforts of United States agencies eventually to achieve this end, but that a peculiarly 'mixed' economy was to develop in which both public and private sectors were to be exposed to and hopefully benefit from the stimulus of foreign investment. Indeed, one of the key paradoxes of Egyptian life since Law 43 is the apparent general support of private Egyptian capitalists for the public sector, which at present accounts for two thirds of industry and much of the rest of the formal economy, with the notable exception of agriculture. Waterbury identifies the building contractors as the 'masters of public-private symbiosis',[4] and they are masters of a large and enthusiastic class.

There are, however, two large reservations. The first concerns food and other subsidies which take up a substantial part of government revenues. This is an extremely important issue but not one that I can pursue here.[5] The second reservation is that the public sector companies claim to suffer from certain disadvantages compared with private sector companies in various important economic areas such as textiles, food processing, metals, chemicals, and engineering. Some of the virtual state monopolies of the Nasser years are part of the open door policy. It was, therefore, a shrewd tactic for the formulators of Law 43 to stipulate that all Joint Venture companies set up under the Law would be treated as private companies, that is exempt from the restrictive regulations governing the public sector, even if the Egyptian partner was a public company. It is not uncommon for governments in other countries to exempt foreign manufacturing industry from local laws within economic zones of one type or another, but the Egyptian idea of automatic privatisation for all Joint Ventures between local and foreign partners appears quite innovative.

Law 43 allows for two categories of foreign investment, governed by different sets of regulations, and within these categories there are different types distinguished. The basic division is between Inland and Free Zone projects. This division, despite appearances, is not geographical, but for the purposes of the Customs authorities. Inland projects are more or less all projects in the country established under the provisions of Law 43. The 1977 Amendment to the Law extended it to cover companies owned by Egyptian nationals as well as wholly-owned foreign companies and Joint Ventures. Free Zones are considered to be outside Egyptian territory (thus *not* Inland) for fiscal, Customs and other purposes. Law 43 empowers the Investment Authority to establish Public Free Zones to house groups of projects, and Private Free Zones to house individual projects, usually near a Public Free Zone and under its supervision.

The incentives for Inland investment projects are familiar to anyone conversant with contemporary Third World foreign investment policies. Law 43 companies have some exemptions from controls on exports and imports of raw materials, intermediate goods, and finished products; they are permitted to maintain foreign currency accounts in Egypt; and they have generous profits tax exemptions for periods of five to fifteen years. In addition, they are guaranteed the best rate of exchange for changing Egyptian pounds into hard currencies, principally U.S. dollars, though this does not always happen.[6]

The reasons why Law 43 was revised in 1977 owed much to the food riots at the beginning of that year and Sadat's struggle to maintain support from other Arab countries as the Camp David process got under way. There was, of course, an economic rationale too. The 1977 Amendment to Law 43 demonstrated a certain flexibility in the Investment Authority and a willingness to respond to what was, clearly, a disappointing first few years. To put it in a nutshell, although there was an enormous amount of foreign and particularly U.S. interest in the Egyptian economy when the *infitah* policy was announced, very little actual foreign investment was forthcoming, and in the case of manufacturing industry, practically none. Waterbury reports that the previous investment law (Law 65 of 1971) had approved 50 projects up to 1974 with a paper value of LE 13m., but not one of these had actually started up; while the Law 43 record from 1974 to the end of 1976 was 66 projects in operation, capitalized at LE 36m., and employing 3,450 people.[7]

The key differences between the 1977 and the 1974 versions of Law 43 concerned the foreign currency situation and the range of activities permitted to foreign investors. Pressure from Egyptian and foreign business representatives, and from within the Egyptian government itself on these points, led the Investment Authority to believe that if these obstacles could be removed then foreign investors would be more likely to commit funds to Egypt. This is all clearly laid out in a report of the New York based Fund for Multinational Management Education, which provides a useful account of the history of Egypt's fdi policies since 1952 and an interesting insight into what U.S. investors wanted from Egypt.[8] Like foreign investors elsewhere, U.S. investors wanted access to the large and rapidly growing domestic market – the population of Egypt grew from 36 million in 1974 to nearly 39 million in 1977. It is now rapidly approaching 50 million people. And they also preferred to operate with the Egyptian private sector rather than the dominant public sector. Legislation and practice surrounding the open-door policy and the implementation and reform of Law 43 had given private capital and its allies inside and outside of the country clear signals that the public sector was increasingly to share the task of economic development with the private sector and, in a sense, the provisions of Law 43 turned all Egyptian–foreign joint enterprises into private sector companies. These signals were also picked up by the forces within Egypt committed to the private sector, and the whole period from 1974 has been characterised by parliamentary and extra-parliamentary controversy between defenders and opponents of the *infitah* policy and, not always the same people, defenders and opponents of the dominant public sector. The debates over *infitah* and the struggles over the ownership of the material base of the Egyptian economy were inextricably intertwined. This makes all the more interesting the misnomer 'Public Free Zone' in relation to 'Private Free Zone'. As I have explained, *all* Free Zone companies are treated as private companies, so the 'Public' can refer only to the fact that the zones are administered by a Public, governmental body, the Investment Authority, and not to ownership. Perhaps the name serves to bemuse some less well-informed potential critics.[9]

The year 1977 was certainly one of frenetic activity by the Investment Authority. Gillespie, in her detailed study of fdi in Egypt, documents the government's haste to improve the foreign investment climate by removing obstacles and speeding up approvals of investment projects. The Investment Authority duly responded by approving 241 projects with foreign participation, the largest total for any one year. On one day alone, March 27, 1977, 65 projects worth LE 400m were approved.[10]

By the end of 1974, the Investment Authority had approved 144 Inland projects involving a capital investment of LE 170m. of which over half was from foreign sources. By the end of 1984, ten times as many projects had been approved – perhaps more significantly, 760 were actually in operation – and both total and foreign capital involved in these actual projects had increased by a factor of 15 over the approved figures. First, two-thirds of Law 43 investment is Egyptian, and most there are three widely recognised problems hidden within the investment figures. First, two-thirds of Law 43 investment in Egyptian, and most of the 'foreign' investment comes from other Arab countries, particularly the oil-rich states. Very little comes from the areas that the open-door policy had originally targetted, namely Western Europe and the United States. At the end of 1984 Arab investment accounted for 52 per cent of total Law 43 foreign investment in operating projects, 23 per cent came from EEC countries, 12 per cent from the U.S., and 13 per cent from other countries. These figures, collated by the U.S. embassy in Cairo, exclude the massive amount of U.S. investment in petroleum. It is not difficult to gain the impression that Egypt is awash with U.S. money, contractors, and consultants, and the fact that of the total Law 43 investment only 4 per cent has come from the U.S. has caused resentment. U.S. agencies in Egypt are now actively promoting more productive investment in the country. Second, the absolute amount of foreign investment in projects actually operating – about one billion dollars at a realistic rate of exchange – is low on per capita and GDP bases, even by the standards of the developing countries. The third problem is that the structure of foreign investment is unsatisfactory in terms of Egypt's perception of its development needs. Of the 19 project categories distinguished by the Investment Authority one alone, Investment and Finance, accounts for more than one third of the total capital in use (LE 936m.). These investment companies and banks have not, as a rule, directed much of their resources towards Egyptian manufacturing industry. If we add to this the second category, of banking, another LE 561m., and the third, tourism, LE 189m., these three non-industrial sectors swallow up more than 60 per cent of total capital investment in Law 43 projects. Therefore, from the point of view of stimulating exports and particularly exports of manufactured goods, the investment programme has clearly not been much of a success.

THE FREE ZONES

The Investment and Free Zones Authority is empowered to establish public and private Free Zones, and is responsible for (i) coordinating policies and planning of the Zones; (ii) acquiring the necessary land; (iii) approving budgets; (iv) acting as and/or appointing boards of directors for each Free Zone; (v) affiliating private zones to public zones (Law 43, Articles 30, 31). The Board of Directors may grant licences to Arab and foreign investors to engage in storage of goods; sorting, clearing, mixing and blending; any manufacturing, assembling, processing etc.; any trade 'warranted by the activities within the free zone or intended for the comfort of the employees of the zone' (Article 35). Anything brought into the zones from outside Egypt or exported from the zones out of the country is exempt from all taxes and duties. Anything coming into the zones from Egypt is subject to normal export taxes and duties, and goods going into the local market from the zones are similarly treated as imports. However, where the local content of such goods constitutes at least 40 per cent of the value of the goods, then duties and taxes are reduced by 50 per cent (Article 37). While Free Zone project profits are tax-free in Egypt, an across the board duty of up to 1 per cent of the value of goods (or up to 3 per cent for purely service activities) is payable to the Investment Authority (Article 46).

Recognition is given to the problems of foreign exchange that bedevil the operations of foreign companies in Egypt, in Article 49: 'Transactions carried out in the free zone or between such zones and other countries shall not be subject to the provisions of exchange control laws'. Law 43 concludes with some general regulations concerning employment, training, labour conditions, and penalties (imprisonment and fines) for violations, the upshot of which is that the Free Zone employees come out with fewer rights but perhaps better pay than those not working in Free Zones.

In addition to Law 43, the Minister of Economy and Economic Cooperation, to whom the Investment Authority was then attached, issued a set of Executive Regulations (number 375 of 1977) covering the operations of Inland investment (50 articles) and Free Zone investment (88 Articles). While there is some repetition of the provisions of Law 43 in the Regulations, they do cover some of the finer details and have been distributed in pamphlet form along with a translation of the amended Law 43 to potential and actual foreign investors as a guide to Free Zone practice.

The Investment and Free Zones Authority makes land available for investors to build their own factories. The rent for the land is fixed at very low annual rates, $1.00 to $1.50 per square metre for industrial use, $3.75 to $5.00 for storage and service projects. The Authority also has purpose built factories available in the zones, for which investors will pay substantially higher rents, negotiated separately for each project. Charges for water, electricity, other fuels, and services are also fixed but, certainly in the case of electricity, the Free Zone investor does not enjoy the subsidised prices of the Inland Egyptian consumer. The investor is also responsible for connecting up the factory or warehouse to the mains supply. All these charges are met in foreign currency.

Table 1 gives the numbers of projects and amounts of capital invested in Free Zones by 1977 and 1984, with 1984 Inland investment for comparison. As can be readily seen, the gap between approvals and actual projects has narrowed considerably, projects in operation on average are attracting larger sums of capital, and most of this capital is foreign, including investment from other Arab countries. In terms of projects in operation, there are three times as many Inland as Free Zone projects, while the total capital employed is five times greater. However, while 99 per cent of Free Zone capital is foreign, just over 55 per cent of Inland capital is foreign. That is, while the Egyptian private sector has

TABLE 1
LAW 43 PROJECTS BY STATUS, TO END 1977, AND END 1984

	Number of Projects			Capital Employed (LEm.)					
				Total			Foreign		
	(a)	(b)	(c)	(a)	(b)	(c)	(a)	(b)	(c)
Public & Private Free Zones									
1977	137	62	59	767	65	87	–	37	–
1984	311	256	34	816	571	45	810	567	45
Inland									
1984	1,326	760	229	5,700	2,804	794	3,136	1,555	465

(a) = approved; (b) in operation; (c) under implementation

Sources: Investment and Free Zones Authority, Report (March 1978); Facts and Figures XIV (Dec. 1984).

invested heavily in Law 43 Inland projects, it has generally avoided the Free Zones.[11]

It is important to recognize that there are systematic differences, both in terms of policy intentions and in concrete reality, between the Free Zones. In 1985, there were four Public Free Zones, at Nasr City, a suburb of Cairo; at Al Ameria, about 30 kilometres from Alexandria; in Port Said; and in Suez. Other zones are being planned, for example in Sinai, but it appears that the government has taken the advice of its critics and will complete the four existing zones before embarking on any new and expensive zone construction. Nasr City Free Zone is located in the general direction of the airport and was intended to attract light industry that could use air transport for import of components and export of finished goods. Al Ameria, by far the largest of the zones, was meant for light and heavy industry, with a mix of capital and labour intensive projects, taking advantage of Alexandria's harbour facilities. Port Said and Suez Free Zones, located as they are at either end of the Canal, would in addition be expected to exploit shipping and petroleum-related business. There is some ambivalence in official publications over the question of whether these zones were ever intended to be export processing zones in the classical pattern[12] although there is no doubt that increasing Egypt's exports, and thus capacity to earn foreign currency, was always a prime goal. A closer look at the first three zones demonstrates how difficult it has been to achieve this goal.

THE COSTS OF FOREIGN INVESTMENT

Nasr City Free Zones

The Free Zone is situated on the eastern fringe of Cairo, just beyond the populous suburb of Nasr City. The Public Free Zone occupies over 330,000 square metres, of which about two thirds are taken up by 27 operating projects. In addition there are four projects in the implementation stage (under construction), and three more approved. The capital actually invested in operating projects in 1985 totalled LE 25.2 m., all but half a million from foreign sources, or mixed local–foreign sources. These enterprises provide employment for over 1,200 people, with prospects of another 300 jobs if all the potential projects actually come to fruition.

The striking feature of the Nasr City Free Zones is that the Private Free Zones have attracted much more investment than the Public Free Zone. The 19 Private Free Zone projects supervised by the Nasr City authorities accounted for over LE 131 m. of foreign investment (out of a total investment of LE 133 m.). This is more than five times as much as the foreign investment in the Public Free Zone, and substantially more than any of the other Public Free Zones.[14] These 19 projects were reported to employ over 2,600 people in 1984. It is clear that the attractions of being near the centre of Cairo outweigh the attractions of the Public Free Zone insofar as the infrastructure, while satisfactory on the whole for the projects already there, is not yet sufficiently developed and the amenities within the zone not sufficient of an incentive to tip the balance between Private Free Zone investment and a commitment to the Public Free Zone.

The Public Free Zone has the appearance of a spacious if as yet somewhat unfinished industrial estate. Of the 27 projects in operation in 1985 nine were manufacturing enterprises. Two were in medical products, two in food, one each in paper and glass, and three in electronics (assembling calculators, watches, and traffic signals).

A brief analysis of the activities of two of these and a third about to begin production will illustrate some of the main problems and prospects of foreign direct investment in the Free Zone system.

Arab Otsuka Pharmaceutical Company is a wholly-owned subsidiary of a Japanese multinational with an annual turnover in the region of two billion dollars. The factory in Nasr City covers 33,000 square metres and began production, mainly of intravenous solutions, in 1979. The company first made the decision to establish a plant somewhere in the Middle East and carried out feasibility studies in Jordan and Iran before looking at Egypt. The proposed site in Iran was not near enough to a suitable water supply, and political problems (of an unspecified nature) ruled out Jordan. The Nasr City Public Free Zone had a good water supply, political stability, and adequate incentives. The company now gives employment to 150 production workers and 20 office and technical staff, a few of whom are Japanese.

Arab Otsuka is a classic case of the conflicts of interests that often arise between the governments of developing countries and foreign investors, leaving the authorities of an export processing zone stranded in the middle of the argument. The company imports almost all of its components – chemicals from Japan, plastics for bottles from W. Germany, some other materials from the rest of Europe – and buys very little from the local market. This the government is prepared to tolerate as Arab Otsuka was set up to export to the Middle East, North Africa, and Nigeria. However, while the company vigorously pursued all potential export markets, it also tried to gain access to the local market and, as most of its business is on a tender basis, it insisted that it be permitted to tender for Egyptian government contracts on an equal footing with indigenous producers. The fact that only 5 per cent of its business is currently with Egyptian customers suggests that it has not entirely been successful in this aim.

One example of Arab Otsuka's experiences with the Egyptian authorities is worth recounting as it does demonstrate, albeit in a rather extreme form, the problems thrown up all over the Third World by such conflicts of interests. The company won a contract from the Egyptian Army to supply a quantity of intravenous solution and, though not strictly permitted by the regulations, the Investment Authority gave its approval for the transaction to be in Egyptian pounds – it will be recalled that all Free Zone transactions are supposed to be in hard (foreign) currency. Two shipments were successfully accomplished, but then the Customs Authority, which controls the movement of all goods into and out of the Free Zones, insisted that the Ministry of Economy had to give permission. This duly took place, but then the Customs insisted that the Import Rationalization Committee (a powerful body set up to decide on what goods may be imported) give its permission. When this was forthcoming, after much argument, the Customs finally insisted that the Prime Minister himself authorise the transaction. Unfortunately, the Prime Minister, Fuad Mohieddin, died in office in 1984 while all this was going on, the Egyptian Army ran out of patience with Otsuka's inability to deliver, and the contract went to an indigenous producer – a government-owned factory.

Another serious problem concerns supplies. The Japanese Managing Director of Arab Otsuka received authorisation for the import of a large consignment of plastic sterile bottles from both the Ministry of Health and the Importation Committee. However, when it was discovered that local producers were also short of these supplies, Otsuka's authorisation was cancelled, no doubt to protect the position of the Egyptian producers in the local market. The Free Zone Authority at Nasr City is bound by Law 43 to play its part in protecting the interests of local industry, but it is also bound to protect the interests of the foreign investors operating in the Zone. Where these interests collide, as they often do, the Investment and Free Zones Authority is, literally, in an impossible position.

This is a problem, in my view, that can never be satisfactorily resolved under the present policies. It is easy, therefore, to understand the frustration of those responsible for the Nasr City Free Zones (and the other Free Zones, as we shall see) when the country is flooded with imported domestic consumer goods, many of which are frankly luxuries, while such obstacles are erected against foreign producers of rather more socially necessary products. In short, it is unrealistic to expect that companies such as Arab Otsuka will refrain from attempting to sell in the large Egyptian domestic market, however much they can export.

Despite these problems, the company is well-established in Nasr City and though it may not be as profitable as planned, it is clearly a viable concern. Labour works out cheaper than Taiwan but dearer than Thailand, and apart from the Japanese factories, the Egyptian plant is the least labour intensive of all the Group's operations. Indeed, apart from the Pfizer company plant in Iran, Arab Otsuka claims to be the most technologically sophisticated manufacturer of its type in the region. This is reflected, to some extent, by a highly structured wage grade system to encourage efficiency at all levels of the work force. There is a twice-yearly profits related bonus system and talk of expansion and a new factory. However, current business prospects, particularly the block on domestic sales, are depressing both of these schemes.

This is all in striking contrast to the expectations of Atlantic Industries Ltd., a subsidiary of the Coca-Cola Export Corporation. Various soft drinks are produced under licence in joint ventures with Egyptian companies by international brands like Cadbury–Schweppes and Canada Dry. Coca-Cola in its Egyptian form is the nearest thing to an 'official government-sponsored' soft drink and for some years Coca-Cola have been supplying bottling plants all over Egypt with imported concentrates, and they in turn have been supplying the local market. The plant in the Free Zone, which is due to go into operation in the near future, will be making up the concentrates from the basic ingredients and thus 'nationalizing' one part of the operation. By doing this, the import content of Coca-Cola is considered to be drastically reduced, despite the fact that all the ingredients (apart from the water), and even the plastic containers for the concentrate, will be imported. The intention is to turn the Nasr City site into the regional headquarters of Coca-Cola responsible for the Egyptian market and for exports to the rest of the area. Adjacent to the concentrate plant, a suite of offices is being built.

This will not be a labour intensive project. The startup team is mainly expatriate, and it is anticipated that the first phase of operations will provide about 25 local jobs. It remains to be seen whether or not the locally mixed concentrates experience any of the problems of the intravenous solutions on their way to the domestic market, and what effect this project has on Egypt's soft drinks balance of payments.

The third project is an altogether simpler operation. The Consolidated Paper Company is a privately-owned joint venture of Syrian, Saudi, and Egyptian partners, with a sales office and storage facility in Saudi Arabia. The factory, which opened in May 1984, brings in 300 kilogram rolls of paper, mainly from Finland, which are chopped into smaller rolls and made up into sheets. The process is largely automated, though the sheets are packeted by hand, and the labour force numbers 48, working in two shifts. As business is expanding – local producers were said to be able to meet only 20 per cent of domestic demand – a further shift and increase in the workforce is planned.

All the machinery is German, and as the manufacturers have an agent in Alexandria, spare parts and servicing have not proved to be a problem (indeed, a German technician was attending to one of the machines during my visit). As the basic raw material, paper, about 80 per cent of production costs, is all imported, there are practically no backward linkages. There are, however, forward linkages to the extent that the company supplies the local newspaper and printing industry – domestic sales account for about 40 per cent of production, and the waste paper from the factory is sold to make egg boxes.

Here, then, is a project that appears to be giving some benefits to all parties. The entrepreneurs are clearly reaping a good return of their investment; the workforce has exposure to some modern, advanced machinery; secure jobs at rates of pay better than average for the locality; the Free Zone Authority has a small, though healthy and expanding tenant; and the country has a firm that supplies a local need that domestic producers have been unable fully to meet, and it earns some foreign currency. This happy set of circumstances is not frequently to be found in Free Zone projects, as we shall see, and the success of the whole Free Zone policy, if not the Investment policy as a whole, largely depends on how many projects meeting all these criteria can be attracted and kept in the country.

THE COSTS OF FOREIGN INVESTMENT

Al Ameria Free Zone
The Free Zone occupies a large tract of land just off the Desert Road that runs from Cairo, and is about 30 kilometres before Alexandria. Construction started on the infrastructure of the zone in 1976–7 in parallel with modest plans to build up the adjoining village of Ameria to house and provide services for those who would work in the zone. The Free Zone was planned in three phases. The first phase of about one million square metres accommodates about 100 factories and warehouses and is in full operation; the infrastructure for phase two is more or less complete; and work on phase three no doubt depends on the occupancy patterns of the already completed areas. Altogether, only about one quarter of the available space has been taken up (something over 635,000 square metres) so the development of Phase Three does not seem imminent.

The Free Zone Authority at Al Ameria, conscious of its distance from the city of Alexandria, has been at pains to provide all the services that investors will require on the Free Zone site itself. A spacious administration building has been built with accommodation for Egyptian and Joint-Venture banks but, as of April 1985, the Minister of the Economy had not yet authorised any banks to operate in the Free Zone. A newly constructed wing of this building will house insurance, shipping, post, and a Customs office – the idea being to turn the Zone into a 'one-stop-shop' for potential and actual investors. Adjacent to the Administration building is a recently completed Exhibition Hall in pink Italian marble, intended to be a showcase for the products of the investors who will be attracted in by the advantages offered in the Free Zone.

Table 2 sets out the recent development of the Public and Private Free Zones administered by the Investment Authority at Al Ameria.

The general infrastructural provisions of phases one and two are, indeed, impressive. A good road system has been built; ample water supply and drainage facilities are available; a 65 megawatt sub-station with a 5 megawatt standby provides electricity; and the telephone system is adequate for present needs, and is being upgraded. A telex system is to be installed by the end of 1985. Altogether, between LE 35 m. and LE 40 m. have been spent on the infrastructure of the Free Zone.

Despite these ambitious steps to make the zone a success, the actual investment record has been very mixed. Although the Free Zone has managed to attract a large number of projects, very few of them are manufacturing enterprises. Indeed, about half of the totals of what are described as 'investment costs', representing capital invested plus a further unspecified sum, have been provided by a group of ten marine and transportation service companies. These are located in nearby

TABLE 2
ALEXANDRIA FREE ZONES, APPROVED PROJECTS AND INVESTMENT COSTS, END 1981 AND END 1984

Activity/Year	1981		1984	
	Projects	Investment Costs ($m.)	Projects	Investment Costs ($m.)
Industrial	27 (22%)	53.7 (17%)	21 (17%)	41.7 (10%)
Storage	85 (70%)	123.2 (38%)	90 (74%)	163.2 (37%)
Services	10 (8%)	145.6 (45%)	10 (9%)	226.6 (53%)
Total	122	322.5	121	431.5

Sources: 1981 = Investment Authority, Alexandria Branch brochure (31 March 1982)
         1984 = Information provided by Investment Authority at Al Ameria (2 April 1985).

private free zones administered by the General Free Zone Authority. If we compare the situation at the beginning of 1982 with that at the beginning of 1985, it is difficult to avoid the impression that a disturbing trend is emerging. Table 2 shows that the efforts of the Authority to shift the balance from non-industrial to industrial projects have met with little success to date. In terms of project approvals – not all of which will turn into actual projects – the proportion of total investment costs taken up by manufacturing projects has declined from 17 per cent in 1981 to 10 per cent in 1984.

Even this, however, is not a totally realistic picture. It appears to be the case that in Al Ameria the default rate between approval and execution of manufacturing projects is very much greater than for storage and service projects. For example, to take the position at the start of 1985, there were approvals for 21 manufacturing, 90 storage, and ten service projects, 121 in all (see Table 2); while the Investment Authority 'Facts and Figures, 1984' brochure gives a figure of 98 projects in actual operation at the year end, without a breakdown by activity. Project approvals for manufacturing split 17 to four with respect to Public and Private Free Zones, 80 projects in all were said to be actually operating in the Public Free Zone, and 16 in the Private Zone. Visual inspection in April 1985 confirmed that, at most, eight manufacturing projects were actually producing in the Public Free Zone, plus one other definitely about to start production, two under construction, and several more somewhere in the pipeline. If we add to this four

Private Free Zone Companies actually in production − 12 projects of an industrial nature in all − then we still have a manufacturing project short-fall of about 40 per cent. Storage and service projects have fared much better. The reasons for this are not difficult to find. Alexandria itself (and to a slightly lesser extent Al Ameria) does have a definite locational advantage as far as services, and particularly the distribution of goods, are concerned. It is a gateway at once into Africa and into Arabia.

The port of Alexandria handles well over three quarters of Egypt's foreign trade, and new port facilities, to relieve the chronic bottlenecks at Alexandria, are being built at Dekheila and Abukir, nearby. Parts of the Public Free Zone do resemble a vast parking lot for new vehicles, and the Investment Authority analysis of commodities for the calendar year 1984 clearly confirms this impression. Of the total value of $255 millions, for stored commodities, $186 millions were motor vehicles (plus $40 millions in petroleum). In addition, the ten service projects already alluded to cater for the substantial marine business in the vicinity. Between them, the service and storage projects account for the vast majority of actual working capital in the Free Zones.

There is a brighter side to the picture, and that is in the key area of employment. Altogether, the Free Zones in Al Ameria have created over 5,500 jobs, somewhat more than half in the Public Free Zone, and almost 23 million dollars were said to have been paid in wages in 1984.[15] There were in March 1985 more than 1,200 employees in industrial projects in the Free Zones, all but 30 being local people. The annual wages of the Egyptian workers averaged out at $1,502 per person whereas the foreign employees earned $5,433 on average each.

This is a clear benefit to the Egyptian balance of payments as these wages are paid in foreign currency (usually if not exclusively U.S. dollars). The other side of the foreign exchange balance-sheet, imports and exports, does not register such a clearcut benefit. Figures from Al Ameria show, on the surface, a fairly serious deficit for 1984. Imports to the zones totalled $365 m., made up of the previously mentioned $255 m. in commodities (mainly stored automobiles), $20 m. in fixed assets (presumably machinery etc.), and $90 m. in raw materials. 'Exports' totalled $290 m., but only $18 m. worth (6 per cent) were genuine exports, the rest actually being 'exported' to the local market. The real situation is, of course, rather more complex than these figures suggest. Just as 'exports' to the local market are hardly genuine exports, though they do earn customs duties, 'imports' of commodities in storage are hardly genuine imports, except where they eventually enter the domestic market. As we saw in the case of the Japanese pharmaceutical company in Nasr City, the Government of Egypt is anxious to prevent the Free Zones being used as a back door into the Egyptian domestic market in competition with indigenous producers. While it is very difficult to quantify, it is clear that this is happening to some, and perhaps a large, extent.

A brief account of three manufacturing projects in the Public Free Zone will indicate the range of projects and their contributions to the local community.

Confection Egyptienne is an Italian garment company with affiliates in Greece and Tunisia — a small Mediterranean transnational — which opened up its factory in Al Ameria in 1981. It imports cloth from its parent company in Italy, cuts it and makes it up into several types of garments, which it then re-exports to Italy.[16] This provides work for around 200 people, mostly young women, who earn $90 per month (paid in dollars) basic wage and an unspecified but probably substantial addition in overtime.

In accordance with the policies of the Investment Authority, there are few expatriates working in the factory, and the products are kept out of the local market. The General Manager and five other staff members are Italian, but the Factory Manager is Egyptian, as are all other employees. As Egypt has its own extensive garment industry, there is a total formal ban on foreign imports, though there are plenty of foreign-manufactured clothes to be seen. There are two explanations for this. First, companies like Confection Egyptienne bring back some of their finished goods via the Free Port at Port Said. Second, there is a considerable degree of smuggling. Clearly, the government is taking a risk by encouraging such firms to produce in Egypt at all. No doubt the jobs they provide are taken to outweigh the damage they may inflict on the domestic sector. It is unlikely that there is any genuine technology transfer in such cases, though there may be some intangible benefit through exposure to 'Italian style'.

Coldalex is a Saudi Arabian firm that takes locally grown speciality vegetables and freezes them. Artichokes, spinach, green beans, okra, and other high value vegetables are grown in a farm that the firm owns near Alexandria and brought to Al Ameria, where they are prepared, blanched, frozen, and packaged. This is fairly labour intensive work, and about 150 people deal with up to 700 kilograms of vegetables every day. Wages are relatively low, averaging around $65 per month for the mainly female manual workers.

There is a cold store with a capacity of 450 tons, and the firm has six refrigerated vans to transport the frozen vegetables to the port, from where they are exported all over the Gulf and beyond. Business appears to be brisk as there is a growing demand for such quality foods and few local competitors in the region. It also fits in well with the policy of the government that Egypt should increasingly be looking to develop such high value crops to capture lucrative markets. These two projects, therefore, are typical of the global export processing sector in that they exist to exploit the low cost labour of women but are nevertheless welcomed by the women no less than the authorities, precisely because they provide the jobs they do.

The third project, Al Mukhtar, is a Libyan-owned printing firm. This factory was in its pre-production stage in April 1985. The owners had a well-established business in Libya and were preparing to begin production in Al Ameria in the near future. Over a period of two years they had set up the factory with a full range of modern printing machinery, including Lasercomp for electronic book and magazine production. The intention was to be able to produce a full range of printed materials, from school exercise books to fully illustrated books.

All the machinery is imported, at considerable expense, but no problems had been encountered in securing its duty-free passage through customs. Likewise, all the paper used is imported, currently from Portugal, and this presented no problems either. The factory itself had been built by one of the many contractors from the U.S. active in Egypt. No backward linkages, apart from the obvious local services and utilities, were anticipated. This project, therefore, is a typical 'enclave' enterprise, cut off as it were from the local economy.

Only on the employment side will the project bring much immediate benefit to the local community. Already there are 30 local workers employed, and it is hoped that full production will bring about 100 more jobs. It is possible that some transfer of technology might take place as the three Libyans who manage the plant train local personnel in the use of the modern machinery, though Egypt itself already has a solid printing industry.

The question of markets is also quite problematic. In the regulations governing Free Zone projects, it is stated that projects that directly compete with domestic producers are not to be encouraged. This is, of course, a contentious issue in an economy as diversified as Egypt. The authorities in a particular zone can hardly be blamed for trying to attract a technically advanced project like Al Mukhtar, even if the potential market for its products, the Arab world, including Egypt, is one that Egyptian producers are trying to serve. This, naturally, applies to many Law 43 projects, as is vividly illustrated in Port Said, to which I now turn.

Port Said Free Zone[17]

The war of 1967 effectively destroyed the economic life of the Suez canal and Port Said, which had become a thriving centre of East–West entrepot trade, suffered great physical damage. The scars of war are still everywhere to be seen. The ceasefire of 1973 and the promise of peace provided the incentive to reconstruct the city, and this was embarked upon in the context of two important structural changes. First, in 1976, Port Said was declared a Free City, exempt from customs duties, import and export restrictions, and exchange controls. This means that within the city limits is available a vast array of consumer and other goods, many of which are difficult to find elsewhere in Egypt, and at a price far lower than anywhere else in the country. The city centre is full of Egyptians on day trips filling suitcases and large shopping bags with all manner of goods. There are customs posts at the bus and rail stations, and at the city limits, where all traffic is stopped and searched. Customs duties are levied on some items being taken back into Egypt, but there appears to be an informal 'personal allowance' in operation. There is also, without doubt, a considerable amount of smuggling. In short, Port Said is a conduit for a vast amount of duty-free imported goods, mainly for personal consumption or resale on the black market.

The second structural change, and the one with which I am mainly concerned here, was the establishment of the Public Free Zone, also in 1976. The Free Zone was constructed, in the first place, to take advantage of the rapid growth of business stimulated by the re-opening of the Suez Canal. The Zone is located adjacent to the Canal and linked to it by junctional canals capable of taking large barges. In general, the Zone is well served for infrastructure and services.

The Zone occupies over three quarters of a million square metres, twice the size of Nasr City, but its occupancy rate is somewhat lower, just under half of its area being presently occupied, though there were more than twice as many industrial projects in the Port Said Public Free Zone as in Nasr City. Most (52 out of 84) of these projects are, as elsewhere, warehousing and what is labelled 'transit trade with complementary operations'; there are also seven cold storage projects, four in the service sector, and 21 manufacturing enterprises. Just south of the main zone and served by a new wharf is an export processing zone which is the object of the next phase of development. The Free Zone Authority hopes to attract export-oriented firms to take advantage of the location and facilities of the port. To date only one factory is operating in the export processing zone, and that is a concrete manufacturer whose total production is sold in Egypt!

THE COSTS OF FOREIGN INVESTMENT

Of the 84 projects approved by the beginning of 1985, 82 were in operation and two were being implemented. The total working capital involved was $132 m., and the total investment costs about $206 m. – industrial projects accounting for about 30 per cent of these amounts. Egyptians owned about 40 per cent of the capital, other Arabs about 30 per cent, and EEC nationals about 20 per cent. The U.S. share was 1 per cent.

As with Al Ameria, the import and export figures reveal the main problem facing the Free Zones in their present stage of development, namely the lack of a genuine manufacturing export sector, and the predominant use of the Zones as launch pads for imports. In 1981, the total amount of imports to the Port Said Free Zones was valued at $378.9 m., the lion's share of which – $189 m. – was accounted for by vehicles, and another $58.5 m. worth of foodstuffs for the five blending and packing plants in the zone. By 1984, the import bill was $223.9 m. – it had declined in each year since 1981 – and most of the decline was in vehicles, down to $58.4 m. worth. Imports of foodstuffs were slightly up to $61.1 m. from a peak of $74.1 m. in 1982, and raw material imports had increased from $20.5 m. (in 1981) to $53.6 m. Exports from the zone have gradually declined from $317.8 m. in 1981 to $271.4 m. in 1984, with 'exports' to the local market also showing a year-by-year decline from $266 m. (1981) to $214.5 m. (1984). However, genuine exports, abroad, have a less regular pattern, $51.8 m. (1981) to $64.6 m. (1982) to $63.6 m. (1983) and $56.9 m. (1984), that is between 16 per cent and 22 per cent of total exports. Clearly a great deal of the goods in storage as well as the products of the manufacturing projects are finding their way, legally, into Egypt. An example of one such company is United Chemical Africa (UCA), a manufacturer of paints, adhesives and varnishes, employing 60 people, ten staff, ten technical, and 40 operatives.

UCA is owned by an Algerian, who has another, smaller, factory in Algeria. When he obtained his licence to begin operating in the Free Zone, in 1977, he was among the first manufacturing companies there, about 30 storage projects being already in business. The first full year of operations was 1981, and the factory has an annual production capacity of 10,000 tons of paint. It is currently operating at only 30 per cent of this capacity because of an unsatisfactory balance, from the firm's point of view, between its access to the local market and its export performance. The original agreement with the Free Zone authorities permitted UCA to sell 50 per cent of its production to the domestic market in 1981, reducing to 20 per cent by 1984. However, the firm argued that it needed to sell 40 per cent of its production in Egypt to keep the business viable. Operating costs were said to be very high and the firm claimed to be paying an incentive wage of up to $350 per month. Male labour is generally very short in Port Said, but this was by far the highest wage I encountered in any Free Zone. Short of examining the accounts of the firm, there is no way that the independent observer (let alone the Free Zone Authority) can judge the merits of such a case; though, as we have seen from cases in Nasr City and Al Ameria, many if not most Free Zone manufacturers will seek entry to the local market as a quid pro quo for exporting effort.

The experience of UCA highlights two further problems of operating in a Free Zone, one specific to Port Said, one more general. To export paints to the Gulf, the obvious market, it is necessary first to get them to Suez, which is an expensive and time-consuming process. The extension and improvement to the harbour facilities at Port Said, promised over the last few years, has not yet happened; the turnaround of ships is very slow, and there is a problem of damage to goods in handling.

The second problem is one of backward linkages. Egypt does have a growing chemicals industry, stimulated recently by the development in petroleum. Domestic manufacturers can and will supply many of the chemicals, including solvents and thinners, that UCA uses. Here, as elsewhere, a minimum of 40 per cent local content will give a 50 per cent reduction on duties levied on sales to Egypt. So, there is a clear incentive for UCA to buy locally where possible. The problem is one of quality and price. The company complained about the quality of the chemicals sold by Egyptian firms, and even more so about the prices charged. Nitrocellulose, for example, was about four times more expensive to buy locally than imported duty free from Europe. There are two aspects to this price differential. Clearly local producers do take advantage of the customs benefits that accrue to Free Zone manufacturers who have high local content in their goods. Further, as Free Zone projects may deal only in dollars (or other hard currencies), they are vulnerable to the exchange rate prevailing for their particular purchases.

The level of discontent is so high at UCA, that the firm is considering a move to another Free Zone, elsewhere in the Mediterranean.[18] The sticking-point is primarily access to the Egyptian market and here the Free Zone Authority is in a real dilemma. While it is bound by law to protect the domestic producer, it also has to respond to investors' requests for some domestic sales while a viable business is being built. The existence of the dilemma does throw doubt on the whole approvals procedure and particularly the feasibility studies that are supposed to ensure the viability of projects. The Investment and Free Zones

THE COSTS OF FOREIGN INVESTMENT

Authority do not publish figures on rejected projects, but the impression given is that very few projects with foreign participation are ever turned down.[19]

Not all firms in Port Said, however, are as unhappy as UCA. The Haniatex Clothes Company, owned by a Lebanese businessman, imports cloth from Taiwan and China and designs mainly from the United States. In the factory about 275 workers cut and make up, in some cases simply copy, garments and about 40,000 pieces (mainly leisure-wear) per month are exported. The average wage for machinists, mostly young women, is $100 to $150 per month, and engineers can earn up to $300. Though the project was approved and land for the factory assigned in 1980, production did not actually start until 1984, but since then business has been booming. Haniatex is the first Port Said Free Zone company to export to the U.S., and a joint venture with a firm in Hong Kong is under way. Like Confection Egyptienne at Al Ameria, this is a relatively problem-free and successful operation that provides jobs but little else for the local economy. The only local purchase is packaging materials.

The Arab Traders Union Coffee Factory, which opened in the Free Zone in 1982, does not even buy its packaging materials locally. It is owned by an Egyptian entrepreneur, born in Port Said, whose multinational activities are headquartered in Switzerland and extend to many projects in Europe and Africa. This company specialises in vacuum packs of fine Raina and Brazilia coffee, in a fully automated factory, the only one of its kind in Egypt. This gives employment to over 100 people. All the machinery and raw materials are imported and the coffee is exported to the Gulf and some permitted to enter the local market. However, as the Egyptian government has a monopoly over this trade, the price is kept down, and the company, while enjoying the benefit of local sales, claims to be making very little profit from them.

Arab Traders Union also owns a cement factory, under the name of Spanish-Egyptian, in the Free Zone. This factory, which started production in 1984, imports clinker from all over the Mediterranean (mainly Spain, Greece and Turkey) and turns it into cement in its 42,000 square metre factory area. This represents a total investment of $10,000,000, one of the largest in the zone, and one of the largest industrial Free Zone investments in the whole country. There are more than 200 jobs in this factory and it is operating on a three-shift system to satisfy the seemingly limitless demands of the local economy.

The construction boom that is in evidence all over Egypt means that Spanish-Egyptian can sell all of its cement to Egyptian, mainly governmental, purchasers. The economics of this particular transaction were not entirely clear but the company is clearly thriving and there is talk of expansion. This appears to depend on the successful resolution of some pressing operating problems. In February 1985, the government put a ban on the direct sale of cement from the Free Zone to Egyptian companies, which forced Spanish-American to set up a company in Egypt (outside the Free Zone) to distribute its cement. It is apparently arbitrary changes such as this in the working regulations that have caused some foreign investors to abandon Egypt altogether.[20]

More evidence of the problems that can arise from inadequate attention to feasibility studies is provided by the experience of the cement factory. Although Spanish-Egyptian had written into their study that they wanted to organise their own barge and handling facilities, they found later that they were unable actually to do this, and have ended up paying the local stevedoring company LE 1.30 to move every ton of clinker.

Port Said Free Zone has had successes and failures and it is tempting to attribute blame for the failures to the government and praise for the successes to the local Free Zone Authority. Insufficient funds have been spent on the infrastructure of Port Said, particularly harbour facilities, and talk of a new international airport, essential if electronic and other low bulk-high value industries are to be developed, has had no tangible result. The four million Egyptian pounds already spent on the Free Zone itself has been recouped, but of the LE 12m. estimated to be necessary to complete the zone, particularly for industrial use, only LE 2.5 m. was allocated in 1985.

The Zone authorities intend to call a halt to non-industrial projects and to concentrate in the next phase on wood industries, textiles, electronics, and marine projects. This is, of course, easier said than done, as there is great competition for such investment from free zones all over the Mediterranean and further afield. It is to the prospects for such investment, and its real economic and social costs and benefits, that I turn in my concluding remarks.

CONCLUSION

More or less everyone who writes on Egypt complains about the bloated bureaucracy, the counter-productive attitudes of decision makers at all levels of public and private life, and the poor quality of local goods and services. No doubt there is much truth in all of these complaints, but it is too easy to lay the blame for Egypt's present problems entirely on internal factors. It is an inescapable fact that the more effort Egypt puts into its promotion of exports, the larger its deficit in foreign trade grows. As this problem has been well-documented[21] suffice it to say that, on World Bank figures, Egypt is one of the 15 countries in the world (out of the 120 for which data are available) who imported more than twice as much (in dollar terms) as they exported, in 1981. The U.S. is Egypt's largest trading partner at present. In 1984 imports from the U.S. totalled $2.7 billion while exports to the U.S. were $182 million, about 60 per cent in petroleum. Egypt's huge trade deficit is kept in check at present by its four main sources of foreign exchange, but two of these (oil revenues and remittances from the millions of Egyptians working overseas) are likely to decline, and the other two (Suez Canal revenues and tourism), though increasing are doing so rather slowly.

While exports have grown, the growth between the mid-1970s and the mid-1980s has been mainly due to petroleum exports, which account for well over half the total. The only other item that accounts for more than 10 per cent is the traditionally vigorous textile industry.[22] The expansion of manufactured exports in the first decade of the *infitah* policy has been very small. The reason for this is obvious, from the evidence of Inland and Free Zone investment alike. Most of the investment attracted by the open-door policy, like banks, trading companies, contractors, storage and warehousing, and services, tend to encourage imports rather than exports. Even the manufacturing projects in the Free Zones, as we have seen, are heavily dependent on imports, and are likely to 'export' their products as much to the Egyptian market (thereby adding to the import bill) as abroad.

As I have already noted, the government of Egypt has been aware of this problem for some time. By 1982 the flood of imports, widely attributed to the open-door policy, had reached such proportions that a high level Committee for the Rationalisation of Imports was established involving the economic, commerce, industrial and infrastructure ministries, plus representatives from the Central Bank, Customs, and parastatal organisations. Decrees modifying import regulations flow regularly via the committee from the Minister of Economy and Foreign Trade and it is claimed that some success in limiting unnecessary imports has been achieved. Nevertheless, the Minister of the Economy, Dr. Sultan Abu Ali, promoted in 1985 from his position as head of the Investment and Free Zones Authority, has specifically highlighted the seriousness of a situation in which 'annual imports eat up 50 per cent of the total national income'.[23] The rationalisation of imports, according to Dr. Abu Ali, is intended to increase exports as a contribution to the balance of payments. The evidence from the first ten years of the Free Zones in particular and the *infitah* in general, demonstrates that there are three main obstacles to the achievement of this aim. First, to repeat, as has long been known by Third World countries following a similar policy, it is usually necessary to import in order to export, and the foreign earnings at the end of the day are often very small. The import bill for intermediate goods for industry is running currently at three and a half billion Egyptian pounds per year and this is said to eat up all the profits of manufactured exports. A debate reported in a Cairo-based economic weekly between the Chairman of the People's Assembly Industry Committee and a private businessman revealed an interesting public sector – private sector difference on the issue. Whereas the former argued that imports must be restricted and Egyptian industry encouraged to produce these intermediate goods for itself, the latter argued that the real problem was that the imports did not go mainly to make up exports at all, but that most of the final goods ended up in the local market. Tariff reform was the proposed solution.[24] The debate continues in Egypt, as elsewhere.

Second, since the late 1960s, any Egyptian with sources of foreign currency was entitled to import goods freely into the country. This, unsurprisingly, has led to enormous 'own imports' of expensive consumer goods and, far from providing healthy competition for domestic producers, has seriously inhibited the development of many indigenous sectors.

Third, the open door that permits the entry of foreign investment in manufacturing industry which may stimulate exports, can also let in non-industrial investment that serves mainly to stimulate imports. There is, of course, no necessity in this latter effect. Law 43 need not have turned Egypt into one of the most heavily 'foreign-banked', 'foreign-contracted', and 'foreign-consulted' countries in the Third World or, for that matter, the largest global recipient of foreign aid.[25] This is, however, what has happened.

The Public Free Zones are tossed about like leaky boats in the turbulent waters of the open door economic policy. The efforts of their staff and even, in some cases, of their investors, may well keep them afloat, and some individual projects can, indeed, bring all-round benefits. But the Free Zones as a whole can do little to stem the flood that threatens to engulf Egypt's economy and society unless present policies are fundamentally revised. For Egypt, like most if not all Third World countries, the awkward question must be posed: what exactly are the benefits for Egypt of its present involvement in the global economy? To those involved in the lucrative import of expensive foreign goods the answer to this question may be clear enough, but the mass of the Egyptian people may be forgiven for taking a more sceptical view.

THE COSTS OF FOREIGN INVESTMENT

NOTES

1 See, for example, Mark Cooper, *The Transformation of Egypt* (London: Croom Helm, 1982), esp. ch. 7; Kate Gillespie, *The Tripartite Relationship* (New York: Praeger, 1984); Malcolm Kerr and El Sayed Yassin (eds.), *Rich and Poor States in the Middle East* (Boulder and Cairo: Westview Press and American University in Cairo, 1982), in particular articles by G. Abdel Khalek (ch. VIII) and N. Ayubi (ch. XI); O. Hamed, 'Egypt's Open Door Economic Policy', *International Journal of Middle East Studies* 13 (1981), pp. 1–9; A. Richards, 'Ten Years of *Infitah*', *Journal of Development Studies* 20 (1984), pp. 323–38; M. Kennedy (ed.), *Social Problems* 28 (April 1981), Special Issue. These are, of course, in addition to a considerable Arabic literature on the subject.
2 Both laws are usefully reprinted in Gillespie, *op. cit.* Appendix A. Hereafter Law 43 refers to this amended Law.
3 'Looking outside, or turning northwest? on the meaning and external dimension of *Infitah*, 1971–1980', in Kennedy, op. cit., pp. 393–409.
4 J. Waterbury, *The Egypt of Nasser and Sadat* (Princeton: Princeton U.P., 1983), ch. 8.
5 For an excellent discussion see ibid, ch. 10. The International Food Policy Research Institute has published several thorough studies on this issue; see, in particular, G. Scobie, *Food Subsidies in Egypt: their Impact on Foreign Exchange and Trade* (Washington, 1983).
6 Egyptian currency regulations are complex, to say the least. In April 1985, there were seven 'official' rates, ranging from LE 0.40 = U.S. $1 (for Soviet bloc trade) to LE 1.40 = U.S. $1 (the floating free market rate).
7 Waterbury, op. cit., pp. 130, 132.
8 Robert Driscoll, P. Hayek, F. Zaki, *Foreign Investment in Egypt* (New York: Fund for Multinational Management Education, 1978).
9 Roger Owen has pointed out to me that the literal Arabic translation of what I refer to as 'Private Free Zone' is 'Special Free Zone'. The official translation of Law 43 issued by the Egyptian authorities refers to it as 'Private Free Zone', and I follow this usage here.
10 Gillespie, op. cit., Table 3.3 and ch. 3 *passim*.
11 The general tendency is for Investment Authorities all over the world to over-represent foreign investment. In this case I suspect that local investment is under-represented, for example, where companies owned by Egyptians are registered abroad. There is a case of this in the Port Said Free Zone, as we shall see below.
12 See UNIDO, 'Export Processing Zones in Developing Countries' (Vienna, 1980).
13 The description and analysis of Nasr City, Al Ameria, and Port Said Free Zones are based on visits made in March and April 1985. I am greatly indebted to the Egyptian Embassy (Commercial Section) in London and to Investment Authority personnel in Cairo and in the Free Zones for making these visits possible and for the level of cooperation extended to me. I do not discuss Suez, which has virtually no industry.
14 There is a large discrepancy in the official figures that suggests that some Nasr City Private Free Zone projects are sometimes counted separately. Compare the Investment and Free Zones Authority publications 'Facts and Figures XIV' (December 1984) and 'Facts and Figures 1984' (n.d.). The latter includes a category – 'The Sector' – accounting for 75 per cent of total Private Free Zone capital and 15 out of a total of 46 projects. Some of these projects and much of this capital appears to be listed under Nasr City Private Free Zones in the former source.
15 This works out to an average of over $300 per month per employee, which seems very high relative to the wages quoted for individual firms. It is probably due to the predominance of the service sector in the private free zones, both tending to higher than average wages.
16 See the similar process whereby German trouser-making has been re-located to Tunisia in F. Frobel, J. Heinrichs, and O. Kreye, *The New International Division of Labour* (Cambridge, C.U.P., 1980).
17 Much of the information in the following section is from an informative illustrated brochure 'Port Said Public Free Zone' (1982?). 1985 data were kindly supplied to me in Port Said.

18 There are several to choose from. Apart from North Africa, Greece and Turkey are vigorously promoting Free Zones as well.
19 The emphasis on speeding-up the approvals procedure since 1977 cannot have helped matters in this regard. F. Shakweer and M. Ghaleb Mourad in 'Cost/Benefit Assessment of Free Zones: a case study on Egypt' (Cairo, May 1981, mimeo) point up the importance of feasibility studies, amongst other matters, in a useful critique of the Free Zones. I am grateful to the Librarian at the USAID Library in Cairo for help in tracing this and other sources.
20 See the cases of Wilkinson's and Massey Ferguson, cited in Gillespie, op. cit., pp. 106–7.
21 Most of the items in note 1 have something to say on this issue.
22 Foreign trade data are taken from Arab Republic of Egypt, *Statistical Yearbook, 1952–1982* (Cairo, CAPMAS, 1983).
23 As reported in 'The Egyptian Gazette' (18 April 1985), p. 3.
24 See *Middle East News* (Cairo), 24 Aug. 1984, pp. 2–3. Dr. H. El-Hinnaway informs me that the chairman of this Public Sector Committee is himself also allied to important private business interests. This reinforces the point above about the public-private symbiosis in Egypt and, of course, elsewhere.
25 For the key role of the United States, and in particular the U.S. Agency for International Development in this process see M. Weinbaum, 'Politics and Development in Foreign Aid: U.S. Economic Assistance to Egypt, 1975–1982', *Middle East Journal*, 37 (1983), pp. 636–55.

8

Labour Migration to the Arab Gulf Region in the Nineteen-Eighties

Masudul Alam Choudhury

The phenomenon of population migration in Arab countries is not just a recent one. The factors contributing to this can be traced back in the work of Ibn Khaldun.[1] It can be inferred from Ibn Khaldun's empirical socio-economic analysis that labour migration in the Arab countries was linked to the natural process of transition of societies from their primitive states to more civilized ones.

In this paper we are interested in the period 1980 to 1985, with projections to 1990. Since the early 1980s a renewed influx of labour to the Middle East was stirred, mainly due to four factors: the sudden unprecedented economic development in the Arab countries following the oil bonanza; the excess labour supply coupled with declining economic prosperity in other Islamic countries; the growing economic protectionism of the West, that has virtually closed the door on foreign labour in the wake of economic recession; and finally, the recent resurgence of conscious institutional forms of economic cooperation among Islamic countries.

The declining flow of manpower from the developing countries to the West, after 1975, can be illustrated in the case of Turkey. Turkey was a country in the Islamic bloc which was fortunate to enjoy the privilege of being an associate member of the European Economic Community and to experience a long-standing flow of guest workers to West Germany. However, the numbers decreased dramatically after 1976, as shown in Table 1.

The tide of labour mobility then started to flow into the labour-scarce, oil-rich Arab countries. It first started as a straightforward flow of skilled, unskilled and semi-skilled Turkish labour to Arab countries. These countries found themselves with an acute shortage of skilled manpower, and their indigenous population structure was oddly poised

TABLE 1
TURKISH EMIGRATION TO EUROPEAN AND MIDDLE EAST AND NORTH AFRICAN REGION
(thousands)

	1971–76	1978	1980	1981
European Countries	*801.0*	2.3	2.8	*1.3*
Middle East & North Africa	24.5	16.5	25.7	57.6
Libya	8.2	7.7	15.1	30.7
S. Arabia	2.6	5.8	5.6	14.4
Other*	13.7	3.0	5.0	12.5

*Mostly emigrants to Iraq and Kuwait.
Source: Central Bank of Turkey (unpublished).

for meeting the immediate and long-term needs of sustained development. What is true of the Turkish labour force is also found to be true of other countries' migrant labour force to the Middle East.

The main objective of this paper is to look at the future prospects of labour migration to the oil-rich countries in the Middle East, with respect to future development trends in these countries. Reference is made in the context of this subject matter to the problems and prospects in the practical implementation of various resolutions passed by the Organization of Islamic Conferences (OIC) in the area of manpower exchange between Islamic countries. This study will be limited to the case of Saudi Arabia, Kuwait and the United Arab Emirates as labour recipient countries in the Middle East. On the other side the labour exporting countries to be looked at will be Egypt, Bangladesh, Pakistan and Turkey, as examples of four Islamic countries whose migrant labour force in the Middle East is characteristic of the predominant manpower mix in the labour recipient countries.

RESOLUTIONS ON MANPOWER EXCHANGE BY THE ORGANIZATION OF ISLAMIC CONFERENCES

Labour mobility between Islamic countries took an organized form during the 1970s. It thus became a ground for Islamic cooperation, and was taken up as an important topic under the various resolutions of the Organization of Islamic Conferences, the political organization of the Islamic countries.

In 1976 the Seventh Islamic Conference of Foreign Ministers for the first time passed a resolution to organize and promote exchange of labour and technical know-how among Islamic states,[2] in recognition of the demand for manpower by rapidly developing Islamic states and the available supply of trained manpower in other Islamic states. Labour migration between Islamic states is therefore to be viewed as an important economic and social aspect of cooperation among the Islamic states.

The Eighth Islamic Conference of Foreign Ministers meeting in Tripoli in 1977, passed additional concrete resolutions to promote the exchange of labour and technical know-how among Islamic countries. The resolutions emphasized the need to collect and disseminate regularly information on labour demand and supply by member states for use by the public- and private-sector agencies in these countries.[3]

The Ninth Islamic Conference of Foreign Ministers meeting in Dakar in 1978 took another positive step towards making the exchange of labour and technical know-how among Islamic countries a reality under the cooperative umbrella.[4] The resolutions proposed the establishment of the now existing Vocational and Technical Training and Research Centre at Dhaka, Bangladesh. This conference called upon the General Secretariat of OIC (Organization of Islamic Conferences) to draw up guidelines from existing agreements concerning labour and social security in order to help member states when concluding bilateral and multilateral agreements. The members further emphasized the need for regular collection and dissemination of information regarding the requirements and availability of manpower and the potentialities for transfer of technology among member-states of the OIC. The existing Statistical, Economic and Social Research and Training Centre established by the Islamic Secretariat at Ankara, Turkey, and the Islamic Centre for Vocational and Technical Training and Research Centre in Dhaka, Bangladesh, were to undertake the above task.

The Tenth Islamic Conference of Foreign Ministers recommended the convening of a meeting of national experts of the member-states on labour to determine the principal guidelines for 'the practical implementation of cooperation in the field of manpower among states'.[5]

The Third Islamic Summit Conference held in Taif, Saudi Arabia in 1981, reiterated the will of member-states of the Islamic countries to organize their efforts in achieving self-reliance and progressive economic interaction among Islamic countries. This was consciously looked at as the medium for enhancing Islamic cooperation by increasing the capabilities for economic development of the member-states.[6]

Later, in October 1981, the OIC experts committee on labour and manpower met at Ankara and proposed the following recommendations for the proper organization of labour migration between member states:[7] all exploitative and dishonest practices of member governments as well as private agencies must be stopped in order to encourage an efficient allocation of manpower across labour-importing and -exporting countries during the hiring process; the working and living conditions of migrant workers must be improved; worker–management relations in employment must be given fair treatment; up-to-date information on labour market prospects in Islamic countries must be continuously monitored through the Ankara Centre for use by their clientele; communal support must be given by member-states to the Technical and Vocational Training Centre in Dhaka, Bangladesh; worker remittances and savings must be allowed to flow freely between member countries of the OIC.

ECONOMIC TRENDS AND LABOUR MIGRATION TO THE OIL-RICH MIDDLE EAST COUNTRIES

The various resolutions of the Organization of Islamic Conferences in the area of manpower exchange and technical cooperation must, however, be viewed with caution. The following analysis shows that the changing pattern of economic development in the Middle East increasingly impeded the future prospects of labour migration from the poorer Islamic countries to the oil-rich countries in the Middle East.

The patterns of economic development in Saudi Arabia, Kuwait and the UAE are similar. The Second and Third Development Plans for Saudi Arabia both recognized the urgent need to diversify the economy, while the economic value of oil was still this country's comparative advantage. The economic plans pointed out that industrial diversification was to be achieved by rapidly using the oil revenues for increased manufacturing development. Likewise, in the case of Kuwait, all industrial growth is related to the predominance of the oil-based economy. With regard to industrial diversification, Kuwait happens to be in a somewhat advantageous position compared to Saudi Arabia. For example, between 1980–81 and 1981–82 development expenditure rose by only 2.8 per cent, reflecting Kuwait's limited domestic needs. Kuwait already had a well-developed infrastructure before the big oil price rise of the 1970s, and with a small population base its requirements had remained small. The main objective of development expenditure in Kuwait was, therefore, to provide better public services and a higher standard of living, and to establish industries which would help to diversify the country's economy. The UAE has excelled in spectacular economic growth following its oil discovery. However, its future economic growth is closely linked to the goodwill and performance of the newly constituted Gulf Cooperative Council. It is to be hoped that the Gulf Cooperative Council will stop the duplication of efforts by its member countries in given projects and instead diversify their individual efforts towards complementary types of development project.

Manufacturing diversification is much needed in the Islamic countries. In the oil-rich Arab states, particularly Saudi Arabia, Kuwait and the UAE, such a development programme would have its own benefits and problems.[8] Some of these are examined now.

One would expect that the problems associated with manufacturing diversification would be dependence on large exports, followed by the effects of international inflation. Initially, there would be large dependence on expatriate labour, followed by wage escalation, out-flow of profits through foreign partnership, finally resulting in domestic inflation.

The positive effects of this development strategy would be the growing reliance on domestic production and a strong incentive towards economic development, particularly in the oil-related secondary industries.

Every sector in these countries has a strong linkage to oil revenues. A method developed by Dr. Stauffer for calculating the non-oil component of GDP in the non-oil sector — by subtracting from the sectoral GDP the contribution of oil revenue through government expenditure — showed almost no non-oil residue. The application of this method to Saudi Arabia showed a contribution of only 6.9 per cent to GDP by real non-oil activity. For Kuwait the estimate was 6 per cent. These are figures for 1979.[9]

Such facts have led some planners to argue that the oil sector in the oil-rich Arab states is to be treated as an exogenous sector in national planning.[10] Therefore, as long as the oil reserves last, there would be a continuing need to sustain a high GDP/energy ratio, while subsequently diversifying the oil-related manufacturing industries. The oil-related energy-intensive manufacturing diversification cannot, however, be considered as the sole goal of industrial diversification in these countries, for depleting oil reserves will tend to make such industries less profitable over time. Therefore, an energy-intensive goal of manufacturing diversification can only be considered as an intermediate step and springboard for other types of economic diversification spilling over into capital-intensive secondary industries. The development of energy-intensive and capital-intensive industries would also interest the oil-rich Arab countries from the point of view of cutting back on expatriate labour and in making such principal industries more productive.

The intention to reduce dependence on expatriate labour is clearly expressed among government circles in Saudi Arabia. The Third

Development Plan, for example, puts a priority on this goal. It states that 'manpower development has the highest national priority since the effective utilization of available manpower is the key element in the whole strategy for the Third Plan'. There are four particular objectives for Saudi manpower development: to increase the total available manpower; to increase the productivity of manpower in all sectors; to deploy manpower to those sectors with the greatest potential for growth and the highest productivity levels; to reduce dependence on foreign manpower.[11]

In Kuwait the resentment against foreign labour is less acute, as they are allowed in some cases to obtain nationality status. However, the expatriate population comprises about 58 per cent of the total population of Kuwait.[12] This poses the problem of integration. Although the labour-force participation rate of the Kuwaitis is increasing more rapidly than that of the Saudis, yet there is a realistic recognition of the fact that dependence on expatriate labour cannot be avoided in the medium run. Table 2 gives the estimates of national/non-national breakdowns of the labour force in these countries for 1980.

TABLE 2

ESTIMATES OF NATIONAL/NON-NATIONAL BREAKDOWN OF THE LABOUR FORCE IN SELECTED OIL-RICH ARAB STATES, 1980
(thousands)

Country	Total Labour (millions)	National Labour	Non-National Labour	National Labour Percentage	Non-National Labour Percentage
Saudi Arabia	4.65	2,650	2,000	57	43
Kuwait	0.71	217	493	30.6	69.4
UAE	0.39	59	331	15.2	84.8

Source: Estimates provided by Statistical, Economic and Social Research and Training Centre (Ankara). *Manpower Exchange & Social Security in Islamic Countries, 1981* (unpublished)

Next let us see whether the substitution of non-national labour either by national labour or by capital is warranted from a labour productivity point of view. It is hoped that gains in productivity will come from the introduction of modern technology, capital–labour substitution or manipulation of workers to work harder and longer for the same remuneration. Clearly, the adoption of the first two methods is feasible for a labour-shortage economy, and this again reiterates our earlier argument, that the trend of future industrial development in Saudi Arabia should be towards more energy-intensive and capital-intensive modes of development. The third option unfortunately is at present being practised in Saudi Arabia with regard to expatriate labour.[13] Based on such a scenario, Table 3 gives the estimates of national/non-national labour force in Saudi Arabia to the year 1985.

TABLE 3
SAUDI AND NON-SAUDI COMPOSITION OF SECTORAL EMPLOYMENT, SAUDI ARABIA, 1980–81 AND 1984–85
(thousands)

Industries	1980–1981		1984–1985	
	Saudi	Non-Saudi	Saudi	Non-Saudi
Agriculture	543	56	479	50
Manufacturing	19	85	31	133
Mining (incl. oil)	25	18	32	24
Gas & Electricity	11	21	17	30
Construction	50	281	37	208
Trade	98	213	107	233
Finance	11	24	14	31
Services (incl. Government)	784	19	904	22
Transport	151	64	193	82
Total	1,692	+ 781 = 2,473	1,814	+ 813 = 2,627

Source: Kingdom of Saudi Arabia, Ministry of Planning, Riyadh. *Third Development Plan*. Statistical, Economic and Social Research and Training Centre (Ankara). *Manpower Exchange and Social Security in Islamic Countries* (unpublished labour report).

In Saudi Arabia, these patterns of development can be seen in the telecommunications sector, agricultural sector, construction sector and certain parts of the manufacturing sector. For example, the electrical generating stations have been converted to less labour-intensive enterprises; the general exodus of the Saudi workforce from the agricultural to the urban sector has made the government embark on increased mechanization here; the major construction projects were planned to come to a close by 1985, leading to a decline in the demand for labour (mainly non-Saudi labour) in this sector. The installation of large petrochemical and hydrocarbon plants in Jubail will lead to capital-intensive technology in the manufacturing sectors. In all, therefore, economic trends projected by the Saudi development plans point towards gains in efficiency expected from the installation of a capital-intensive mode of production.

These facts are also applicable to countries like Kuwait and the UAE. In all these countries there is a need for rapid industrialization, using oil revenues, in the face of limited indigenous skilled labour force, in order to increase these countries' economic efficiency. Besides, in the face of the dual constraints of restricted immigration of expatriate labour and monopsonistic competition with neighbouring oil-rich Arab countries to attract trained labour, the need for capital and energy-intensive modes of production will continually increase. The expressed goal of the development programme for Kuwait can be summarized in the following words of the Under-Secretary of the Ministry of Finance, Ali Khalifah al-Sabah:[14]

> I can't imagine that Saudi Arabia, Kuwait or any other oil-producing country in a similar situation would undertake industrial projects merely for the sake of providing employment. The truth is that every additional job provided by a project will have to go to a non-national, and this will in turn entail considerable added investment in services and infrastructure ... I would hate to see a series of white elephants draining the economies of the oil-exporting countries under the guise of industrialization.

Present economic, social and political trends in the oil-rich Arab countries limit labour migration between Arab countries and sound policies will need to be developed and implemented by the national and trans-national agencies of Islamic countries to better organize and facilitate labour migration between these countries as an important factor of cooperation.

The worsening effect of future trends in economic development in oil-rich Middle East countries on labour migration to this area can be further studied with respect to the manpower requirements profile of major projects in the oil-rich Arab states. To this we now turn.

1. United Arab Emirates

First we examine the major projects profile by sectors. This is the most direct way of estimating the medium term demand for labour resulting from the development of new capital projects.

Table 4 gives the summary of some major capital projects in the UAE started during the eighties. Assuming the labour component of capital expenditures to be about 40 per cent, which is a liberal view

TABLE 4
MAJOR CAPITAL PROJECTS PROFILE IN THE UNITED ARAB EMIRATES

Projects	Capital Expenditure	Starting Date	Nature
Oil & Gas Sector: Abu Dhabi Marine Operating Co. (ADMA-OPCO)	N.A.	1980	Drill 34 wells
Abu Dhabi Co. for On-Shore Oil Operations (ADCO)	$750 million	1981–84	2 production stations, 6–60,000 cubic meters storage tanks, 350 staff houses, floating quay, loading terminal, 103 kilometers of piping.
Zakum Development Co.	$4000 million	1980	Increase production.
Tahama Gas Field	$300 million	1980	Development.
Fluor Mideast	$26 million	1981	Construction & Management of treated gas.
Abu Dhabi National Oil Co. & Dubai Aluminium		1980	100 km pipeline.
Abu Dhabi Marine Operating Co.		1980	Exploratory drilling for gas.
Dubai Natural Gas Co.		1980	Gas fractionator.
Abu Khaki Gas Liquefaction Co.	$320 million	1980	Development
Zakum Development Corp.	$550 million	1980	Development
Construction			
Emirate Planning	$206 million	1980	Road expansion, flyovers, widening, etc.
Arab Contractors Co.	$67 million		Ring road.
Abu Dhabi Water & Electricity Dept.		1981	Large power and desalination schemes, gas turbines.
Al-Ain Airport	$327 million		—
Abu Dhabi Central Souk	$50.4 million	1982	—
Zayed Sports City	$43.5 million		—
Corniche Clock Tower	$95 million	—	—
Central Food Lab	$18 million	1982	—
Dubai Underpass	$81.7 million		—
Dockyard	$26.8 million		Dredging scheme.
City Department	$550.3 million	1980	Sewerage, parks, shops and markets.
Road to Al-Ain	$16.3 million	1982	—

Source: *Middle East Economic Digest* London. 1981 (First Quarter).

in labour-intensive production, we find that this would amount to $593 million in wages and other worker compensations on projects shown in Table 4, and which are to be completed not before 1990. Now by assuming average annual wages and fringe benefits to be $12,000 and escalating this by 7 per cent annually, a total capital expenditure of $593 million would create approximately 4,942 jobs per year on the average, to the year 1990. The picture on new manpower requirements based on major capital projects will not be improved in the late eighties, as few new major projects have been put on stream following the world oil glut.

The specific areas of capital expenditure shown above mean a significant increased demand for skilled labour. Owing to extremely keen competition for contracts in construction projects, supply of such skilled labour will be forthcoming. This has its good as well as depressing effects for the Islamic countries: Turkey has a reputation for its highly productive construction workers; therefore, construction contracts could be usefully directed to Turkish contractors or sub-contractors; however, countries like Bangladesh, Pakistan and Egypt still lack the highly skilled construction workers required for modern projects. With wages of skilled labour remaining high, because of high productivity, keen competition among prospective contractors will divert construction contracts to non-Islamic countries. For the UAE the principal construction contracts are found to go to the United States, the United Kingdom, West Germany, and Canada in this order. This state of affairs would have to be considered in the various manpower and technical assistance agreements formulated by the OIC. These were referred to earlier in this paper.

Estimates of the inter-country breakdown of construction workers employed in the UAE can now be seen in Table 5. These estimates indicate that, although some large capital projects are to come onstream in the UAE, they will not significantly step up fresh demand for migrant labour. In Dubai the amount of construction activity has significantly declined and large schemes are not foreseen soon enough.[15]

From the pattern of demand for migrant workers in construction activity shown above, the pattern of demand for labour in other sectors of economic activity in the UAE can be estimated. Estimates of employment in construction are about 32 per cent of the total employment in the UAE. The next highest percentage of total employment will be in community, social and personal services (29 per cent), where indigenous labour has always been picking up. The other sectoral shares will be around 2–8 per cent.[16] In conclusion therefore, it appears that the best days of labour migration to the UAE from Islamic countries are over.

TABLE 5
ESTIMATES OF THE INTER-COUNTRY BREAKDOWN OF CONSTRUCTION LABOUR DEMAND FOR THE UAE, 1980

Country	Percent	Number (thousands)
Egypt	5	247
Pakistan	40	1,977
Bangladesh	1	49
Other*	54	2,669

Source: The percentages are those for the total labour force. Birks, J. A. & Sinclair, C. A. *International Migration and Development in the Arab Region* (International Labour Organization, Geneva, 1980).

* 'Other' here gives all other countries' labour demand in construction activity in the UAE.

The principal causes for this, which have been established above, are the sectoral trend towards capital intensiveness and the increasing competition among contractors to win the highest bids on the basis of their ability to provide productive labour and management. This picture is expected to perpetuate in the labour market scene in the Middle East in general, following their present depressed economic condition.

2. Saudi Arabia

We now turn to look at the prospective demand for labour by sectors in Saudi Arabia and its effect on labour migration. Most of the information is gathered from the Saudi Third Development Plan,[17] while the estimates are derived by the author.[18]

The pressing need for industrial diversification has never been more greatly stressed than in the Third Saudi Development Plan. The oil sector, again, plays an intrinsically central and peculiar role in Saudi national development. Because of its key role in economic development, the oil sector becomes an exogenous one in the Saudi economy. As long as the oil reserves last, there is continuing need to sustain a high GDP to energy input ratio, while subsequently diversifying the oil-related industries on the basis of comparative advantage for this nation.[19] The oil-related secondary diversification cannot, however, be considered as a long-term goal, because the depleting reserves of oil will make such industries less profitable over time. As has been said above, a secondary diversification is only an intermediate step, to serve as a springboard for other types of economic diversification spilling over into capital-intensive secondary industries, and subsequently, into the service sector.

The picture of industrial development vis-à-vis employment growth for Saudi Arabia shows that the service sector has grown much faster than the goods-producing sector. This is mainly due to the growing number of non-Saudis already employed in the construction industry and management occupations, compounded further by the influx of Saudi labour migrating from agriculture into the trade sector. One might question whether the heavily oil-related industrial diversification which has been planned is the most desired one for Saudi Arabia. The problems lie on two fronts. First, the service sector and infrastructure management – particularly construction, transportation and utilities – are very labour-intensive. To expand growth in these sectors with labour-intensive technology would perpetuate the Saudi government's dependence on foreign manpower. The second problem arises from the inability quickly to train and transfer control of an increased amount of capital-intensive technology into the Saudi hands, particularly in the oil-related secondary industries. The alternative of having capital-intensive technology in most sectors in Saudi Arabia can be an attractive one considering the relatively smaller manpower needed in these capital-intensive industries.

To tackle these problems linked with the liberal expansion of the industrial sector and concentrate more on a fuller development and utilization of indigenous manpower, the Third Development Plan aimed at a structural change of the economy, increased participation and social welfare in development, increased economic and administrative efficiency. In this range of objectives manpower development has the highest national priority. These goals of development planning are expected to continue into the next decade for Saudi Arabia.

The trend in manpower development, manpower requirements and utilization by sectors can be viewed by looking at the sectoral pattern of development envisaged by the Saudi Third Development Plan which among all the existing plans highlights the central issue of manpower development and industrial diversification.

Table 6 gives the financial requirements for economic resource development under the Third Development Plan. Principal capital projects in the Agriculture and Water sector include the on-going projects sponsored by the Ministry of Agriculture and Water (MOAW), namely, (1) construction of a large dam for irrigation purposes at Wadi Jizan; (2) cultivation project at Wadi Bish and Wadi Haly; (3) construction of an irrigation and drainage system in the Eastern Region managed by Al-Hassa Irrigation and Drainage Authority; (4) establishment of a reclamation project to encourage Bedouin settlement in Haradh; (5) construction of a dam for flood control

TABLE 6
FINANCIAL REQUIREMENTS FOR ECONOMIC RESOURCE DEVELOPMENT UNDER THE SAUDI THIRD DEVELOPMENT PLAN

Sector Components	Total Capital Expenditures (Millions of SR. at current prices)	Recurrent	Project
Agriculture and Water	72,085	12,767	59,318
Energy and Mineral	93,523	14,014	79,509
Manufacturing Commerce	95,602	3,643	91,958

Source: *Third Development Plan* (1980–1985), Ministry of Planning, Riyadh, Saudi Arabia.

and irrigation in Wadi Najran; (6) Wadi al-Dawasir project in the Central Region using water from the Wajd aquifer.

In the agricultural sector there were to be ten new directorates, 25 new branch offices, seven animal quarantine stations and 25 storage depots. Other service developments in the agricultural sector include land development programmes, agricultural services programmes and agricultural research programmes, as well as a support programme in manpower training which was expected to take on 3,731 new trainees by 1985.

The key policy note of the Saudi government in all such programmes is to minimize labour and water inputs and bring about public–private sector cooperation in realizing the goals of agricultural development. It is to be noted, that while the UAE and Kuwait traditionally had a small agricultural base, the labour force in Saudi Arabia until recently was concentrated in this sector; it was 24 per cent of the total labour force in 1980 and was expected to come down to 20 per cent in 1984.

Migrant labour in the primary agricultural sector was negligible and was expected to remain so in the years to come. However, out-migration of Saudi labour from the agricultural sector will be significant. This out-migration will put pressures on other migrant non-Saudi employment in the service sector. Between the years 1980 and 1984, Saudi labour in agriculture was expected to decline by 12 per cent from its level at 543,000 in 1980. In the service sector, Saudi labour was expected to increase from 784,000 in 1980 to 904,000 by 1984, while non-Saudi labour would increase from 19,000 in 1980 to about 22,000 by 1984. These figures are shown in Table 3.

Let us now turn to the energy sector. Here, the planned inventory of major capital projects included those launched by ARAMCO, Arabian Oil Company, Getty Oil Company and the Ministry of Petroleum and Minerals (PETROMIN). The type of projects included development of new production wells, maintenance of existing plant and equipment, exploration programmes and the construction of pipelines.

In oil-refining, the principal programmes under the Third Development Plan included expansion of domestic refinery capacity, export refinery capacity, development of Yanbu crude oil supply, Lubeoil projects in Jeddah, Jubail and Ryadh. Crude oil refining is also linked to natural gas development. In the natural gas industry, the Saudi government has a programme to develop the East West gas pipeline system, which will require maintenance and replacement.

The energy sector by its very nature is capital-intensive. Furthermore, the present and expected medium term shortfall in the demand for crude oil and the lower extent of development in the energy sector in Saudi Arabia, signify a lower derived demand for expatriate labour. Based on the figures given in Table 6, a 30 per cent labour component of capital expenditure in the energy and minerals resources sector would yield SR. 8,056 millions in labour cost. With an estimate of SR. 5,000 per month in total labour compensation, the estimated number of jobs created would be 14,013 by 1985. This compares well with an alternative estimate of labour demand of 13,000 in the energy sector in 1985.[20]

Next, we turn to the manufacturing sector in Saudi Arabia. The oil-related manufacturing sector, which is the principal one in Saudi Arabia, is divided into the hydrocarbon sector and the non-hydrocarbon sector. These are again distributed in the private and public sectors. In the public sector Saudi Arabian Basic Industries Corporation (SABIC) has programmes for conversion of separated associated gas into industrial petrochemicals. In the private sector, programmes include joint ventures in the conversion and utilization of gas feedstock and fuel; development of methane utilization projects; development of ethane utilization projects.

In the non-hydrocarbon manufacturing sector, programmes include maintenance of existing industrial estates and provision of new ones at Medina and Abha; development of adequate sewerage and treatment plants; continued operation of existing flour mills, animal feed concentrate mills; new grain storage; joint venture steel mill projects between SABIC and Karf Stahl and so on. The private sector planned five new cement production plants in Riyadh, Hofuf and Jeddah; industrial gas plants at Jubail and Yanbu, basic petrochemical production plants at Jubail and Yanbu.

Referring to Table 7, here one sees the state of labour demand by sectors in Saudi Arabia. The demand for labour in the manufacturing sector was expected to be 60,000 by the year 1985; of this about 48,000 would be non-Saudis. The large number of non-Saudis in the manufacturing sector indicates a good prospect for labour migration in the medium run, during the period when Saudis are training their own nationals in the manufacturing trades and occupations. Manpower training programmes are being established at Yanbu, Jubail by the Saudi government and by SABIC, PETROMIN, ARAMCO, and others jointly with the private sector. The replacement of expatriate labour by trained Saudi labour would eventually follow in the manufacturing sector in the years to come.

Let us now look at a labour demand picture for the construction sector in Saudi Arabia. The construction industry has been a productive part of the non-oil sector. In 1980 the industry contributed 21 per cent of the total non-oil gross domestic product, the employment level was 330 man-years and this comprised 13 per cent of the total labour force. Of this 85 per cent constituted the non-Saudi share and 15 per cent the Saudi share. By the year 1985, construction-employed labour forces were expected to decline to 245,000 – 208,000 non-Saudi labour and the remaining 37,000 Saudi labour. This indicates a decline of 26 per cent in foreign labour. These estimates are derived from Table 7.

In the commercial sector comprising the wholesale and retail trades, transportation, financial institutions and personnel and community services, the percentage rate of growth in employment will be low in the near future. This profile is shown in Table 7 by a breakdown between Saudi and non-Saudi labour in these sectors. A large concentration of Saudi labour in this sector was explained earlier by the fact of labour migration from the agricultural sector to the service sector. However, in the probable absence of the requisite level of training and occupational diversification, increasing the labour intensiveness of this sector by national labour may not increase labour productivity, which is already low in the service sector in Saudi Arabia.

The aforementioned labour demand profile by various sectors in Saudi Arabia shows that labour migration from Islamic countries, although promising, will be cut back considerably. The causes for this have been pointed out as the development of capital-intensive industries in the primary and manufacturing sectors, the influx of Saudi labour into the labour-intensive industries, especially in the commercial service sector, and the decline in construction activity which was forecast for 1985.

TABLE 7
ESTIMATED LABOUR DEMAND PROFILE BY INDUSTRIES AND OCCUPATIONS, SAUDI ARABIA, 1980–1985
(thousands)

Industries	Saudi	Non-Saudi	Total
Agriculture	−64	−6	−70
Mining (including oil)	7	6	13
Manufacturing	12	48	60
Utilities	6	9	15
Construction	−13	−73	−86
Transport	42	18	60
Trade	9	20	29
Finance	3	7	10
Services (incl. government)	120	3	123
Total	122	32	154
Occupations			
Professionals	27	7	34
Clerical	32	5	37
Salesmen & Labourers	75	19	94
Farmers	−64	−6	−70
Service Workers	50	6	56
Total	120	31	151

Source: *Saudi Third Development Plan*, 1980–85. Statistical, Economic and Social Research and Training Centre (Ankara). *Manpower Exchange and Social Security in Islamic Countries* (unpublished Labour Report).

3. Kuwait

We now turn to the profile of labour demand and migration resulting from sectoral development trends in Kuwait. In Kuwait as in Saudi Arabia and the UAE the need for industrial diversification is considered a priority, although the oil sector continues to contribute the most to the gross domestic product. Between the years 1975 and 1979 the oil sector contributed 65 per cent to the GDP of Kuwait. The intermediate industries contributed only about 6 per cent to GDP. Non-metallic mineral products industries contributed 9.7 per cent to GDP, while foodstuffs, beverages and tobacco and manufactured metallic products contributed about 7 per cent each. The lumber and wool products industries contributed about 6 per cent. (These are per annum figures.) The agricultural sector is small and the trend here is towards increased modernization, employing capital-intensive technologies.[21]

Kuwait's programme of economic diversification is based upon (1) development of the oil industry and various economically viable industries dependent on oil, gas and their by-products, through the use of sophisticated technical means of production; (2) establishment and development of such substitution industries as might prove to be economically viable within the framework of the Kuwaiti economy.[22]

Since 1980, Kuwait has begun to expand oil refineries and to construct petrochemical plants. Among the major construction projects are Doha West power station, a 681 million dollar desalination complex, and 256 million dollar steam and generator installations. There has also been vigorous construction activity in marine and port expansions and in public housing projects.

Sectoral development is found to follow a balanced trend for Kuwait. This is so because development expenditure here has been fairly stable in recent years, reflecting Kuwait's limited domestic needs. Kuwait already had a well-developed infrastructure before the big oil price increases of the 1970s and in the following years the small Kuwaiti population base put less pressure on the need for infrastructural development. Thus, the main objective of developmental expenditure in Kuwait continued to be the provision of better public services so as to keep the people's standard of living high, and establish industries that would diversify the national economy away from oil. Besides, Kuwait, having a traditionally small agricultural base, does not experience the influx of its labour force out of agriculture and into the service industries of the urban sector which has taken place in Saudi Arabia.

Because of the more balanced pattern of infrastructural and industrial growth, and less friction between the national and non-national labour force in the absence of any significant internal migration, Kuwaiti international labour migration should remain stable in the medium run. However, as seen for Saudi Arabia, job bidding towards development and management of modern projects, construction and other business contracts will go to countries like Japan, West Germany, South Korea and a number of other industrialized countries. Possible sub-contracting, and hiring of workers and personnel from the Islamic countries will remain totally at the discretion of the principal contractors. The implications for OIC manpower and technical assistance agreements among Islamic countries are, again, to be considered in the light of these facts.

CONCLUSION

The analysis of this study indicates that the intensity of labour migration to the Arab Gulf Region will soon decline. The causes can be attributed to the deliberate will of these governments to substitute capital-intensive technologies, particularly in the primary and manufacturing sectors, the natural influx of national labour leaving the agricultural sector and flowing into the service sector, and the decline in construction activities as most of the major capital projects and infrastructures near completion by the end of the eighties.

Reduced labour migration, particularly from Islamic countries, could follow pressing demand for highly qualified and productive labour to man the sophisticated capital-intensive industrial projects. This will also result from the increasing number of contracts going to the industrialized countries. The oil-rich Arab states, which are under pressure to rapidly diversify and develop their economies while the oil revenues are still flowing in, will press for high performance and efficiency from their contractors. The contractors will, therefore, have to look for skilled and more efficient manpower in order to accomplish their contracts on time, at lower cost and higher output. Part of this could be accomplished through capital-intensive technology, the rest will depend upon the productivity of labour at work. Neither of these may be forthcoming as desired from countries like Bangladesh, Pakistan and Egypt. Turkey, however, enjoys a special advantage, particularly in the construction sector. But there too the bulk of Turkish construction workers in the Middle East countries is found to be associated with Turkish contracts, which at present are few and small in Saudi Arabia, Kuwait and the UAE. Faced with such requirements, the oil-rich Arab countries would prefer to award contracts to partners from industrialized countries.

It has been observed elsewhere[23] that capital-rich Arab countries are increasingly preferring Far Eastern labour to labour from other countries for their construction projects. The reasons are attributed to lower costs and to the readiness of Far Eastern labourers to live in enclaves of work camps. Also, companies from South-East Asian countries are found to complete their contracts within deadlines and then return their migrant enclaved workers to their home countries. This feature offers an overriding social and political advantage to the oil-rich Arab states in hiring Far Eastern workers. These facts are supported by the labour demand trends by different nationalities shown in Table 8. It appears that, although immigration of Asians (Pakistanis, Bangladeshis and Indians) was estimated to maintain

TABLE 8
ESTIMATES OF LABOUR DEMAND BY NATIONALITIES IN THE CAPITAL RICH MIDDLE EAST COUNTRIES, 1975-1985
Labour Demand
(thousands)

Nationalities	1975 Number	1985 Number (Projections)
Total Labour Demand	3,320	5,213
Migrant Workers:	1,649	3,056
Arabs	1,237	1,927
Asians	278	500
Orientals	15	490
European & American	34	70
Iranian	86	70

Sources: Birks, J.S. & Sinclair, C.A., *Arab Manpower* (London: Croom Helm, 1980).

its percentage share of total migrant labour to about 16.4 per cent, the orientals (Far Easterners) were estimated to increase their share from one per cent in 1975 to about 16 per cent in 1985.

NOTES

1. Rabi, M.M., *The Political Theory of Ibn Khaldun*, Luden: Netherlands, 1967.
2. Resolution No. 5/7-ELS, 'The Promotion of Exchange of Labour and Know-how Among Islamic States', Seventh Islamic Conference of Foreign Ministers Meeting in Istanbul, Republic of Turkey, 12-15 May 1976.
3. Resolution No. 4/8-E, 'The Promotion of Exchange of Labour and Know-how Among Islamic Countries', Eighth Islamic Conference of Foreign Ministers Meeting in Tripoli, Socialist People's Libyan Arab Jamhiriya, 16-22 May 1977.
4. Resolution No. 6/9-E, 'Promotion of Exchange of Labour and Know-how Among Islamic States', Ninth Islamic Conference of Foreign Ministers Meetings in Dakar, Republic of Senegal, 24-28 April 1978.
5. Resolution No. 7/10-E, 'Promotion of Exchange of Labour and Know-how Among Member States', Tenth Islamic Conference of Foreign Ministers Meeting in Fez, Kingdom of Morocco, 8-12 May 1979.
6. Resolution No. 1/3-E(IS), 'The Plan of Action to Strengthen Economic Cooperation Among Member States', Third Islamic Summit Conference Meeting in Makkah Al-Mukarramah, Kingdom of Saudi Arabia, 25-28 Jan. 1981.
7. Statistical, Economic and Social Research and Training Centre for Islamic Countries (Ankara), *Report of the Expert Group Meeting on Manpower Exchange and Social Security in Islamic Countries*, 26-28 Oct. 1981.
8. Crane, R.D., *Planning the Future of Saudi Arabia*, New York: Praeger Publishers, 1978.
9. Barker, P., *Saudi Arabia: The Development Dilemma*, Economist Intelligence Unit, Report No. 116, 1982.
10. Cleron, J.P., *Saudi Arabia 2000*, London: Croom Helm, 1978.

11 Ministry of Planning (Riyadh, Saudi Arabia), *The Third Development Plan, 1980–1985*.
12 Ministry of Planning, Central Statistical Office, *Annual Statistical Abstract: State of Kuwait*, 1980.
13 Birks, J. S. and C. A. Sinclair, *Arab Manpower*, London: Croom Helm, 1980.
14 Birks, J. S. and C. A. Sinclair, op. cit.
15 *Middle East Economic Digest*, London, First Half of 1981.
16 *Middle East Economic Digest*.
17 *Third Development Plan, 1980–85*, Ministry of Planning, Riyadh, Kingdom of Saudi Arabia.
18 Choudhury, M. A., *Manpower Planning and Policies for Saudi Arabia*, Memorial University of Newfoundland Press, Dec. 1982.
19 Crane, R. D., *Planning the Future of Saudi Arabia*, New York: Praeger Publishers, 1978.
20 *Third Development Plan, 1980–1985*, Ministry of Planning, Riyadh.
21 *Quarterly Economic Review of Kuwait*, Annual Supplement, Economist Intelligence Unit, London, 1981.
22 Central Bank of Kuwait, *The Kuwaiti Economy in Ten Years* (1969–1979).
23 Birks, J. S. and C. A. Sinclair, op. cit.

9

Saudi Arabia's Industrialization Strategy: A Question of Comparative Advantage

Robert E. Looney

INTRODUCTION

In almost every country, industry is the glamour sector of economic development. People look to industrial development to provide much needed employment, to generate higher individual and national income, to relieve balance of payments constraints through import substitution, to open up markets for primary products such as those from the mining and fishing sectors, to give the country greater economic independence, to generate new tax revenues, and to furnish an important source of national pride.[1] By and large, these hoped for benefits of industrialization are realistic – provided a country makes sensible choices.

Until recently, investment in Saudi Arabia has concentrated on infrastructure, light manufacturing and construction materials. Most of the major products in transportation, communications, health, education, electricity, and water that were initiated in the 1970s are completed or nearing completion. Since the mid-1970s, attention has centred on industrial development, primarily in the downstream activities of the petroleum sector and on import substitution.

In fact, one of the most intriguing question marks concerning the kingdom's development strategy centres precisely around the government's selection of industries. A steel plant, fertilizer plants, domestic and export-oriented refineries, and a series of major petrochemical complexes form the basis of the government's attempt to diversify the economy. What is the rationalization for this strategy and is all this too ambitious for a country with virtually no previous industrial experience?[2]

As Yannis Stournaras[3] has recently noted, the whole rationality of this policy has been seriously questioned. The main purpose of this paper is to examine in some detail the basic arguments for and against the industrial strategy adopted by Saudi Arabia. The aim is to provide some general explanations rather than a detailed cost–benefit analysis of specific projects.

COMPARATIVE ADVANTAGE

The existence of under-exploited gas reserves in the kingdom has been one of the strongest arguments for developing gas-based heavy industries. Gas — especially the dry gases, methane and ethane — is an expensive product to transport, thus making it sensible to look for more productive uses for its exploitation.

International trade theory is capable of rationalizing a gas-based industrialization strategy. For example, according to the Heckscher–Ohlin theory of international trade, a country tends to have lower comparative costs in the commodity that uses the largest amount of the relatively cheapest factor in its economy. These considerations provide the fundamental rationale for specialization.[4] In general terms, the theory indicates that Saudi Arabia should establish and promote industries primarily based on natural gas and/or oil. These are the industries, everything else aside, that are most likely to be efficient and successful. Fortunately for the Saudis, these industries are not only energy intensive but also capital intensive. Thus, they tend to utilize its abundant financial surplus as well as gas and oil.

Once oil has been produced at an optimal rate, there is an excellent theoretical argument for developing gas intensive industries around it.[5] These can either be chemical industries, which use the gas as a feedstock for conversion into higher value and more easily transportable chemical products, or they can be energy intensive industries such as steel or aluminium production, where the gas can be used as a reasonably cheap source of energy.

Few observers would quibble with these general observations. The planners' task in identifying precisely those industries best suited for the kingdom has not been as easy as it might appear at first sight, however.

Because the country had virtually no heavy industry or industrial experience to speak of in the early 1970s, the Heckscher–Ohlin predicted pattern of trade had not been established and the price system had not developed to the point where it was capable of giving the planners the correct signals as to the best areas of investment. In addition, a number of less obvious considerations surrounding the introduction of heavy industry into the country have made it extremely difficult to design procedures capable of identifying the most effective methods of allocating the country's resources. Although financial capital may not be a constraint, especially in the short term, the kingdom has to face other constraints to industrial development. Physical bottlenecks, manpower shortages and inflation have proved to be real impediments to the absorptive capacity of the economy. In particular, the impact of these negative factors has often been most severe in the very developmental activities intrinsic to a successful diversification policy.

GOVERNMENT INVESTMENT IN INDUSTRY

A number of potentially profitable projects have been identified by the government for its investment programme. These are industries which conform to the Heckscher–Ohlin theory of trade by using relatively large amounts of the kingdom's relatively abundant factors of production, oil, natural gas and capital. These industries appear attractive because not only do they mesh into the present structure of the economy, but also should logically fit the next phase of development by providing competitive exports with which to pay for future imports.

Because the capital cost of these industries is immense, the private sector is unable to undertake investment in them at this time. Instead, the Saudi Basic Industries Corporation (SABIC) was founded by the government to initiate development of the kingdom's heavy industries.

The Saudi Basic Industries Corporation was set up in 1976 with a capital of SR10 billion to undertake investments in operation and marketing of products in the basic industries, using local hydrocarbon and mineral resources and other complementary and supporting industries.[6] SABIC has so far set up and developed 14 industrial companies in Jubail, Yanbu, Heddah and Dammam and work is progressing on the establishment of two new companies. By the first quarter of 1986, all of these companies were in operation except for one of the new companies, which is expected to begin production in 1988[7] (Table 1). With these facilities, Saudi Arabia is capable of producing between four and five per cent of the world's primary petrochemical output.[8]

The features of these industrial operations and planned industrial development have emerged sufficiently to allow us to characterize the future industrial structure and industrial employment of Saudi Arabia.

In August 1985, the government announced that more than SR16,000 ($4,384 million) is to be spent on expansion of SABIC during the current development plan (1985–90). According to SABIC, more than half the new investment will be channelled into building more downstream petrochemical plants and just over 20 per cent of the total will be devoted to further plastics and rubber industries.[9]

TABLE 1
SABIC: DOMESTIC HEAVY INDUSTRY PROJECTS

Project	Joint-venture partner(s)	Signature date	Production start-up date	Location	Feedstock	Products	Annual capacity (tonnes)
Saudi Arabian Fertilizer Company (Safco)	Saudi private sector (including Safco employees — 59%)	1965	1970	Dammam	Methane	Urea Sulphuric acid Melamine	330,000 100,000 20,000
Saudi Iron & Steel Company (Hadeed)	DEG (West Germany — 5%)	March 1979	1983	Jubail	Iron ores, limestone, natural gas, scrap iron	Steel rods and bars	800,000
Jeddah Steel Rolling Mill Company (Sulb)	Hadeed subsidiary (100%)	May 1979	1981	Jeddah	Steel billets	Steel rods and bars	140,000
Saudi Methanol Company (Ar-Razi)	Japanese consortium led by Mitsubishi Gas Chemical Corporation (50%)	November 1979	1983	Jubail	Methane	Chemical-grade methanol	600,000
Al-Jubail Fertilizer Company (Samad)	Taiwan Fertilizer Company (50%)	December 1979	1983	Jubail	Methane	Urea	500,000
Saudi Yanbu Petrochemical Company (Yanpet)	Mobil Oil Corporation (US — 50%)	April 1980	1984	Yanbu	Ethane	Ethylene Linear low-density polyethylene High-density polyethylene Ethylene glycol	455,000 205,000 91,000 220,000 260,000
Al-Jubail Petrochemical Company (Kemya)	Exxon Chemical Company (US — 50%)	April 1980	1984	Jubail	Ethylene	Linear low-density polyethylene	
Saudi Petrochemical Company (Sadaf)	Pecten Arabia (subsidiary of Shell Oil Company — 50%)	September 1980	First unit ethylene, 1984 Last unit styrene, 1985	Jubail	Ethane Salt Benzene	Ethylene Ethylene dichloride Styrene monomer Crude industrial ethanol Caustic soda	656,000 454,000 295,000 281,000 377,000

Company	Partners	Date	Location	Feedstock	Product	Capacity
National Methanol Company (Ibn Sina)	Celanese Corporation (US — 25%) Texas Eastern Corporation (US — 25%)	February 1981	Jubail	Methane	Chemical-grade methanol	650,000
Arabian Petrochemical Company (Petrokemya)	None	May 1981	Jubail	Ethane	Ethylene	500,000
Eastern Petrochemical Company (Sharq)	Mitsubishi-led Japanese consortium (50%)	May 1981	Jubail	Ethylene	Linear low-density polyethylene Ethylene glycol	130,000 300,000
National Industrial Gases Company (Gas)	Saudi gas companies (30%)	February 1983	Jubail	Air	Oxygen Nitrogen	438,000 146,000 300,000
National Plastic Company (Ibn Hayyan)	Lucky group (South Korea — 15%)	December 1983	Jubail	Ethylene Ethylene dichloride	Vinyl chloride monomer Polyvinyl chloride	300,000 200,000
Saudi European Petrochemical Company (Ibn Zahr)	Arab Petroleum Investments Corporation (Apicorp — pan-Arab — 10%), Neste (Finland — 10%), ENI (Italy — 10%)	December 1984	Jubail	Butane Chemical-grade methanol	Methyl tertiary-butyl ether Butadiene Butene-1	500,000 125,000 80,000

Source: Sabic

As noted, most of these plants are sited at Jubail and Yanbu, located respectively on the East and West coasts of Saudi Arabia. Both are new industrial cities that represent enormous undertakings. Jubail is expected to grow to a city of 280,000 by the year 2010, and Yanbu will have a population of 100,000–200,000 persons. All infrastructure had to be planned and provided. Much of the new industrial investment in petrochemicals will be located in these two cities.[10]

The private sector is strongly encouraged to participate in the country's industrialization, through utilizing the output of the SABIC industries, this being one of the major objectives behind the kingdom's industrial development strategy. Among the incentives provided to the private sector are:[11]

1. Exemption from import taxes on imported machinery, spare parts and raw materials;
2. Protective tariffs or quotas against competing imports;
3. Financial assistance on very easy terms (primarily through SIDF financing);
4. Long-term leasing of industrial sites at nominal rents ($0.03/sq.m. for building lands);
5. Electricity at heavily subsidized rates ($0.02 per KWH, although it appears likely that the cost will have to be increased in line with 'rationalization' policies;
6. Preferential treatment for locally manufactured goods in government procurements;
7. Assistance in the identification of viable projects through cheap feedstock and guaranteed supplies of crude for 15–20 years (500 b/d for every $1 billion in investment, although the government is reported to be reneging on some agreements, and in some cases, the 'cheap' price was set when oil prices were at a peak, making the terms far less tempting in today's market).

In sum, the government has tried vigorously over the last decade to expand the industrial base of the country. This has been undertaken through encouraging and subsidizing private sector industrial projects and by initiating the development of large-scale industrial projects in the public sector. The government's motives for promoting industrial expansion include:[12]

1. The desire to exploit Saudi Arabia's natural resources in as efficient (and profitable) a way as possible. Thus, large public sector projects and joint ventures draw on crude petroleum and natural gas (much of which used to be flared) as raw materials.

An added advantage of this form of industrial development is that it increases the vertical integration of the newly Saudized domestic oil industry, giving it more influence in world markets.
2. The desire to diversify the economy. It is recognized that petrochemical and other energy-related projects contribute little in this respect, insofar as their performance is strongly related to demand conditions in the international energy markets. Light industries which are the domain of the private sector are more useful in increasing the level of economic diversification, although the scope for their expansion is limited.
3. The desire to ensure a greater degree of regional balance by positioning industries in a number of different locales, so as to provide employment for underemployed labour, distribute the kingdom's wealth more widely, and consolidate the kingdom's physical structure.
4. The desire to enhance the role of the private sector, especially as the public sector continues to expand. Light industries are regarded as an eminently suitable avenue for the utilization of private capital.
5. The desire to offer local banks the opportunity to assume a greater degree of oversight risk, to ensure the integration of the financial sector into the mainstream of domestic economic activity.

Despite the massive amounts of investment in Saudi Arabian industry — $10 billion in refinery projects and another $10 billion in plants using ethane and methane as feedstock to produce products such as ethylene, polyethylene, ethylene glycol and methanol — the contribution of the industrial sector to GDP, although growing, has been fairly limited. The contribution of manufacturing to GDP was 5.0 per cent in 1980, but by 1985 this had increased to 8.1 per cent. This pattern is fairly typical of the Gulf Cooperation Council (GCC) countries (Table 2).

Saudi Arabia's development plans for the Fourth Plan period (1985–90) place great emphasis on continued industrialization, human resources development and increased use of local products and services.[13] Associated with these goals is the development of a more appropriate financial system that would facilitate channelling private capital to productive projects. Emphasis is moving from infrastructure building to production. There are priority shifts as well within the infrastructure from construction and transportation to operations and maintenance and from physical to social and educational infrastructure. These are being paralleled by directional changes in the

TABLE 2
CONTRIBUTION OF MANUFACTURING SECTORS TO GDP IN THE GCC COUNTRIES, 1980–1985

	1980	1982	1983	1984	1985
Saudi Arabia	5.0	4.3	5.8	7.5	8.1
Kuwait	5.9	6.6	6.4	6.3	6.6
UAE	3.8	8.2	8.7	8.7	n.a.
Oman	0.7	1.4	2.3	2.8	n.a.
Bahrain	11.5	11.3	11.5	11.8	n.a.
Qatar	3.3	5.0	6.0	6.0	n.a.

Sources: Various National and Regional Sources Including: *Unified Arab Economic Report*, 1985, edited by The Arab Monetary Fund

area of production from construction materials to basic industries and manufacturing.[14]

In sum, the Saudi government hopes that the development of heavy industry in the petrochemical sector will spawn a wide range of manufacturing activities. There are two major reasons why the kingdom can rationalize reversing the more typical experience of developing light manufacturing first and heavy industry second. With 40 per cent of world crude oil reserves, Saudi Arabia has the resource endowment to support an efficient petrochemical sector, and it is natural that petrochemical facilities be established to process this crude. Initially, Saudi Arabia will export most of its primary petrochemical output, but over time chemical and plastics enterprises can be established locally to process increasing proportions of primary petrochemical output. Second, with a relatively small labour force and relatively large amounts of capital (government foreign exchange assets exceeded $150 million in 1983), capital intensive operations are consistent with relative factor endowments in Saudi Arabia.[15]

THE CASE FOR PETROCHEMICALS

In addition to the availability of gas, several additional characteristics associated with petrochemicals have made investment in this industry especially attractive to the Saudi government.[16]

Capital Intensity
This industry enjoys one of the highest capital/labour ratios in the world. In fact, investment per new job created is estimated at $20,000 to

$100,000. Also, larger amounts of investment are required as the stage of production advances from basic products to intermediaries to finished products and finally to the consumer stage. In fact, the investment required for the transformation of finished products into consumer or industrial products (third manufacturing phase) is two or three times higher than that necessary for the production of intermediate products (second manufacturing phase) and five times higher than that necessary for the production of basic products (first manufacturing phase).

Economies of Sale

Investments do not vary in proportion to the capacity, but rather according to a power factor generally lying between 0.6 and 0.85. This is the reason why it is advantageous to build large capacity units which cost proportionately less than small or medium capacity units. Manpower as well as general and plant overhead also appear to have proportionately lower expenditures with larger plant size.

Given Saudi Arabia's abundant endowments of both the raw materials and capital needed to finance large-scale investments, petrochemicals seem to be an ideal sector around which the country could build its industrialization programme.

SOME POLICY ISSUES

There are at least two main issues[17] related to industrialization in Saudi Arabia. One is that the existing and anticipated expansion of industrial activity implies considerable strain on the government and private enterprise. It also means accentuating the disadvantages in factor proportions that are critically vital for self-sustained industrial growth, namely, skills and markets.

The second important issue relates to the diseconomies of competition. There is little doubt that the lack of coordination in the Gulf, until the recent past, over industrial projects had led to wasteful duplication and lowered the returns on investments. In these cases, the problems are the same: short production runs, high fixed costs in relation to total costs and diseconomies of scale.[18]

More specifically, the problems and constraints facing the kingdom's industrial development schemes can be detailed as follows:

1. The kingdom's most ambitious industrial objective, to become an international force in the production and marketing of petrochemicals, has involved it in disputes with its trade partners in Western Europe and the United States. The market

for petrochemicals is currently depressed and the current (1987) potential for producing $3 billion (or more) worth of petrochemicals requires that the kingdom continue to fight for a major share of the international market. The EEC and the United States are likely to intensify the degree of protectionism currently in effect to protect their petrochemical industries, citing as pretext the heavy subsidization of feedstock in Saudi Arabia (where the government charges producers $0.50 per million BTU, compared with $4.50–5.00 in Western Europe and $3.30–3.50 in the United States).[19]

2. Regardless of how emphatic Saudi Arabia planners are about promoting private sector participation, the Saudi economy is largely driven by government expenditure,[20] the level of which is to some extent (not totally) dependent on the level of oil revenues, which fluctuate as oil prices vary and as world markets continue to be depressed. This results in complications for the industrial sector inasmuch as:

(a) The heavy petrochemical industrial projects require considerable capital allocations, and their scale cannot be easily adjusted up or down. As fiscal pressures intensified with the recent oil revenue declines and planners became aware that they could not count on nearly infinite supplies of capital, they became more reluctant to invest in 'megaprojects', cancelling some which had already been planned and slowing down payments to others. This tends to shake the confidence of foreign partners and has complicated marketing plans.

(b) Private sector (mostly light) industries are sensitive to the level of government spending, since government-funded or supported projects provide the basis for demand for many light industrial projects. By the end of 1984, for instance, over ten private sector factories had closed and some 40 enterprises were reporting serious problems in meeting financial obligations or launching marketing campaigns.[21] One major manufacturer estimates that his total sales declined by over 50 per cent during 1984 and 1985. One of his responses has been to cut employment by over one-third.[22]

(c) Government subsidized loans by the Saudi Industrial Development Fund (SIDF) have decreased significantly. SIDF was a major source of industrial investment funds during the 1970s and early 1980s. Private investors have been more reluctant to commit funds as domestic spending has slowed. Domestic investors are accustomed to the high rates of return on investment realized during the period of rapid growth from 1974 to 1982. Foreign investors too made highly profitable investments during this period. Some foreign investments were made to ensure supplies of crude and this incentive no longer applies. As a result, some investments in secondary and light industries have been postponed or cancelled. These are the industries associated with lower capital/labour ratios.[23]

3. As in nearly all sectors of the economy, the manpower shortage is a serious constraint. Not only does the scarcity of skilled and unskilled workers translate into higher labour costs, but the adoption and implementation of proper management and marketing techniques in the industrial sector is sometimes hampered by the lack of adequate expertise. University education at home and abroad is slowly filling the upper echelons of management with well-trained Saudis, but the prospects for filling middle management positions with qualified Saudis are problematic.

4. Despite modest success in building industrial estates outside the major industrial centres of Jeddah, Riyadh, Damman, Yanbu and Jubail (with partially completed industrial centres in Qassim province northwest of Riyadh, at Hassa in the Eastern Province and at Mecca), the prospects for additional industrial expansion in the provinces are limited. The need for budgetary austerity necessitates the rethinking of spending priorities, a process likely to penalize projected investment in localities distant from major market outlets and requiring substantial infrastructural investment. While additional estates are planned at Asir, Medina, Hail and Tabuk, earlier projections of provincial industrial growth are being scaled down in size and geographic scope.

5. The domestic market is too small to absorb enough production to make economies of scale a factor in most cases. The prospects for foreign markets for Saudi products are limited, and the possibility of GCC integration expanding the scope for Saudi industrial output is circumscribed by the lack of coordination and duplication in industrial effort among GCC members. In this regard, Saudi Arabia is favoured. Crude (a primary factor of industrial production) is produced more cheaply and on a larger scale in Saudi Arabia than elsewhere. At the same time,

Saudi Arabia has a far larger population than other GCC countries. Gains from integration (in terms of generating demand for locally produced goods) may accrue to other GCC countries – initially at least.

Concentrated efforts at regional cooperation and coordination appear absolutely essential for Saudi Arabia, given the fact that the kingdom's neighbours have similar resources and industrial aptitudes. Unless development is coordinated, it is likely that there will be major duplication between states in the energy-based industries. Awareness of these problems has led to a good deal of consultation and contact in the region, as is illustrated by the following examples:[24]

1. One of the recommendations approved by the Arab Gulf Co-operation Council called for the establishment of an industrial cooperation committee with a view to promoting greater co-ordination and interaction;
2. Steps are being taken to constitute institutional apparatus for coordination of petrochemicals industry so as to (a) achieve product specialization, (b) prevent harmful duplications, and (c) evolve a regional strategy;
3. Institutions, such as the Gulf Organization for Industrial Consulting, have been created to encourage coordination between and among the states of the region in their respective plans for economic and industrial development. Here again, the intent was to avoid unnecessary duplication of projects;
4. At the project level, Saudi Arabia has acquisitioned 20 per cent of equity holding in the ALBA (Aluminium Bahrain), and has dropped its plans of having its own aluminium smelter.

LESSONS LEARNED

Several general lessons have emerged from Saudi Arabia's initial attempts at industrialization.[25] The most important is that there is no industrial option open, even including petrochemicals, to the country which gives anywhere near the kind of returns provided by successful investments in the oil sector. This implies that while the country may be choosing to restrict production levels for the benefit of future generations, it is still not absolved from the responsibility of ensuring that oil is produced as efficiently as possible. That means ensuring that existing oil fields are exploited with the best techniques, with growing attention to enhanced recovery and to the exploration necessary to replace declining production in existing fields.

In countries like Saudi Arabia, prudence may dictate the building of pipelines designed to give greater commercial flexibility. With oil prices still far above oil production costs, the country's planners would be extremely unwise not to start by ensuring they are getting the optimal returns from the oil sector before turning their attention to diversification strategies.[26]

Second, it appears that there is not a very strong case for investing in export-oriented refining capacity. The bulk transportation of crude oil will always remain cheaper than transporting oil products, so the best the kingdom can do is maximize the efficiency of its refineries. However, the comparatively greater cost of transporting oil products rather than crude is still very small in comparison to the final market price of oil. It is, therefore, perhaps at least possible to defend the decision to increase refining capacity.

Third, before utilizing gas in industry, Saudi planners should first ensure that they have used it as productively as possible in prolonging the life of oil fields (through gas ejection) or in substitution for oil in the domestic economy (thus releasing high value crude for export). The returns from exporting oil are so much more than exporting gas or its derivatives that there is an overwhelming logic in substituting gas for oil in such areas as electricity generation, oil refinery powering and desalinization.

Fourth, simple generalizations about the comparative economics of petrochemicals are difficult to make since a project which may make economic sense in a tight market may be unjustifiable if its products are in global oversupply. However, it appears that the creation of gas-based industries in the kingdom makes sense if the relative cheapness of the country's gas can be used to overcome some comparative disadvantages which the country currently faces:

1. Construction costs are high in Saudi Arabia for the current generation of plants under construction. Costs may be at least a quarter more expensive than in the United States or Western Europe.
2. The country is a long way from the richest world markets (North America, Japan and Western Europe). Its export-oriented industries will have to be particularly competitive if they are to break into these established markets. The alternative strategy is to aim for markets in Africa and Asia where the country may be closer as a supplier than the established competition in the advanced industrial countries. However, there are limits to how far the country can concentrate solely on Third World

markets, which are by definition relatively poor and unsuitable for the more sophisticated chemical products.[27]

Fifth, it must be emphasized that regional cooperation is essential, not only as a means for securing access to the wider regional market for the growing petrochemical industries, but also as a vehicle for coordination and harmonization with the other oil producers' plans for the development of petrochemicals and various energy and capital intensive industries. This type of cooperation is particularly necessary to prevent duplication, waste and harmful competition.[28]

Finally, a number of different factors have combined to form a bias against the conversion of oil revenues into productive industrial output and employment. It has been much easier to create direct government employment than industrial employment. To develop public sector jobs it is only necessary to build a room and put a desk in it; to develop a job in the modern industrial sector involves importing machinery and finding a skilled work force. The easiest activity for the government to promote has been construction, and the authorities have been notably successful in this area. Most of the jobs in this sector, however, have gone to foreigners.

The underlying reasons accounting for so few Saudis employed in modern industries are, in addition to those mentioned above, numerous, complex and interwoven. They include:

1. The great distances between regions and the poor communications connecting many parts of the kingdom;
2. Many government loans and grants to small farmers with the objective of aiding their mechanization and modernization are not spent on farming activity, but instead are considered additional income by recipients and spent on consumer goods — the result is to raise the opportunity cost of leaving the rural sector;[29]
3. The high value that rural men in Saudi Arabia place on leisure reinforced by the utilization of women in activities not permissible in urban areas;
4. Various government payments for social welfare contribute significantly to rural incomes;
5. Supplemental incomes earned by many in agriculture from patronage, traditional obligations and loyalties, and rents from family properties and land;
6. The high financial and social costs of moving into cities; rents are high, properties difficult to acquire.
7. Conditions in towns are relatively poor, meaning that the

standard of life in the cities for lower and middle income Saudis is lower than in rural areas;
8. Even at unskilled manual levels at which Saudi nationals are unwilling to work, foreign labour which is most cost effective is easily available.

Given the virtually unlimited amount of financial resources, the existence of large amounts of low or underemployment in Saudi Arabia is somewhat surprising. It has been shown, however, that this condition is the direct result of a complex mix of economic and social factors. One additional factor is the phenomenon of socially induced voluntary underemployment because Saudi workers are biased against types of work which they consider socially inferior.[30]

Labour theory suggests that the unwillingness to accept socially undesirable employment can be overcome by payment of a premium over the wages in the more desirable occupations. The market equilibrium wage would then be established by the simultaneous interaction between the strength of demand and the distribution of tastes. It appears, however, that in Saudi Arabia the social factors are so strong that, given the limited size of internal markets and the inefficiency of labour and capital in the modern industrial sector, the wage gap is not large enough to draw Saudi workers into the formal sector. The extended family, subsidized loans, and the existence of the informal sector enabling occasional work to supplement other income allow Saudi workers to set a high reservation wage.[31]

There should be a large enough positive compensating wage differential to overcome the reluctance to accept socially inferior jobs. It appears, however, that in Saudi Arabia, because the income incentive is so weak, even excessively high wages are not sufficient to entice Saudi workers into the industrial work force.

As a result of this interaction of economic and social factors, numerous Saudi workers have not gained appreciably from economic development. In most cases, their move from country to city involves a horizontal move from one low productivity job to another. Underemployment continues to exist because the planners have failed to provide the right types of government opportunities given the existing cultural environment. Again, in time this problem may be overcome. It is hard to predict at this point, however, whether Saudis will eventually be more inclined to join the industrial work force. The outcome may depend on how successful technology transfer to the kingdom is during the next decade or so.

TRANSFER OF TECHNOLOGY

Within the framework of Saudi Arabia's industrial strategy, attention is being closely paid to the selection of new technology and the means of innovating the existing technology. The concept of technology transfer used here is expanded to apply to the transfer of technological know-how internally between various industries and scientific R & D organizations and also internationally from similar institutions in other countries.

True industrialization is achieved not only through production but also through the development of national design and application capability so that an increasing number of products can be conceptualized and realized in Saudi Arabia. There are at present many areas where such capability has already been developed: progress is being made with acquired maturity.

It may be opportune to point out that the course of the transfer of technology has never been a smooth one. Among the major obstacles that the Saudis have had to overcome in their attempt to absorb new technology are:

1. Lack of industrial infrastructure and an industrial tradition;
2. Lack of skilled manpower, particularly on operational levels (e.g., skilled workers and technicians), and
3. The reluctance of many foreign companies to cooperate sincerely in the transfer of technology.

In the past decade, the Saudis have begun to adopt a cohesive effort to tackle the issue of technology transfer. The most important measures which have been taken are:[32]

1. Introducing advanced technical subjects in vocational schools and universities;
2. Establishing contact with technical and scientific organizations of international repute, and
3. Sending many students and researchers to institutions of higher education abroad in the various branches of science and technology.

It is recognized that sustained growth of the technological base is almost directly correlated to the quantity and quality of research and development work being carried out. Therefore, the Saudi Arabian government has been investing heavily in its institutions of higher learning, and at the same time establishing the real data base which indigenous research requires.[33]

CONCLUSIONS

It is still too early to say with much certainty what success the kingdom will have in its industrialization effort. The country is still going through an experimental period in which it is finding out exactly what future its oil and gas sector has and which kinds of industrial diversification make the most sense for its society. One lesson which will probably emerge is that it is pointless to push ahead too fast wtih such a diversification.[34] It takes time to build up an industrial culture, and there may be no point in developing industries which have to be run by more expatriates than the indigenous society can tolerate. At the same time, we really do not know if the Saudi workers will choose to dedicate themselves to mastering manufacturing skills. It may well be that they will prefer to continue settling for desk jobs, in which case the kingdom's strategy should continue to be to develop a limited range of capital intensive hydrocarbon processing industries, firmly leaving the labour intensive operations for other countries.

Based on its factor endowments, the private sector in conjunction with government guidance has been wise in selecting techniques of production which make maximum use of available energy and/or capital resources. Government investment in petrochemicals, cement, and steel are examples of energy and capital intensive industries. In other industries catering primarily to the local markets, such as the building materials industry, capital intensive techniques of production must be chosen to combat acute labour shortages prevalent in most of these countries. Unlike labour surplus economies unable to draw extensively on existing modern foreign technology because it is labour saving, Western technology is particularly suited to the factor endowment of the kingdom. The employment of capital intensive and sophisticated techniques of production requires, however, skilled and scientifically trained manpower. Thus, the upgrading of human resources will become a critical factor in expanding the capital absorptive capacity of the economy.

Few other countries would consider or could afford to consider the industrial programme taking place in Saudi Arabia. There is a genuine concern for the educational, social, and ethical development of the Saudi citizen, from a current low base. Much has been accomplished in the last ten years, but standards are still not high. Much more will be done in the coming decade, but without satisfying employment prospects, a contradiction between talents and expectations on the one hand and opportunities on the other must inevitably arise.

NOTES

1. Cf. Sharif S. Elmusa, 'Dependency and Industrialization in the Arab World', *Arab Studies Quarterly* (Summer 1986), pp. 253–67.
2. A question also asked by Louis Terner, 'Industrial Development Strategies in the Arab Gulf States', in May Ziwar-Daftari, ed., *Issues in Development: The Arab Gulf Strategy* (London, M.D. Research Services Limited, 1980), pp. 210–11.
3. Yannis Stournaras, 'Is the Industrialization of the Arab Gulf a Rational Policy?', *The Arab Gulf Journal* (April 1985), pp. 21–8.
4. J.L. Ford, *The Ohlin–Heckscher Theory of the Basis and Effects of Commodity Trade* (New York: Asia Publishing House, 1965), Ch. 1.
5. Cf. the argument given in B.I. Mohyuddin and R.Z. Karam, 'Arab Petrochemicals – Supply and Demand', *Arab Gulf Industries* (Dec. 1986), pp. 8–38.
6. Saudi Consulting House, *A Guide to Industrial Investment*, 7th Edition (Riyadh: Saudi Consulting House, 1986), p. 42. This is an excellent source of information on the Saudi government's industrial policies.
7. 'Proposals for Expansion Reflect SABIC's Confidence', *Middle East Economic Digest Special Report: Saudi Industry* (Nov. 1985), pp. 7–8.
8. Donald Wells, 'The Effects of Saudi Industrialization on Employment', *The Journal of Energy and Development* (Spring 1986), p. 274.
9. 'Proposals for Expansion Reflect SABIC's Confidence', op. cit., p. 7.
10. Wells, op. cit., p. 274.
11. Middle East Research Institute, University of Pennsylvania, *MERI Report, Saudi Arabia* (London: Croom Helm, 1985), pp. 80–9.
12. Ibid., pp. 85–6.
13. Cf. Kingdom of Saudi Arabia, Ministry of Planning, *Fourth Development Plan, 1985–1990* (Riyadh, Ministry of Planning, 1985), especially pp. 196–213.
14. Henry Azzam, 'Investment Climate in the Gulf: Opportunities and Constraints', *The Arab Gulf Journal* (Oct. 1986), p. 26.
15. Wells, op. cit., pp. 274–5.
16. Cf. Louis Turner and James M. Bedore, *Middle East Industrialization* (Farnborough: Saxon House, 1979), Ch. 6, for an excellent elaboration of these and other related issues.
17. For an analysis of the Gulf as a whole, see Nasif Dabdab and Badr Mohyuddin, 'Industrialization in the Arab Gulf', in M.S. El Azhary, *The Impact of Oil Revenues on Arab Gulf Development* (London: Croom Helm, 1984), pp. 91–106.
18. Ibid., p. 102.
19. Arab–British Chamber of Commerce, 'Saudi Arabian Petrochemicals Exports', *The Arab Gulf Journal* (April 1985), pp. 9–20.
20. Cf. Robert Looney, 'The Impact of Petroleum Exports on the Saudi Arabian Economy', in Robert W. Stookey, ed., *The Arabian Peninsula* (Stanford, Ca.: Hoover Institution Press, 1984), pp. 37–64.
21. Michael Field, 'Weathering the Storm', *Financial Times* (21 April 1986), p. 1.
22. *Wall Street Journal*, 28 April 1986, p. 1.
23. Wells, op. cit., p. 282.
24. Dabdab and Mohyuddin, op. cit., pp. 103–4.
25. Cf. Robert Looney and P.C. Frederiksen, 'The Evolution and Evaluation of Saudi Arabian Economic Planning', *Journal of South Asian and Middle Eastern Studies* (Winter 1985), pp. 3–19.
26. Louis Turner, 'Industrial Development Strategies in the Arab Gulf States', op. cit., pp. 215–19.
27. Ibid.
28. Based on questions of economies of scale and efficiency of plant size, cf. M.M. Metwally, 'Market Limitation and Industrialization in Arab Countries' (mimeo), 1979.
29. J.S. Birks and C.A. Sinclair, 'The Domestic Political Economy of Development in Saudi Arabia', in Centre for Arab Gulf Studies, University of Exeter, *State, Economy and Power in Saudi Arabia* (Symposium, 4–7 July 1980), p. 7.

30 See Ramon Knaverhase, 'Social Factors and Labor Market Structure in Saudi Arabia', Yale University Economic Growth Center, *Discussion Paper No. 247* (May 1976) for an elaboration of this thesis.
31 Ibid.
32 See Joseph Szyliowicz, 'The Prospects for Scientific and Technological Development in Saudi Arabia', *International Journal of Middle East Studies* (Aug. 1979), pp. 355–72, for a discussion of these issues.
33 Ibid.
34 Turner, op. cit., p. 219.

10

One Arab State, Many Arab States: The Impact of Population Growth and Oil Revenues

Gad G. Gilbar

From the early 1920s, when the institutional foundations of separate Arab nation-states in the Middle East were being laid, until the present day, the Arab world has existed in a tension between the conflicting pulls of Pan-Arabism and particularism. Several factors have determined the actual course of events that has unfolded between these two poles – between the creation of a single united Arab state, on the one hand, and the existence and consolidation of a number of distinct Arab nation-states, on the other. I shall concern myself here with the effect of two specific developments – one of them demographic and the other economic – upon the tension between Arab unity and particularism. The two developments I shall be considering are, first, the high rate of natural increase of the populations of Egypt and of Iran; and, second, the influence exerted by the substantial revenues received from the export of crude oil in the period 1974–81. The interrelation between these developments, and their impact on the situation of the separate Arab nation-state, will also be examined.

The growth rates of the Arab population in the Middle East remained at a high level in the last generation. Indeed, in some of the Arab countries not only was there no drop in the natural growth rate, but it actually rose significantly. And whatever may be our reservations concerning the reliability of the demographic data furnished by some of the governments in the region, a natural growth rate of 3.0 per cent and more appears to have existed throughout the 1960s and 1970s in Syria, Iraq, Jordan, Libya and apparently in the oil states of the Arabian Peninsula as well (see Table 1).

TABLE 1
THE MIDDLE EAST – NATURAL INCREASE RATES, 1960 and 1982

	Birth rate		Death rate		Natural increase	
	1960	1982	1960	1982	1960	1982
Sudan	47	45	25	18	22	27
Yemen, PDR	50	48	29	19	21	29
Yemen, AR	50	48	29	22	21	26
Egypt	44	35	20	11	24	24
Morocco	50	40	21	15	29	25
Tunisia	47	34	19	9	28	25
Lebanon	43	29	14	9	29	20
Syria	47	46	18	7	29	39
Jordan	47	45	20	8	27	37
Algeria	51	47	20	13	31	34
Iraq	49	45	20	11	29	34
Oman	51	47	28	15	23	32
Libya	49	45	19	11	30	34
Saudi Arabia	49	43	23	12	26	31
Kuwait	44	35	10	3	34	32
United Arab Emirates	46	28	19	3	27	25
Iran	53	41	19	10	34	31
Turkey	43	31	16	9	27	22
Israel	27	24	6	7	21	17

Source: The World Bank, *World Development Report 1984*, t. 20, pp. 256–7.

An evident case in point is the recorded rise in the natural growth rate in Egypt, from a figure of 2.2–2.3 per cent early in the 1970s to about 2.7 per cent in the late 1970s and early 1980s.[1] Moreover, Egyptian demographers are now predicting that a further rise can be expected for the second half of the 1980s.[2] In Egypt's case, these high population growth rates are expressed in very substantial absolute figures. We need only note that between 1952 and 1985 Egypt's population increased from about 21 million to about 48 million, and that by the end of the present decade its population is expected to reach about 54 million.[3] Put another way, in the first ten months of 1986 the population of Egypt grew by about one million, and in 1990 only seven to eight months will be required for the population to increase by a million souls.

Egypt is one of the two Arab states in the Middle East (the second being Sudan) whose rapid expansion of population has become a serious economic and social problem. This increase in the country's population during the last generation created mounting pressures on available resources. During a number of years (1966–8 and 1972) in which GNP growth rates were low, per capita growth rates in real terms were negative as a result of the high rates of population increase.[4] The gravity of the problem posed by this rapid population growth is brought home by the fact that the increase in the Egyptian population in the last generation was one of the major factors responsible for the failure of the repeated efforts to achieve self-sustained economic growth. The Egyptian government had been aware since the mid-1950s, and possibly earlier, that the pace of increase of the country's population made it necessary to take vigorous steps to change the structure of the economy and to stimulate the process of economic growth.[5] Moreover, Abd al-Nasser soon realized that unless Egypt received large-scale aid from abroad, no real long-term economic growth could be achieved. There have been only a small number of countries with the economic capacity and the political interest to offer large-scale aid to Egypt. Over the past 30 years Egypt has received economic aid from the following groups of countries: the Soviet Union and the East European states; the United States and some countries in Western Europe; and the Arab oil-producing states, chief among them Saudi Arabia.

Oil revenues of the Arab oil-producing countries were considerable even before the 1973 'energy crisis'. By 1969 the oil incomes realized by the most prominent of these countries, Saudi Arabia and Libya, came to more than a billion dollars each. These revenues cannot of course be compared to those attained in the 'good years' between 1974 and 1981. The total income accruing to OAPEC countries (Saudi Arabia, Iraq, Kuwait, Libya, the United Arab Emirates, Algeria, and Qatar) from the export of crude oil totalled US$865 billion in the years 1974–81, and US$1,279 billion in the period 1974–85. And Saudi Arabia, as we are aware, is distinguished among these countries for having the highest income – with US$622 billion flowing into its coffers from its export of crude oil in the course of 1974–85 (see Table 2).

These incomes were in excess of both the immediate needs of these economies and the opportunities available to them for short-term spending on consumption and investment; the result was that these countries began to accumulate reserves in enormous amounts. At the end of 1981, the monetary reserves of the Arab oil economies totalled US$321 billion. In the same period, Saudi Arabia's accumulated reserves were estimated at about US$160 billion.[6]

Thus in the last two decades we have witnessed the emergence of a deepening economic gap between populations on either side of the

TABLE 2
MIDDLE EAST OPEC – GOVERNMENT OIL REVENUES, 1972–1985

	1972	1973	1974	1975	1976	1977	1978	1979	1980	1981	1982	1983	1984	1985[a]
Saudi Arabia	3.1	4.3	22.6	25.7	33.5	38.6	34.6	57.5	102.0	113.2	76.0	46.1	43.7	28.0
Iran	2.4	4.1	17.5	18.5	21.1	21.6	20.9	19.1	13.5	8.6	19.0	21.7	16.7	13.8
Iraq	0.6	1.8	5.7	7.5	8.5	9.8	9.6	21.3	26.0	10.4	9.5	8.4	10.4	12.1
Kuwait	1.7	1.9	7.0	7.5	8.5	7.9	8.0	16.7	17.9	14.9	10.0	9.9	10.8	9.0
Libya	1.6	2.3	6.0	5.1	7.5	8.9	8.6	15.2	22.6	15.6	14.0	11.2	10.4	9.4
United Arab Emirates	0.6	0.9	5.5	6.0	7.0	9.0	8.0	12.9	19.5	18.7	16.0	12.8	13.0	11.2
Algeria	0.7	0.9	3.7	3.4	3.7	4.3	4.6	7.5	12.5	10.8	8.5	9.7	9.7	8.6
Qatar	0.3	0.4	1.6	1.7	2.0	2.0	2.0	3.6	5.4	5.3	4.2	3.0	4.4	3.5
Total OPEC	8.6	12.5	52.1	56.9	70.7	80.5	75.4	134.7	205.9	188.9	138.2	101.1	102.4	71.8
Total ME OPEC	11.0	16.6	69.6	75.4	91.8	102.1	96.3	153.8	219.4	197.5	157.2	122.8	119.1	95.6

Sources: *Petroleum Economist*, May 1977, p. 167; June 1981, p. 232; July 1985, p. 236.
Petroleum Intelligence Weekly.

Note: [a] Provisional

Red Sea: the population of the Nile Valley and that of the Arabian Peninsula (excepting the southeastern corner). The impact of the various aspects and manifestations of this gap has been considerable, having been responsible for the weakening of the forces calling for Arab unity, or – if one prefers – the enhancement and institutional entrenchment of the separate Arab nation-states. A number of developments connected with, and arising from, the processes we have been considering tend to reinforce this view.

Egypt's need to turn to Arab oil producers for aid, initially for the purpose of arms procurement and later in order to finance economic projects, forced the country's leadership as early as the late 1960s to desist from various activities that might have undermined the stability of regimes that did not regard themselves as obliged actively to advance the cause of Arab unity – and most especially not a union under Egyptian leadership. The decline in Egyptian Nasserist activism of the late 1950s and early 1960s made it possible for regimes such as Saudi Arabia and Jordan, which sought to foster the development of the distinct nation-state, to pursue their ends. Moreover, the failure of Nasserism – particularly as regards the vision of Pan-Arabism – weakened Egypt's ideological rejection of the existence of separate Arab states.[7]

The expanding incomes that the oil states realized were responsible for enhancing, quantitatively and qualitatively, those groups and strata which had a vested interest in the existence of a distinct nation-state. Two groups that obviously benefited from their increasing numbers, and their growing share in the power that was available within the political systems, were the members of the bureaucracy and technocracy, and the officer corps. The public sector as a whole, too, gained in a similar fashion.

The enormous investments of the Arab oil economies in economic development since 1974 – in the way of infrastructure, industry, agriculture, and human resources – were mainly carried out by means of the public sector. This required a very considerable expansion of the number of workers employed in the public services. According to one estimate, the number of persons employed in the civil service in Saudi Arabia (Saudi nationals receiving a monthly salary) grew from 20,000 in 1960 to about 184,000 in 1980. The number of Saudi teachers in the country's school system increased in the same years from 2,413 to 37,954.[8] These groups identified themselves with the Saudi state (although not necessarily with the regime or its policies). They derived their economic and social power from the Saudi political entity and from the various economic, social and political institutions that this state had established in recent generations.[9]

In Saudi Arabia, as in the other oil economies, there developed a broad stratum of businessmen alongside the public sector – particularly merchants and suppliers of various services. This group joined the economic system that had been developing steadily since 1974. Additionally, the number of people employed in the services branch of the economy – principally in trade and finance – rose at a significant rate from the early 1970s on. The total figure for persons employed in the services in the private sector increased from 253,000 in 1967 to 685,000 in 1979.[10] The incomes of these socioeconomic groups, especially of those on the upper levels, rose in both absolute and relative terms after the Saudi government initiated its first five-year plan for economic development (1970–1975).[11] It stands to reason, then, that these groups too should have developed a strong interest in the existence of a separate Saudi state.

Clearly, the Saudi elite, like its counterparts in other oil-producing states in the Arabian Peninsula, was reluctant to share the economic resources at its disposal with the elites of other societies or states, even if they were Arab. Obviously, the greater the extent of such resources, the more reluctant was the elite to surrender control of it.

The rapprochement of Egypt and the oil states of the Arabian Peninsula, and their concentration on achieving economic growth during the 1970s and 1980s, very soon exerted an influence on the relations of Egypt with the oil-producing states. At the heart of the relations in the years 1974–7 was the issue of the scale and conditions of economic aid. It may be recalled that the oil-producing Arab states, principally Saudi Arabia and Kuwait, were already extending aid to Egypt as early as 1967, as a consequence of the Khartoum summit.[12] But aid in significant amounts, of over a billion dollars annually, was granted to Egypt only after the October War and the attendant precipitation of the 'energy crisis'.

The sudden increase in incomes from oil exports at the end of 1973 and the beginning of 1974 created among the Arab countries which were not major oil-exporters, and most particularly in Egypt, high expectations of receiving generous amounts of economic aid from Saudi Arabia and Kuwait. These expectations were encouraged by pan-Arab ideology, to the extent that it claimed, at least implicitly, that whatever natural resources were available in the Arab homeland had to be placed at the disposal of the whole Arab nation.[13]

There were additionally other factors that nourished the Egyptian leadership's expectations of comprehensive economic aid. First, Egyptian spokesmen argued that the steep rise in the price of oil on the international market in October 1973 was to a large extent due to a war that had been initiated and led by Egypt. Second, for years, Egypt had been in the forefront of the Arab struggle with Israel; and in the course of that conflict Egypt had paid very dearly in blood – more than any other Arab state. Moreover, the economic cost to Egypt had been substantial. Indeed, in estimating the direct cost to Egypt of this long drawn-out war, Egyptian leaders cited figures of US$12–15 billion, for which Egyptian society deserved to be equitably compensated. Third, the major countries in the Middle East that were geographically close to Egypt had since 1971 invested heavily in developing their economies (the amount running into tens of billions of dollars in each of the oil countries), with the result that they had undergone very tangible and extensive social and economic transformations. This circumstance made it even more incumbent on Egypt to keep up with them in its own development, and on a scale that would require economic aid from them.[14]

Egypt received quite large amounts of Arab aid in the period between the October War in 1973 and the Baghdad foreign ministers' meeting in 1979. According to my calculations, this aid – part of which was allocated to defence expenditures, and part intended for civil uses – came to a total of roughly US$11 billion.[15] The aid estimates published by various sources on behalf of the Arab oil-producing states in 1979, when the relations of these countries with Egypt were deteriorating, are rather higher – amounting to as much as US$17 billion.[16] However, the last figure would seem to be excessively high. The unavailability of data makes it difficult to come up with accurate figures of the relative share of military and defence aid in the total Arab aid made available to Egypt: a rough estimate would be 40–50 per cent of the total (or about US$5 billion of the US$11 billion received).[17] Economic aid for civil purposes, taken all in all, reached its peak in 1975, when it came to a total of more than US$2.0 billion.[18] In the course of all of the years in which Arab aid was extended to Egypt, the principal donor was Saudi Arabia. In the years 1973–8, total Saudi aid amounted to about US$7 billion.[19] Other major donors were Kuwait and the United Arab Emirates.

The aid officially extended to Egypt by Arab governments ended in 1979 in reaction to Sadat's peace initiative. However, a crisis had already been brewing for some time in Egypt's relations with the countries from which she had been receiving aid, in particular Saudi Arabia. As early as the end of 1974 and the beginning of 1975, Egyptian statesmen began to complain about the meagreness of the aid that was being offered by Arab oil-producers. And in the course of 1975–6 Egyptian disappointment deepened. This took place against a background of the Egyptian government's hopes that the oil-producing states of the Arabian Peninsula would offer Egypt aid to the amount of US$10–12 billion for development projects connected with Egypt's five-year plan for 1975–80.[20] The five-year plan was supposed to give new life to the Egyptian economy, which had been in a state of stagnation, in terms of gross investment and per capita growth rates, since the middle of the 1960s. The response of the rulers of Saudi Arabia and the Kuwait was to establish GODE (the Gulf Organization for the Development of Egypt) in April of 1976. This organization committed itself to providing Egypt with loans (rather than unilateral transfers) amounting to no more than US$2 billion, which was to be paid out over a period of five years.[21]

In January of 1977 Egypt was struck by a wave of protests and demonstrations, known as the 'food riots', which seriously threatened the stability of the Sadat regime.[22] But even these events failed to bring about any real change in Saudi attitudes on the matter of economic aid to Egypt. Newspapers in Kuwait even claimed that the 'food riots' had been instigated by the Egyptian government itself in order to bring pressure to bear on Arab oil states to increase their aid to Egypt, and that the riots therefore could not be taken seriously.[23] Indeed, already in 1976, aid to Egypt had been scaled down significantly, and the conditions attached to it made more stringent.[24]

The position taken by the rulers of Saudi Arabia and the other oil-producing states of the Peninsula in 1976–7 left a considerable residue of resentment and bitterness among Egyptian government circles. It had already become patently clear to Egypt in this period that Arab economic aid was steadily being reduced. The forecast that had been prepared by the Egyptian Ministry of Finance before November 1977 predicted a continuing decline in aid in 1978, and anticipated that by 1979 aid would be reduced to a mere US$300 million per annum.[25]

This, therefore, was the setting in which in 1977 (before November of that year) Egyptian statesmen accused Saudi Arabia and its partners in GODE of arrogant and humiliating conduct, unbecoming to relations between two Arab states.[26]

All of the evidence published in recent years would seem to indicate that in the months following the January 1977 'food riots', and possibly even earlier, Anwar al-Sadat reached two conclusions concerning the economic future of Egypt and its relations with the oil-producing states of the Arabian Peninsula, and concerning the implications deriving from both of these issues. The first was that unless the country could achieve a sufficiently high economic growth rate, not only would the 'New Egypt' – that is Egypt after the Free Officers' revolution – fail to fulfil the people's expectations, but the very regime whose foundations the Free Officers had laid would be doomed. And second, the economic aid which had been furnished by the Arab oil states, and which in 1973–4 had been regarded by the Egyptian government as of crucial importance for Egypt's economic and social recovery, would no longer play the major role that had been anticipated for it in the process of the country's renewed economic growth. It would seem, therefore, that the Egyptian leadership reached the conclusion that the Saudi and Kuwaiti elites had no interest in a fundamental change in the Egyptian economy.[27] This being the case, new sources of aid on an appropriate scale would have to be sought elsewhere. As has already been pointed out, these developments took place at a time when considerable monetary reserves were being accumulated by the oil-producers – principally by Saudi Arabia. It is also worth mentioning that Saudi Arabia's total aid to Egypt (about US$7 billion) accounted for 4.4 per cent of her total oil revenues in the years 1973–8 (US$159 billion). The total aid (about US$11 billion) of the three main donors – Saudi Arabia, Kuwait and the United Arab Emirates – accounted for 4.7 per cent of their total revenues in the same years (US$237 billion). Taking the whole period since the first 'energy crisis' (1973–85) into account, we find that in the case both of Saudi Arabia and of the three donors together, the aid given to Egypt accounted for 1.1 per cent ($7 out of $626 billion, and $11 out of $986 billion respectively).

The policy of Saudi Arabia and Kuwait on the issue of economic aid appears to have reinforced the awareness of the Egyptian leadership, as well as of other social groups in the country, regarding the limits of putting the idea of pan-Arabism into practice. And once such a conclusion had been reached, there no longer remained any serious impediments, including those of an ideological nature, in the way of violating a fundamental imperative of Arab nationalism: namely, neither to recognize nor come to terms with the existence of a Zionist state in the Middle East. In other words, from the moment that the limits of pan-Arabism stood revealed, the Egyptian elite chose to commit itself to working on behalf of the advancement of Egyptian national goals, and in practice gave only marginal consideration to other demands.

Thus, the dramatic increase of incomes from the export of crude oil, and the expectations that this development had awakened on both sides of the Red Sea, merely served to bring into sharper focus a fact of political life that had always been there: where interests are concerned, everyone looks to his own – Egypt no less than Saudi Arabia.

ONE ARAB STATE, MANY ARAB STATES

The relations of the Arab oil states of the Persian Gulf (chief among them Iraq and Saudi Arabia) with Egypt in the years following the Camp David accords, and the Baghdad meeting of foreign ministers of 1979, are also instructive in regard to the issue we are considering. The response of most Arab states to Sadat's peace-making was one of rage, and in March 1979 they took the decision to ostracize Egypt from the community of Arab states by suspending her membership of the Arab League, breaking off diplomatic relations, and imposing an economic boycott.[28] At the time, Egypt maintained economic relations with Arab countries in a broad and varied range of fields, which included the exchange of goods and services (tourism and communications), and private and public investments. Even so, had the sanctions in these areas been fully enforced, they would of themselves have been insufficient to create a real economic crisis, although they certainly would not have smoothed the course of Egyptian economic development. There was one way, however, in which the Arab oil states could deal the Egyptian economy a very severe blow: they could shut their doors to Egyptian migrant workers.

In 1979 the number of Egyptian workers employed in the oil economies had reached a total of about 1.5 million.[29] In the same year, the official remittances to Egypt by these workers came to US$2.2 billion.[30] If we add to this figure the net increase of foreign currency deposits attributed to the remittances of migrant workers, and to remittances that found their way to Egypt through unofficial channels, the total contribution in foreign currency to the Egyptian economy was actually higher. Even the sum of US$2.2 billion, which is the figure ordinarily cited in Egyptian publications, would represent an undeniably substantial contribution. Indeed since 1976, a year in which such remittances already totalled US$755 million, they had been an important factor in financing the deficit in the balance of trade.[31]

At the end of the 1970s, Egyptian migrant workers were concentrated in four oil economies: Saudi Arabia, Libya, Kuwait, and the United Arab Emirates. Not only did their number not decline as a result of the decisions taken at the Baghdad meeting of Arab leaders, they actually doubled over a two-year period: by 1982 there were about 3 million Egyptian migrant workers, the principal increase having taken place in Iraq.[32] Concurrently there was also an increase in the flow of remittances: their official total for the Egyptian fiscal year 1983–4 came to more than US$3.9 billion.[33] Unofficial estimates put the total of remittances arriving by both official and unofficial channels and the increase in personal foreign currency deposits and of goods sent home by migrant workers at US$5–6 billion.[34]

205

Even if we accept the official figure of US$3.9 billion, it is clear that the contribution of remittances to the economy was great. They were the most important item of income in foreign currency in 1983−4. They constituted 33 per cent of the total income from the export of goods and services (US$11.8 billion), 76 per cent of the trade deficit (US$5.1 billion), and 13 per cent of the GNP (US$30 billion).[35]

In other important fields as well, Egyptian economic relations with other Arab states remained on a normal footing after 1979. So, for example, foreign currency deposits maintained in Egyptian banks by Arab private and public sectors in 1979 amounted to roughly US$4.0 billion. And, except for some isolated instances, these deposits were not withdrawn.[36] Nor was there any drop in tourism from countries such as Saudi Arabia, Kuwait and the United Arab Emirates. Rather, tourism from these countries increased between 1977 and 1984.[37] Even as regards trade, the damage done to the Egyptian economy, when measured in absolute terms, was very slight indeed. Thus, although exports of goods to all Arab states fell from a total of US$161 million in 1978 to US$88 million in 1980, they rose again to US$126 million in 1981 and to US$170 million in 1984.[38]

For the Arab states that continued to maintain their economic ties with Egypt, there were alternative options available in all of the relevant fields. This is particularly evident in regard to their employment of Egyptian workers, whose numbers, as we have noted, increased markedly. The other alternatives were less desirable, whether for political reasons, or because of economic or social considerations. This is to say that the economic relations maintained by Iraq with Egypt, or by Saudi Arabia with Egypt, were determined in the main by the particular self-interest of Iraq, Saudi Arabia, and the rest. As has been pointed out, in the tensions between pan-Arabism and particularism, it was the claims of the latter which proved to be decisively superior. Especially striking in this regard is the fact that it was in the very years in which Egypt committed the most serious infraction in its history against the imperatives of Arab nationalism − a separate peace with Israel − that Egypt's economic ties with other Arab countries actually assumed a greater scope and significance than ever before. I am of course referring here to the issue of migrant labour. It is however true that this development is to a large extent connected with a deterioration that took place in another arena and in regard to another conflict between two national movements in the Middle East.

Developments in Iran and Iraq since 1973−4 have also been affected in many ways by the impact of population growth and expanding revenues from crude-oil exports. In this part of the Middle East, too, the course of social, economic, and political events has had a far-reaching impact on the fate of Arab unity – or, viewing the matter from another perspective, has been of great significance in accounting for the situation of the separate Arab nation-state.

Iran is the only country in the Middle East which has both a considerable population and an abundance of oil. In 1985 the population of Iran numbered about 45 million, and its natural rate of increase in the course of the last generation has been very high indeed – over 3.0 per cent (see Table 1). Current forecasts predict that the population will reach 53 million in 1990.[39] Until 1979, Iran had been the second largest oil-producer in the Middle East, surpassed only by Saudi Arabia. Its total income from oil exports in the period between 1974 and 1979 came to US$119 billion (see Table 2).

The increased income from oil exports in the 1970s gave rise to, or precipitated, a whole range of social and economic changes, some of which created serious problems: accelerated migration from the countryside to the big cities which was neither controlled nor planned; deepening economic disparities in Iranian society; and, most important of all, the disappointment among the lower strata of Iranian society in their expectation of an improvement in their living standards.[40] Additionally, there may be solid grounds for the claim that in the 1960s and 1970s income inequality generally increased.[41]

A number of factors have been proposed by students of contemporary Iranian history to explain the collapse of the Pahlavi regime and the emergence of an Islamic (theocratic) government in Iran. One such factor was the Shah's failure, socially and politically, to ensure a broader distribution of the expanding resources that had been at his disposal between 1974 and 1977. And one of Khomaini's principal messages was that of the necessity of social justice for those who felt themselves to have been deprived of a fair share in the nation's wealth under the Shah's rule. Indeed, among the very first acts of revolutionary government in 1979 was a demonstrative transfer of resources, particularly urban and rural land, from the upper classes to the lower classes.[42]

Nevertheless, in the years since the revolution, it has become increasingly evident that neither Khomaini nor the Islamic Republican Party has any satisfactory solutions to offer for dealing with the problems of dislocation, economic disparities, and expectations that were created by, and in the presence of, conspicuous abundance in a society having to cope simultaneously with a rapid population growth and the complex processes of modernization. The economic difficulties of Iran have become even more severe since the revolution, and not merely as a consequence of the war with Iraq.[43]

The country that started the war in the Gulf was Iraq; and the country that has so far refused to end it has been Iran. Both the commencement of hostilities and their continuation derive from – among other factors – internal considerations having to do with the consolidation of a distinct national framework in the case of Iraq, and the regime's increased solidarity in the face of its actual and potential enemies in the case of both Iran and Iraq.

As regards the subject under review in this paper, what stands out in the Gulf War is the tipping of the scales in favour of particularist over pan-Arab interests. Consider the case of Iraq, a state which has for years been ruled by a Ba'th regime, whose key men are Sunni Arabs. For all of the twists and turns of events, Iraq had since 1963 been squarely in the camp of the more radical of the Arab states in its international, regional, and pan-Arab orientation. The same state has been embroiled for years in an armed conflict with a non-Arab state for the control of a territory which the Arab national movement regards as part of the Arab homeland – namely Arabistan (Khuzistan). In the course of this war – a war which has been the longest, the most highly escalated, economically the costliest, and the bloodiest in the history of armed conflicts between nation-states in the Middle East – Iraq has on more than one occasion since 1982 found itself in serious military difficulties. And yet Syria and Libya, two of the most militant spokesmen of the pan-Arab cause in the last two decades, have chosen to back Iran in this contest. Nor have they confined their backing of Khomaini's Iran to mere declarations, but have assisted that country both economically (Libya) and militarily (Syria and Libya).[44]

Since 1974 the vision of pan-Arabism – both in its maximalist version of complete political union and in its minimalist version of inter-Arab solidarity on issues of common interest – has been dealt a number of severe blows. Two of the hardest have been, on the one hand, Egypt's separate peace with Israel and, on the other, the support by Syria and Libya of Iran in its war against Iraq. There can be no doubt that particularism, as it has become manifest in the continuing development and consolidation of the separate Arab nation-state, has received a considerable boost in the process. This trend has come into its own since the latter half of the 1970s, when Arab states began actively to pursue a policy of advancing their own interests, even when that policy was in obvious contradiction to the ideals, principles, and aims of pan-Arab ideology. The origin of this circumstance can be traced at least in part to the fact that, at the same time as some Arab states were prospering, the social and economic problems of other states, Arab and non-Arab, became exacerbated as a result of the accelerated pace of population growth. Put another way: as the economic disparities grew, they assumed the guise of political differences that became increasingly more marked as time went on. In recent years this development has also had its ideological manifestations in several Arab states, for example Egypt, Iraq and Saudi Arabia.[45]

Thus, the call for closer economic ties among Arab states, to the point of economic integration, upon whose foundations progress could be made toward greater political cooperation,[46] would seem to be a quest after the unattainable. The profound disparity in the economic domain among the various political entities in the Arab world is ultimately responsible for driving them apart politically. This difference, the essence of which is economic, is one of the 'givens' of the contemporary Middle East.

NOTES

This article is based on a paper submitted to the Leonard Davis Institute's international conference on 'The Future of the Nation State in the Middle East', which was held at the Hebrew University of Jerusalem in June 1986. My thanks go to Dr. Herbert Silbermann for his kind assistance during the preparation of the article.

1 *Al-Ahram al-Iqtisadi*, No. 572, 15 June 1979; Arab Republic of Egypt, CAPMAS, *Statistical Yearbook 1952–1981*, Cairo, 1981; UN, *Demographic Yearbook 1983*, New York, 1985, p. 156.
2 D. MacKenzie, 'Tackling Egypt's Baby Boom', *The Middle East*, Oct. 1985, pp. 51–2; A. Charnock, 'Simple Solution Saves Lives', *The Middle East*, Dec. 1985, p. 54.
3 For a somewhat different projection, see The World Bank, *World Development Report 1984*, Oxford, 1984, Table 19, p. 254.
4 GNP growth rates in constant 1965 prices were: 0.6 per cent in 1966, – 1.2 in 1967, 1.6 in 1968, and 1.9 in 1972. See The World Bank, *World Tables 1976*, Baltimore, 1976.
5 J. Waterbury, *The Egypt of Nasser and Sadat*, Princeton, 1983, pp. 51–3.
6 For detailed data on the monetary reserves of the Arab oil countries in the years 1974–84, see OAPEC, *Secretary General's Eighth Annual Report 1981*, Kuwait, 1982, p. 66; IMF, *World Economic Outlook 1983*, Washington D.C., 1983, p. 187; *Petroleum Economist*, June 1985, p. 196.
7 See for example, Haikal's article, *al-Ahram*, 18 Oct. 1968; and Abd al-Nasser's address on the occasion of July Revolution Day, *al-Ahram*, 24 July 1969.
8 M. Heller and N. Safran, *The New Middle Class and Regime Stability in Saudi Arabia*, Harvard Middle East Papers, Modern Series, no. 3 (1985), pp. 29–34.
9 Al-Hegelan and Palmer's conclusion that the low level of salaries explains inadequate incentives for enhanced performance of the Saudi bureaucracy need not mean that Saudi nationals employed in the public sector do not identify with the Saudi state. See 'Bureaucracy and Development in Saudi Arabia', *MEJ*, vol. 39 (1985), pp. 48–68.
10 Kingdom of Saudi Arabia, Central Planning Organization, *Development Plan A.H. 1390 (1970–74)*, p. 81; J. Chamieh (ed.), *Saudi Arabia Yearbook 1980–81*, Beirut, 1980, p. 266.

11 R. M. Kavoussi, 'Economic Growth and Income Distribution in Saudi Arabia', *ASQ*, vol. 5 (1983), pp. 71–8.
12 *al-Ahram*, 2 Sept. 1967; *al-Hayat*, 31 Aug.–2 Sept. 1967. See also A. Sela, *Unity within Conflict in the Inter-Arab System* (Hebrew), Jerusalem, 1982, p. 79.
13 See, for example, A. Abdel-Malek, *Egypt: Military Society*, New York, 1968, pp. 285–7.
14 On these and additional arguments see *al-Ahram*, 30 Jan. and 22 May 1975, 2 and 14 May and 27 July 1979; *al-Ahram al-Iqtisadi*, no. 586, 15 Jan. 1980, pp. 6–9; M. El-Beheiry, 'Egypt and OPEC', in R. A. Stone (ed.), *OPEC and the Middle East*, New York, 1977; D. Dishon, 'Inter-Arab Relations', in C. Legum et al. (eds.), *Middle East Contemporary Survey*, vol. 3 (1978–9), New York and London, 1980, p. 231.
15 This figure includes all kinds of government-to-government aid (grants and loans). Most sources mentioned below do not give estimates regarding military and defence aid. See The World Bank, *Arab Republic of Egypt: Economic Management in a Period of Transition*, Washington D.C., 1978, vol. 4, p. 48; *Al-Nahar Arab Report and Memo*, 23 April 1979; K. Ikram, *Egypt*, A World Bank Country Economic Report, Baltimore and London, 1980, pp. 350–1; J. Wieh, *Saudi-Egyptian Relations: The Political and Military Dimensions of Saudi Financial Flows to Egypt*, Santa Monica, 1980, pp. 47–60; The World Bank, *World Development Report 1981*, New York, 1981, table 16, p. 165; OECD, *Aid from OPEC Countries*, Paris, 1983, table II.8; UNCTAD, *Trade and Development report 1983*, New York, 1983, pp. 61–76.
16 *al-Qabas*, 14 April 1979; ARAMCO, *World Magazine*, 1979, pp. 2–3. See also *MEED*, 6 April 1979.
17 N. Ayubi, 'OPEC Surplus Funds and Third World Development: The Egyptian Case', *JSAMES*, vol. 4, no. 4 (1982), p. 46.
18 OECD, *Aid from OPEC*, table II.8.
19 *The Middle East*, June 1979.
20 *al-Ahram*, 22 May 1975; *Middle East New Agency*, 26 July 1976.
21 *MEED*, 7 May 1976, p. 17; Ikram, *Egypt*, pp. 345–6, 364.
22 For some details on the 'food riots', see *al-Ahram*, 19, 20, and 21 Jan. 1977; *MEED*, 28 Jan. 1977, pp. 5–6, 13.
23 Waterbury, *Nasser and Sadat*, p. 419.
24 The World Bank, *Arab Republic of Egypt*, vol. 4, p. 48; OECD, *Aid from OPEC*, table II.8; *Ruz al-Yusuf*, no. 2652, 9 April 1979. In early August 1976, Sadat told delegations of Egyptian students in the U.S.A.: 'the Arab aid fund [GODE], amounting to two billion [US dollars], is not sufficient. Our Arab brothers ought to appreciate our situation ... they ought to reconsider this fund, because two billion are not enough.' Radio Cairo, 3 Aug. 1976.
25 Ayubi, 'OPEC Surplus', pp. 54–5.
26 *al-Ahram*, 4 Aug. 1976 and also 3 April 1979.
27 J. Waterbury, *Hydropolitics of the Nile Valley*, Syracuse, 1979, pp. 172–3; F. Ajami, *The Arab Predicament*, Cambridge, 1981, p. 103; M. H. Kerr, 'Introduction: Egypt in the Shadow of the Gulf', in M. H. Kerr and E. Yassin (eds.), *Rich and Poor States in the Middle East*, Boulder, 1982, pp. 9–10.
28 Sela, *Unity within Conflict*, pp. 183–8.
29 *al-Ahram*, 18 Sept. 1978. See also G. Feiler, 'Workers Migration to the Arab Oil Economies, 1974–1983' (Hebrew), unpublished M.A. thesis, University of Haifa, 1985, pp. 27–8.
30 The World Bank, *World Tables*, vol. 1, *Economic Data*, Baltimore and London, 1984, p. 283.
31 Ibid.
32 *al-Ahram*, 5 Aug. 1982, 13 Aug. 1983, 12 Oct. 1984.
33 IMF, *International Financial Statistics*, Dec. 1985.
34 For data on personal foreign currency deposits, see National Bank of Egypt, *Economic Bulletin, 1982–1983*, various issues.
35 These calculations are based on IMF data. See *Direction of Trade Statistics, Yearbook 1985*, p. 163; IMF, *International Financial Statistics, Yearbook 1985*.

36 Ayubi, 'OPEC Surplus', p. 54.
37 Government of Egypt, General Authority for the Promotion of Tourism, *Tourist Statistical Information, 1975–1984*, Cairo, 1985; Y. Meital, 'Economic Relations between Egypt and Israel, 1980–1984' (Hebrew), unpublished M.A. thesis, University of Haifa, 1986, pp. 70–4.
38 IMF, *Direction of Trade Statistics, Yearbook 1985*, p. 164.
39 The World Bank, *World Development Report 1984*, table 19, p. 255.
40 L. Binder, 'Iran', in Joint Economic Committee, Congress of the United States, *The Political Economy of the Middle East: 1973–78*, Washington D.C., 1980, pp. 157–66.
41 M. Parvin and A. N. Zamani, 'Political Economy of Growth and Distribution: A Statistical Interpretation of the Iranian Case', *Iranian Studies*, vol. 12, nos. 1–2 (1979), pp. 43–78; F. Kazemi, *Poverty and Revolution in Iran*, New York and London, 1980, pp. 89–91; R. E. Looney, *Economic Origins of the Iranian Revolution*, New York, 1982, pp. 247–53. For a different conclusion see N. Momayezi, 'Economic Correlates of Political Violence: The Case of Iran', *MEJ*, vol. 40, no. 1 (1986), pp. 71–6. Momayezi ignores available data which do not support his main point – i.e., that there was hardly any increase in income inequality during the concluding years of the Pahlavi regime.
42 S. Bakhash, *The Reign of the Ayatollahs*, New York, 1984, pp. 185–9, 197–200.
43 A. Ashraf, 'Bazaar and the Mosque in Iran's Revolution', *Merip Reports*, no. 113 (March–April 1983), pp. 15–18; H. Razavi and F. Vakil, *The Political Environment of Economic Planning in Iran, 1971–1983: From Monarchy to Islamic Republic*, Boulder and London, 1984, pp. 108–10; J. Tagavi, 'The Iran–Iraq War: The First Three Years', in B. M. Rosen (ed.), *Iran Since the Revolution*, New York, 1985, pp. 75–6.
44 A. R. Taylor, *The Arab Balance of Power*, Syracuse, 1982; D. Dishon and B. Maddy-Weitzmann, 'Inter-Arab Relations', in C. Legum et al. (eds.), *Middle East Contemporary Survey*, vol. 7 (1982–83), New York, 1985, pp. 193–5.
45 For manifestations of distinct (*watani*) national identity in elite-initiated ideologies of the 1970s and 1980s see R. A. Hinnebusch, Jr., *Egyptian Politics under Sadat*, Cambridge, 1985, pp. 116–76; A. Baram, 'Mesopotamian identity in Ba'thi Iraq', *MES*, vol. 19 (1983), pp. 426–55; idem, 'Culture in the Service of *Wataniyya*: The Treatment of Mesopotamian-inspired Art in Ba'thi Iraq', in G. Warburg and G. Gilbar (eds.), *Studies in Islamic Society*, Haifa, 1984, pp. 265–313; J. Nevo, 'Religion and National Identity in Saudi Arabia', Paper delivered at the 15th Congress of the International Association for the History of Religion, University of Sydney, August 1985.
46 In 1981 the late Professor Malcolm Kerr wrote:

> As for the implications of the oil boom for public policy in the Arab states, perhaps the most important are the steps that may be taken towards regional economic integration. This is by no means a new idea, but the sudden accumulation of revenues in several Arab states has made it possible for the first time to consider many development schemes that once seemed beyond reach. In many other respects, government planners and private entrepreneurs are now reminding themselves of all the ways in which the potential for regional cooperation had already been present but has not been implemented. And for many Arabs, economic unity looks like a possible short cut to the long-elusive goal of political unity. ('Egypt in the Shadow', p. 2)

For Product Safety Concerns and Information please contact our EU representative GPSR@taylorandfrancis.com
Taylor & Francis Verlag GmbH, Kaufingerstraße 24, 80331 München, Germany

www.ingramcontent.com/pod-product-compliance
Lightning Source LLC
Chambersburg PA
CBHW062224300426
44115CB00012BA/2211